THIS IS A STORY ABOUT GHOSTS

Anne Champion

Poetry by Anne Champion

Hunted Carrion: Sonnets to a Stalker
The Good Girl is Always a Ghost
Book of Levitations
Reluctant Mistress
She Saints & Holy Profanities
The Dark Length Home

THIS IS A STORY ABOUT GHOSTS

Anne Champion

ISBN Paperback: 979-8-9904315-0-8

ISBN Hardcover: 979-8-9904315-1-5

Cover and interior design © 2024 Anne Champion Author photo © 2021 Anne Champion

For any inquiries, please don't hesitate to get in touch. Am-champion.com/contact

To anyone told your feelings were weakness.
To anyone told it was your fault.
To anyone made to feel orphan.
Or alien.
Or object.
Or prey.

I

1

When I knew I'd commit suicide, it didn't feel like a decision: it felt like something I'd been running from had caught up with me, like a shadow that trails behind you in an alley, only to bloom massive in front of you as you pass a streetlamp. It towered over me as I sunk to the floor in a corner, ready to drape over my body, swallow me whole.

I looked at my shadowed reflection—I didn't see the worn woman I was used to: the gaze from the mirror went through my center like a flaming sword.

She had a psychopathic glee in thinking of destroying me. She knew I deserved it.

Who'd she look like?

I spent a moment arrested in a glare-off.

Mother.

I dipped my brush in foundation, began to paint over her face. But she was there all day: it was in the eyes.

November 2020. I'd protested racism all summer. Covid-19 barreled through with such a disorienting speed that it was impossible to process and impossible not to heft the new weight of grief. I'd lost my job. I was in debt. Desperate, I took a teaching job in rural Texas. It was a tense election. Each party had its rabid following. I no longer trusted any politicians.

I hadn't been hugged in a year.

I hadn't had sex in four years.

The person who couldn't stand me most, however, was myself.

Death was building its nest in my ribcage, waiting for my body to settle in.

Only two students came to class that morning—the Covid new normal. They weren't interested in discussing English. They talked about hunting, "Do you have a gun?"

"I don't know anything about guns."

"If your record's clean, you could have one this afternoon."

A door. It was the beginning of the plan.

Plagued by insomnia, I imagined shooting myself.

Should it be the temple or the mouth?

It'll be over so fast, the voice soothed.

I had a therapist. I lived week to week like a child scaling playground monkey bars whose arms were losing strength. I'd tried EMDR, medication, yoga, meditation.

I drove past gun shops; I'd imagine walking in and cheerfully saying "hello!" so as not to give away I was a suicide.

I had 20 days in which I wrote things in my journal that made me unlovable. RAPE is scrawled all over pages in angry, stark scribbles.

I was just shy of 40.

I took a bath, sunk my head underwater, thought admiringly of Virginia Woolf, drowning with rocks in her pockets.

Then, as if a mouth pressed to my ear: "Anne."

I jolted from the water.

I knew that voice.

I hadn't heard it in 23 years.

"It's time," he said.

That's how the ghost of my childhood boyfriend who committed suicide shattered my grey world.

By morning, it was technicolor.

My life was saved.

2

"And ghosts must do again what gives them pain."

—W.H. Auden

O r I'd lost my mind completely.

As a child, I saw a woman on TV with silky ringlet curls and vapid doe eyes collapse into the arms of a vampire who draped his erect fangs over her neck.

I've been hooked on monstrous men ever since.

Some of us live an undead life obliviously—waking up and walking out of the grave to the place where that wound took us out.

Some lives are a cyclone that spirals incessantly around the same tragedy—unbearable, unsurvivable—yet, something compels us to do it again, to replay what killed us. We do that until some living soul informs us we're dead.

We startle to realize we've been dead this whole time, tripping cluelessly into the same quicksand of the same betrayal.

3

When Officer Derek Chauvin kneeled on George Floyd's neck for 9 minutes and 29 seconds, Floyd called out, "Mama!" His mother had been dead for two years.

I think of George Floyd's passing as a release from a haunting, a return to source.

The dead one is the killer.

It happens to some of us—whole swaths of humanity stillborn due to the history that precedes us, the dead who raised us.

If you say "Bloody America" in a mirror three times in darkness, the spitting image of your ancestors' corpses will transform your face. Are you brave enough to look directly at their truths?

Each of us will have to confront our ghosts and bury them; examine our bones, inspect for damage; hunt for other dead versions of ourselves wandering our passageways. Padlock the rooms where the evils occurred. Cover the mirrors. Save the child calling out for its mama.

4

Racism and sexism: a two-headed snake that slithered through our days growing up in 90s Midwest suburbia; some let it lurk in their garden, while others were attacked, poisoned, paralyzed.

The first time I heard, "You look like a girl who'd date black guys," it was from my mother, the daily terrorism of her domestic orbit. She scanned my body up and down, spat, "N**** Lover. You'll be pregnant at 15. Then we'll put you on the streets."

I'd always been a nerd—glasses, buck-teeth, my nose in a book. I believed I'd never be beautiful enough to think about love. But by the time I was 9, I was in a bra. This prompted teasing by bra-snapping boys.

I knew little about sex—my parents, in a cult-like conservative fervor, kept me out of sex education until I was 15. They weren't religious—this denial of access to knowledge was a punishment for being born girl.

By my teens, my mother's insults were expertly aimed arrows. As long as I could remember, she'd used "I hate you" as her sharpest weapon, but the more I developed, the more places she found to target. "Ugly slut," "fat whore," and N**** lover" became the most frequent refrains.

She wasn't the only one who speculated about what sort of girl I looked like. I'd not yet kissed a boy, but other students said, "You look like a girl who'd date black guys."

I was obsessed with Madonna, her face plastered over my walls. I stood in front of each poster like they were funny mirrors, marveling at her chameleon-like beauty. No matter her hair color or style, she commanded worship. Draped in crucifixes and anointed in hair dye, I found nothing quite as holy. I crimped my hair, wore short skirts, collected crosses and sunglasses.

In 1989, she released, "Like a Prayer." In black negligee, straps falling down her shoulders, rosary skipping across her breasts, she bounces in front of flaming crosses. She watches as a group of white men stab a white woman and run away. When a black man finds the stabbed woman and cradles her, police arrive and he's arrested. Madonna prays to a black Jesus statue that cries tears. She kisses his feet. He comes to life. He kisses her forehead. She dances with wild abandon in front of an all black choir. She falls to her knees, writhing with the music. The frame switches and she's on her back, the black man on top of her—they kiss on the lips.

"Why can't a white and black person kiss?" I asked my parents.

"You wouldn't fall in love with an animal, would you?"

Madonna was the type of girl who'd kiss black men. Perhaps that wasn't so bad.

I was forbidden from listening to black music. I'd go to neighborhood garage sales and buy Janet Jackson tapes. I learned how to unblock BET from my TV when my parents weren't home. My sister and I put on dance shows in the living room, as Puff Daddy, Mase, and The Notorious B.I.G. shimmied the Harlem Shake in front of neon backdrops. Hip hop injected my spirit with joy. When I shoplifted 2Pac's single, "How Do You Want It," staring at his tattooed abs, I knew that what my mother accused was correct.

But a white girl wasn't supposed to like black boys.

In 1992, the white cops bludgeoning Rodney King on television made that clear.

"Why are they beating him like that?" I asked.

"He's a criminal."

"They could arrest him."

"He must have done something really bad. He's black," my mom shrugged.

After the not guilty verdict, after the city of L.A. went up in flames, we watched as a group of black men pulled a white truck driver

14

out of his vehicle and beat him. My mom gasped with an empathy she didn't express for King.

Soon after, we watched as police chased a white Bronco, as the newscaster described how Nicole Brown Simpson had been nearly decapitated by her ex, O.J. Simpson. "That's what happens to n**** lovers," my mom warned.

First Lady Hillary Clinton spoke of "super predators:" black children born so depraved that there was no hope. Destined to become criminals, she advocated for tougher laws on children to "bring them to heel."

You look like a girl who'd date black guys.

Maybe we wore the look of wanting to be uncaged.

At 13, I sat in the school lobby with a friend waiting for our ride. Two black boys came out of basketball practice and sat next to us, casually draping their arms across our shoulders. One cupped my breast in his palm.

"Hey," he said, "what's your name?"

5

The groping boys aren't the story—the story is the girls on that bench.

The relationships girls have in childhood is our first dabble at love. We spend our youths together learning how to perform love and how to lose it, all while feeling certain we've never known love—doubting we're even worthy. We're trained to pine for boys, imagine scenarios in which they fall for our beauty on sight.

When girls hurt each other, they split wide open on impact like the gasp of a razor slash.

Traumatized girls find each other: there's an unspoken, unconscious recognition, a gravitational pull, a reliable, inseparable orbit. I orbited Dee.

We obsessed over glossy teen magazines. We recreated outfits from movies like *Clueless,* pantomiming ditziness. We wore plaid skirts and carried makeup Caboodles full of feather pens. Both of us were chubby enough to be insecure, but developed enough to garner attention.

My traumas were caused by my parents; Dee's by a babysitter when she was four and her stepbrother as a preteen, but I didn't know about either until later, after she hurt me with the sharpness damaged girls wield.

Before that happened, we flipped through magazines, cut out pictures of our crushes to tape on our walls. I was in love with Christian Bale, she with Chris O'Donnell.

16

A conversation happened amongst white girls often: would you date a black guy? Answers varied from *I don't want a mixed baby* to *Maybe.*

Dee and I both had magazine posters of Aaliyah. When our parents weren't home, we flipped the posters over to the R&B group, Immature—a group of teenage boys who crooned about love.

Those glossy pages were our porn and our teachers. The headlines guided our insecurities and self hate: How to lose weight fast; Dating disasters; Boyfriend snatchers; Celebrity crushes; How to tell if he's the one; Makeover 101; What to do about his mom/his friends/your friends hating you; How boys think; and Quiz: What kind of girl are you?

Dee and I boiled everything down to a single plight: fat. The beauty standard of the 90s was impossibly withered-to-bone skeletons who stared glossily with dead-eyed glares and gaunt cheekbones that made us imagine cocaine-infused parties crowded with adoring men. They were so perfectly frail.

Dee and I were known for our breasts: we were eager to rid ourselves of them. We wore oversized Nike T-shirts; we dieted with more focus than our studies.

We figured that if dieting was good, starving was better. We plotted how to survive only on Saltine crackers, debated what foods would be best for low calorie but good for energy. We started to fail, finding ourselves salivating while huddled near the microwave heating nachos. We became skilled at inducing vomiting.

In 8th grade, Dee asked me to go on a church bike trip. The trip involved biking along the coast of Lake Michigan and camping on the beach. Boys would be there. We were hopeful we were going to get our first kisses.

We weren't in shape to bike 60 miles a day, and we weren't well. We saw the trip as a way to lose weight, so we were trying not to eat calories we'd burned. Most days, we survived on a single banana or power bar. We fainted, we vomited, we cried—sometimes we had to ride in a truck.

When it was over, we both lost 15 pounds and had boyfriends.

When we started high school after, it was like walking into a glossy-paged new life. We had our first kiss, our first cigarette, our first drink. We rode high on a life of firsts. There were so many firsts to come. She was my first heartbreak.

6

Four years separated my little sister and I, but we were also separated by my mother's rage and our inability to cope with it. I coped quietly and obediently, but Cassie came out of the womb defiant. She split the stale air of our authoritarian house with her screams.

Her worst fear was being locked in her room. I couldn't understand it—I got more physical violence than my sister, who I perceived as getting off easy: she received excessive favoritism, attention, and gifts from my mom, who seemed to want my sister to be her clone, even giving her the same initials, rhyming names, and the same middle name. I found my room to be a safe haven in which I could absorb myself in books during long punishments, but, as early as toddler years, my sister couldn't endure it. My mother had my father turn the locks on her door so she could be locked in, and they never tired of alternating between showering her with adoration and then shoving her into isolation.

My mother doled extreme punishments: being grounded for one to six months was not unusual, and she also paid keen attention to how to hurt us most. There was no telling what would set her off. It could be that the shampoo ran out. It could be that her coupon for the grocery store expired. If the stoplight turned red for too long, we might get nails across our cheeks. Life with her was navigating impossible booby traps. She had no friends and a contentious marriage lacking physical or emotional affection. She usually only left the house once a week for groceries and didn't have a job until I was in high school. Being raised in her world was claustrophobic and confusing.

My sister's room became such an unendurable prison that she started head-banging. *BOOM, BOOM, BOOM…* heavy, consistent, haunting punctuations to her terror. I was sure, every time, this would be the time that her small head would develop some brain damage she couldn't return from. My parents did nothing, other than occasionally yell or enter her room and whip her with a yardstick, which only made it worse. She'd head-bang until she passed out at her door. Hours later, she could be found in fetal position with eye crust and snot on her face, disoriented and eager to scurry out, trembling like a wounded doe in my arms.

A long wooden ruler hung in my father's workshop. My parents said that my father's domain was work while my mother's was home. This meant that my mother decided punishments, and my father doled them when commanded. She mostly did it herself, but she knew my father hit harder, so she'd sometimes ask him to contribute. My father had his own rage, and his fights with our mother were explosive. Cassie and I were equally afraid of both, but our father worked evenings, so most of our time was spent navigating our mother's anger.

My first suicide attempt was at 8 years old. I wrapped a blanket around my neck and tried to tie the other end to the ceiling fan.

When I fell, I thought even God rejected me.

Soon after, I began to scrape scissors against my wrist, light candles and run my fingers through them until they blistered, relieved as the skin would turn pink, part like lips, and release my silent pain.

Where I had self harm, Cassie had rebellion.

One day, my father went to his workshop to grab the stick and came back with a look of astonishment, "Someone broke it."

My sister, only four years old, looked directly at him with the defiant rage of an abused, growling kitten.

The idea of breaking the stick had never crossed my mind; I would've been too fearful of repercussions. My sister was a baby: how had she thought of this and had the courage to carry it out?

My parents replaced the stick with a metal ruler, and my sister eventually replaced her head-banging with other forms of hurt. She paced around the kitchen table. She picked at the skin on her fingers until her fingertips were bloody.

I hid the marks of their fists and my own hand. But my sister wore her bruises so plainly that teachers noticed: Child Protective Services came. My parents explained that my sister was easily bruised and liked to lie, and my sister and I agreed, terrified of becoming orphans.

We were often pitted against each other. My mother chose one of us to target, usually me; the other became the favored child, usually my sister. This tactic worked for many years. As long as one sister was getting beaten, the other was safe. My sister often participated in hitting me with my mother, starting to mirror her as a toddler.

One day, I was crying when I heard a knock coming from inside my closet. I got up, opened the door, crawled inside, and listened.

"Sissy?" My sister whispered on the other side. Our closets shared a wall: she'd crawled inside to talk.

"What are you doing?" I whispered back, "You're going to get in trouble."

"I feel bad," she said.

In those moments, we were pouring the foundation that we would ultimately need to survive—as allies. But it took until she was 11 and I was 15.

I used my pen to cope with emotional neglect, scribbling poems, journals, stories. In 4th grade, I tested at a 12th grade reading level and was allowed to read adult books. I read everything I could. I searched for words for pain. I needed to name it. I always thought that if I could name it, then I could understand, and if I could understand, perhaps I could fix it.

One night, I heard a familiar smack against my window. The neighborhood boys had started to come around like strays sniffing for a cat in heat. Bad boys who'd previously paid no attention to me began throwing rocks at my second story window. Their presence could've gotten me a beating; I rushed to the window, begged them to leave.

My sister walked in. I quickly turned away and pretended nothing was happening, but rocks started to hit the window again. I knew if she found out, she'd have ammunition to direct my mother's vitriol, but I couldn't think of a lie.

"It's boys," I blurted. "Please don't tell mom."

My sister's eyes went wide. "What do they want?"

"For me to come outside."

"Do you have…a boyfriend?"

"No, a crush."

"Have you ever…like…kissed a boy?"

"Yeah," I shrugged. I basked in this forbidden knowledge, just like my friends' teenage sisters used to when I was her age.

Cassie laid down, transfixed, "What's it like?"

After that, we stayed united against my mother for the rest of our childhood.

7

Most horror movies have a moment you can pinpoint as the nightmare's beginning—some lapse of good sense where some naive girl let the ghosts in.

Maybe she was the girl who thought the Ouija was a harmless toy. Maybe she was a powerful witch lashing out at a rival for her lover's affection. Maybe she was the serial killer's next victim, an airhead who stumbles towards strange noises rather than away. Maybe she's the love interest of a vampire, eager to collapse into starved arms.

Maybe she's just the girl who spread her legs—that's the easiest way for the devil to enter.

You watch the madness and keep that moment in your head as the nightmare reveals potholes: if only she hadn't let the ghosts in.

They're at the door. I'll have to let them in if I'm going to tell the story.

I could hold my breath, stay still, wait for them to leave. They must have others to haunt.

They aren't going away.

They've been here all this time.

I hold onto the wall as I stand. I take a breath. I can smell death on them. I reach for the handle.

I let the ghosts in.

Come in. Have a seat. We need to talk.

Don't touch me.

I said sit, goddamn you.

22

8

I worked at a trendy clothing store in the mall. I'd be straightening clothes when I'd be startled by a hand on my ass, a grip around the waist, or the sound of my name, commanded.

"You have a break soon?" They'd ask.

There were a few of them. They were friends. All races. I cycled through crushes based on who was paying attention to me. I knew nothing about sex and less about love.

We'd walk out of the store and into elevators.

Boys seemed to understand desire in ways I couldn't. I had no idea how I was supposed to act, what was supposed to happen, what boys wanted, what I wanted.

I was so shamed by my mother's obsession with me as a sexual object that I grew up disconnected from my body. I was fearful of my vagina, believing it dirty. I never touched myself: I found out later this was abnormal. I'd never had an orgasm. I had no idea what to do.

I did what smart prey does: I went slack.

The boys would hit the emergency button.

They'd press my back against the mirrors.

Their hands became seagulls, diving into my waters to feed. Up my shirt, into my bra, down my pants, into my vagina.

I didn't understand that this was supposed to feel good. I thought it was something that must feel good for them—an ego triumph. I endured.

I hoped that giving them what they wanted would make me lovable.

The elevator would ding. I'd rush to button my jeans.

I'd go back to work wondering if I'd given enough. I'd go home, sit by the phone, wait patiently for love to root.

Whispers at school began. I'd always been invisible, but I became the faint outline of a ghost taking form, hovering quietly through the hallways, never flinching or speaking as girls hissed, "Slut."

The boys treated me differently: they conjured me, gathered in covens and manifested me in bathroom stalls, in elevators. They had many spells.

All of them left me dizzy.

9

A boy in gym class. Popular, tall, black. A red jacket with my name on it—Champion— along his wide shoulders. He sits alone at the top of the bleachers as I walk around the track with Dee. His stare undresses like a casting agent scrutinizing a hopeful actress. It penetrates like a bullet that settles amongst brain tissue. It remains no matter what I do, no matter how long I look away.

Grayson asks me to skip. I tell my teacher I have to visit my guidance counselor. I meet him in the hallway. We run out the front doors, into the woods behind the school. He sees a pile of branches, says, *Our bed.*

He wants to have sex. I say I'm not ready. He asks me to sit on his lap. I do. He rocks me back and forth. *It'll be just like this,* he says. I tell him I'm not a slut. *Of course not.* He kisses my neck. He asks me to take off my shirt. I feel fat. He sticks his head up my shirt and pulls down my bra and kisses me. *Can I see it?* He tugs at the top of my jeans. I say no. He asks to touch it. *Have you ever heard of blue balls?* His fingers probe. He's not gentle. I say I'm not losing my virginity until I'm in love. *I love you,* he whispers. *Just rock in my lap.* He moans, shivers, falls backwards.

When we walk back, Dee hangs out of a window, "Annie!" The rumor mill begins its faithful churn.

Later, I watch Grayson in a group of boys, offering his hand, "Smell my fingers." Dee hears and shoves him so he spills Gatorade. *Lick it up, slut,* he says.

When Grayson asks to be my boyfriend, I say yes.

25

No one had ever held me with love. To this day, I still bloom under the slightest caress, even with no love attached, even though every man who's ever touched me has been artificial light. All my life, every pore of my body has been the gaping beak of a newborn bird, helpless, blind, and insatiably hungry, swallowing every filthy worm whole, begging for more, more, more.

10

This is a story about girls, *those girls,* girls who'd pass intricately folded notes written in rainbow ink. This is a story about girls who had sleepovers and played with each other's hair, every strand tingling along the scalp as it was braided. This is a story about girls who'd watch movies while drawing on each other's backs, giggling when they discovered sentences being traced up their spines. *Anne Loves Grayson. Dee Loves Shawn.* This is a story about girls who took debate, putting an L to their foreheads with their fingers and glaring at boys after being declared winners. This is a story about girls who sat in the front row of history because Mr. Moon was so hot.

This is a story about girls who made pacts to starve, who sat with each other in the bathroom as they trained their gag reflexes to weaken, jamming toothbrushes down their throats, cheering when McDonald's came up. This is a story about girls who thought about sex and obsessed over perfection, whose world revolved around the boys who groped them.

This is a story about girls with no boundaries.

This is a story about girls with no boundaries because they were never taught they had a right to their own bodies, whose borders were trespassed young by adults. This is a story about girls who had no agency because they were used to their bodies belonging to those who took them.

This is a story about girls with landmines planted in their flesh by people who touched them who shouldn't have. This is a story about girls growing up in a way that one misstep activates an explosion and their minds splatter.

This is a story about girls like Dee and me, who didn't understand sexual power, so we wore it inside out. This is a story about a culture so obsessed with girl's bodies that whenever we walked through the halls, students flocked like press, shoving us, asking, *Is this true? Is that true? Will you fuck us too?*

This is a story about girls who gasped to find that their backpacks had "slut" inked in permanent marker.

This is a story about sluts. This is a story about how Dee got on her knees behind a 7-11 to give Shawn what he wanted most. This is a story about girls so devoid of love that they kneel and give, swallow and bury, and bury.

This is a story about how Grayson declared that he had "hit that;" how he reached into his mouth, pulled out a wad of gum, chucked it; how the gum was lodged into my hair so I had to leave school; how Dee gently massaged peanut butter through it; how we were a balm to each other's wounds, a shield against poison-tipped arrows.

This is a story about how Grayson and Shawn asked Dee to run a train, and she did.

She did.

She had sex with my boyfriend.

This is a story about how I cried whole nights, gulping the darkness, how no pain had ever hurt like that, how her parents begged me to stay her friend, how her mother confessed that she'd been raped by several people, how she moved through a world of hurt that many couldn't understand, how badly she needed attention and to be loved.

I thought, *rape is no excuse.*

This is a story about ghosts.

11

When you have no love growing up, when you have no sense of ownership over your body, when your sense of safety is trespassed by those who say they love you—by those tasked to keep you alive—then you're like a seed growing with no light. Even a sliver of artificial light beneath a door might as well be the sun: you bloom overnight like a dandelion.

You bloom in lawns—the worst place to bloom—a public intrusion, a shame, a gaping yellow mouth screaming in the green.

Men run their bladed machines over you, eager to uproot you, to sever bloom from body.

It happened to Dee. It happened to me.

When we weren't wilting, we were weeds.

We're the children of ghosts; we're the bad seeds.

12

I stopped being friends with Dee and answered Grayson's calls—I let him tell me he loved me and beg to be my boyfriend, but I didn't take him back. I wanted him to prove it.

After Dee lost my friendship, she was ostracized. Dee's bullying was intense before, but it became so cruel that I wince to recall it. In my pain, I participated. Those memories are an abyss in which I hear the cacophonies of "slut, hoe" reverberate back relentlessly.

Dee quit school, moved to Las Vegas, had a child. Rumors were rampant that remade her into tragic movie cliches: prostitute, stripper, drug addict, AIDS.

Dee and I were girls who absorbed the lie that we were unlovable —we crafted that lie from the wreckage of pain left behind after being taken against our will and spat at by our peers for existing in bodies that were vulnerable to taking, bodies unloved by our families. Painfully, in dabbling at loving each other, we reinforced that lie: she taught me I wasn't lovable enough for loyalty, and I taught her that she wasn't lovable enough for forgiveness.

Violating a girl is a boring horror story.

The real horror lies in the silence shame creates.

13

In the 90's, the word AIDS sent a jolt. I was too young to understand the full scope of it politically or historically. I understood it as something associated with gaunt gay men with body sores turning skeletal. I absorbed the traumatic national consciousness of fear.

I took a sewing class in middle school. Our teacher announced that we'd be making a square for the AIDS quilt. When I told my mother, her eyes went wide.

My mother explained that she couldn't have her daughter making a quilt for homosexuals. My family didn't go to church. It's not exaggerating to say that their religion was Ronald Reagan. The party masked its bigotry through religion and an obsession with homosexuals. Ironically, my teacher was extremely religious: her decor theme was the crucifixion.

To quell the outrage, we made a square for a little girl who died of AIDS with a religious theme: Noah's Ark.

Growing up with this backdrop meant growing up in a world where sex was consistently aligned with death, taboo, and sin, yet where selling it was a major pillar of the economy; a world where sex meant pleasure, but could as easily mean illness, pregnancy, or shame.

Our pop culture pulsed with this: TLC danced with condoms taped to their sunglasses. *The Real World* introduced us to a young gay man with AIDS, Pedro, who we watched die. Parents threatened that our only choices were abstinence or Hell. The most cutting edge teenage shows, like *Melrose Place* and *My So-Called Life*, featured gay characters and

31

their profoundly hard lives in a culture with rampant homophobia. Teachers pulled streamers of rainbow condoms out of their bags like magicians, "Take however many you want."

I'd latched onto a new favorite person, Loralee. Loralee replaced Dee: she was traumatized, sexually active, slut shamed, and in need of a shield in the form of a friend.

Loralee tore off a handful of condoms. We shoved them into our pockets.

The condoms came into our lives like Chekhov's gun—our thoughts revolved around when they'd fire, who'd hold the weapon. We carried them so our parents wouldn't find them.

Then my mom broke open my chest of journals.

I came home from school and she was on the computer. The internet was new, and my mom was addicted to chat rooms. Her addiction was good for us, because it kept her entranced, though it tied up the phone line. Usually, I could go upstairs unnoticed. This time, she swung around, "Are you having sex?"

"No!"

"Show me what's in your pockets, slut." She stood, walked towards me, and began to grab my jeans. I pulled away. She charged, grabbed the waist, and grasped onto the button. She began to fiddle it. She unzipped them. I was crying. I didn't know why she needed to undress me. But I kept the pocket with the condoms out of her grasp, punching and kicking. Finally, I scrambled into the bathroom, locking it. She banged on the door. She said not to think about flushing them because I'd clog the toilet. I dug them out of my pocket, shoved them into my sock, flushed the toilet, and prayed.

I came out and showed my empty pockets. My mother rushed in to search the trash and plunge the toilet. I hid the condoms. She made me stay up until my dad returned; she told him she'd found my journal, that I was planning to have sex with one of the n*****s.

To have my sexuality paraded in front of my father before I had sex rattled me beyond anything I'd experienced. I'd idolized him when young. He was abusive, and he never protected me, but still, I loved him.

I felt love turn into a hard pit when his gaze fell on me, and he called me a "n***** loving whore."

It was one of the only times I saw my father cry. He sobbed high-pitched sobs that turned his voice into a wailing violin played by a child's hand. I could barely make out his sentences. He called me "kinky." He screamed, "I went to the military with those monsters! Do you know what they think? They think you're holes! For their dicks!"

When your father looks at you and calls you a hole, something foundational breaks.

He looked me in the eyes, "No white man will ever love you."

To my father, this meant no good man will ever love you.

To me, this meant *no one* will ever love me.

14

He was a handsome boy. He always had on name brand t-shirts: Nike, Adidas, Fila. He played basketball, had a lean but muscular physique, the flashiest shoes. He was Mexican; his tan shimmered as sweat beads rolled down his back. He wore Tommy Hilfiger cologne. I'd go to the mall and ask for samples so I could smell him.

I was smothered before he ever touched me.

In Human Growth and Development, we were given plastic baby dolls that cried sporadically; we took them home and had to stop whatever we were doing to stick a key in its back until it stopped. This was supposed to teach us how parenthood robs time and sleep. I chose a doll with a tan complexion. Some boys mocked me. "Of course you would," they scoffed. I named it Damien. I pretended it was his, that I wasn't a virgin, but a woman who went to bed nightly with the worth that must come from being pinned underneath a man's body. I held the key in the baby for hours, patiently, knowing my husband put baby after baby into me because he loved me—I'd sacrifice anything for it. I'd lose sleep, leap out of the shower covered in suds to attend to his child. I could be good. I could be.

He stared when I walked by—an intense, unblinking glare that began at my chest and moved up. He never spoke. Somebody told me I named my baby another name for the devil. His dark eyes severed my motor skills. He was a boy, so to a girl he was a god.

15

His name was Miguel, a popular boy.

When I remember, I see his thick eyebrows.

I see the way they arched in a shape that scared me.

When he wanted something, they arched.

The eyebrows were severe.

His muscles were severe.

I don't remember him smiling. In photos, he's as stoic as the dead.

When his voice emerged from the cave of him, it was deep, unnerving, full of commands.

Whispers dashed through hallways like skittering mice: *rapist*.

I thought they meant underage sex, statutory rape. I thought some girl probably didn't want her parents to know she had sex, so she said rape.

A rapist wouldn't be handsome. Wouldn't be popular. Wouldn't be dressed well. Wouldn't play basketball. Wouldn't be him.

Everyone seemed to agree. The girl in the center of the whispers was bullied.

He was a boy, so to a girl he was a god.

16

This is important. He was a boy, not a man. This was a boy who did this to me. He was younger by a year. That would make him 14. That would make him just a boy. That would make him just a child. When I taught 14-year-olds as an adult, they were so small, like fragile china dolls. They needed delicate care. A cruel word could slug them so hard they'd sob for an hour during lunch, question if life was worth living. A little love on them was promptly soaked up like the thirst of droughted soil. He was 14, so he was a boy, so he was a child—do you know what that means? I can barely face it. I didn't for the next 25 years. It means that a cold bulb took root in him as a baby. He couldn't bloom. He must've been planted in a dark room. What are we doing to our boys that they can only love with venom? I want to show you how his poison paralyzed me for decades, that when he took me to his room, it went dark and I never left. I couldn't bloom. I almost died. He was a boy, so to a girl he was a god.

How could a god?
How could a boy?
How could a boy?

17

I remember different versions, a different boy at different times.

Actually, I don't always remember a boy.
Sometimes I remember a wolf.

Always I remember ghosts.

18

Growing up, I had a toy called a View-Master. It resembled bulky 3-D glasses. You held it to your eyes and put a cardboard disk inside that had film negatives. You'd click the button on the side to turn the reel, instantly transported into a colorful 3D landscape.

I flip through my memories like that now. *Click,* his arched eyebrows, *click,* my lungs filling with his Tommy cologne, *click,* his hand reaching for my back pocket, *click,* pulling me by my jeans into a room, *click,* his smooth, bare torso writhing over me, *click,* The Notorious B.I.G.'s "Fucking You Tonight," *click,* blood, *click,* Loralee and a boy, *click,* Loralee's anger, *click,* the next reel is empty. *Click,* empty, *click,* empty, *click.*

There's nothing else.

That would be how I remembered losing my virginity for the next twenty five years, until I cracked open my journals like Pandora's Box.

19

As teenagers in the 90s, we mixed ancient with innovative. We sought psychics in AOL chat rooms, found spells on websites, bought ritual materials at Target, hovered over a homemade Ouija board with a lip gloss lid as planchette.

Loralee and I were told we looked like witches. We weren't trying to: we wore baggy jeans and coveted name brand t-shirts. I wore my hair straight and long. She wore hers straight and chin length. We both dyed our hair blonde with hydrogen peroxide. What likely cinched the witch accusations was our burgundy matte lipstick—the hot shade of the 90s—and our stoicism.

We were routinely bullied. Having become sexually active thrust us into a vicious rumor mill no child is prepared for. We responded like steel. We glared at anyone who said anything. When groped, we learned not to flinch, to keep walking, to not show emotion. No one could see us hurt.

We were hurt in ways we didn't even know how to admit.

We survived through friendship and avoiding or numbing our pain.

The Craft came out the year I lost my virginity. The movie is about four high school outcasts who seek witchcraft to enact revenge on their abusers. Loralee and I didn't consciously connect our traumas to the screen. We'd never heard the words "slut shaming," and we were in denial about the injustice of our bullying: we were just regular girls in a regular world that wasn't kind to regular girls.

But something unconscious was ignited by witches. For so many girls coming of age while lodged in the jaw of patriarchy, the figure of the witch speaks to longing: a power beyond what boys had. A power to control boys.

We'd walk through the hallways and hear people say: "Don't they look like the girls from *The Craft*? Don't they look scary?"

For Halloween, we decided to dress like them: short black skirts, knee high socks, form-fitting collared shirts, thick lines of black eyeliner.

It's one thing to look like trendy witches, but we wanted magic.

Loralee was not my only friend, though at school and outside we were inseparable. The tie that bound us was our race. The girls who accepted us were the other girls who were overly sexualized, slut shamed, and harassed: girls of color.

I've thought a lot about how I ended up one of the only white girls in a clique of girls who were black, biracial, Latinx, and Middle Eastern. At the time, it seemed like it just happened: one day I walked into drama class in middle school and sat next to a beautiful girl with long braids sitting alone. I thought perhaps I'd befriended her as rebellion towards my parents. But nothing racial in America is by chance: we were living out a history we were wholly unaware of. The past and the present are constantly commingling in the racial realities of our lives.

There are other things we had in common: racists looked at us with disgust and we had large breasts. With the latter came harassment. All of us were known as sexual girls before we had sex.

I was a white girl attracted to boys outside of my race, and I had a body shape that matched more closely with my black girlfriends than any of the 1990s white beauty standards that our white supermodels flaunted. As such, we got lumped into a vicious racial history of thought that stretched hundreds of years before us, one that we were wholly ignorant of, one that made us into oversexualized myths in our school hallways, one that turned us into training ground for the sexualities of boys. What tormented us most was why we weren't lovable.

We had no answers, so we'd search desperately for magic.

One glance at the cafeteria made the racial politics of the white suburbs clear—the few girls of color sat in the doorway of the cafeteria on a bench. Most students who weren't white seemed to be automatic friends. Being one of only a few white girls accepted into their inner circle was an insulation, as the girls generally stuck up for us when we were bullied, having zero tolerance for any disrespect towards them or their friends.

One day, a Mexican girl, Mandy, invited me over after school. We sat at her computer trying to get on the internet. In those days, you kept trying until you heard a satisfying beep and scramble sound that meant you'd entered into a magical universe. We went to chat rooms: *Does anyone have a love spell?*

We got a spell that was simple and required things we had around the house. We followed directions carefully, ending up on our knees in her backyard, burying ashes of paper we'd burned with our crushes' names written in lipstick with our kisses.

Mandy's crush was Robby, a new Mexican boy with curly hair and a penetrating stare who was seamlessly absorbed into the popular crowd. He never spoke to us, but he stared at us and sometimes spanked us as we walked by.

The next day, I stood with Mandy and Loralee at Mandy's locker when Robby walked up. He looked at Mandy, grabbed her by the waist, pressed her up against the locker, and kissed her. The bell rang and he walked away, leaving Mandy disoriented and swooning.

In class, I sat behind Mandy, "Do you realize what this means?"

"You think it was the spell?"

"He didn't even say anything! A trance!"

Robby continued to pounce Mandy in the hallway for weeks; they eventually had sex. He stopped talking to her shortly after. We couldn't understand what went wrong. We fervently did more spells. Nothing worked. But we held onto Robby as proof of our power, if only we could harness it.

We had no idea: boys take their power. They don't need charms to manifest it.

20

Boys take their power—in that taking, they take other things with them.

One day, I walked into driver's ed, and a boy belted out, "I saw your videotape!"

When I remember this, I can viscerally feel my body as if it's suspended in air because the ground has vanished. Disoriented, I responded, "What?"

"Did you and Loralee go to Miguel's yesterday?"

We had.

"Did you have sex with Miguel?"

I did.

"Did Miguel say, 'What's my name?'"

I sat down, dizzy, a wave of nausea overcame me. The whole class had their eyes on me. I suddenly felt naked. Had they all seen me? Had they all seen my imperfect body having sex for only the second time in my life?

The rest of the day was a whirlwind of trying to discover if the videotape was a rumor. Our calls to Miguel went unanswered, but finally a sympathetic boy agreed to call my ex, Grayson, on three-way calling while I listened.

Grayson gleefully admitted that he watched us have sex from inside Miguel's closet, how when he heard I'd lost my virginity, he got angry that it wasn't to him, so he reached out to Miguel and orchestrated revenge. He brought his mother's camcorder, propped it next to the computer, and sat in the closet as Miguel performed—slapping me and instructing me to say his name. I stammered like the inexperienced child I was, "Miguel, your name is Miguel." Grayson explained how I wanted to keep my shirt on, and how Miguel had pulled it up to ensure they all got "the view." Anyone could see it for $2.

Boys take their power, and sometimes they take things we can never get back.

I remember the fear the next time I walked into school, as if everyone was looking at me, as if they'd all seen my naked body and found me disgusting. I put myself on auto-pilot and walked robotically through the hallways, betraying no emotion, no fear, and no shame, but inside, my body was a hurricane, a torrential downpour was lifting off the roof of any shelter of self respect I'd known.

In my journals, I say, "What can I do?" I write a lot about Dee, about missing her, about wanting to tell her everything, about wanting to show her my new journal, about wondering if she missed me too. The experience of revenge porn, on some level, made me understand we were more alike than different.

The videotape would follow me all through high school. Even boys from middle school, lured by older boys, would walk by the store I worked at and point, "It's the girl from the video!" They'd erupt into an echo of laughter and run off.

Then one day a boy recognized me and put his eyes on me in such an intense way that I never wanted him to stop watching me.

His name was C.D. 24 years later, his ghost would save my life.

21

The second day of 10th grade. Loralee and I did our regular hallway pacing. "Hi Logan!" Loralee paused, looked at the boy next to him.

"Hi C.D."

They walked past. "Who's *that*?" I asked.

"C.D. He's a freshman. Boy, has he grown."

I looked back—the thickness of his chestnut brown hair, perfectly styled with gel; the sheen of his flashy blue shirt; the loose folds of his baggy jeans; the softness of his light brown eyes; the glow of his tan. I was entranced.

She gave me a look that said, *Snap out of it.*

Days later, we ran into them again.

"Hi Logan," I said. "And...what's your name?"

He smiled so big that it startled me.

"C.D."

"Isn't your name Carl?" I'd looked him up in Loralee's middle school yearbook.

"Yes," his smile continued to pour into me.

"What's the D for?"

"My middle name."

"Cool," I said. "Does anyone have a dollar? I'm thirsty."

They nodded apologetically.

The next day, I ran into C.D. again. "Hey, are you still thirsty?"

I looked at Loralee, confused. "No, I eventually got a pop."

C.D. looked disappointed. "Well, I asked my grandma for a dollar for you." He pulled the dollar out of his pants and thrust it at me.

From that day on, C.D. stopped me daily either to give me a soda or a dollar. "He's strangely obsessed with your hydration," Loralee said.

I thought it was strange too— I'd never had a boy be kind towards me. My journals are peppered with references to the way he smiled, the way his eyes sparkled, the way his gentle voice quivered when he said my name.

22

How to resurrect the dead? How to watch them walk across your pages like you're a voodoo priestess controlling them? You can make them whoever you want. Take away their flaws, exaggerate their kindnesses. But love needs no exaggeration in the heart of the grieving. When I put C.D. back together on the page, it's as if I'm taking a weapon out of my body and bleeding out memories that could kill me. I don't want to be that girl again, because if I inhabit her, then I have to recognize all the ways she was hurt that were beyond her wisdom to cope with. I have to admit that it wasn't just C.D. who died, that his death was an atomic bomb and none of us standing close to him survived. All of us died in different ways. I'm not just resurrecting him: I'm attempting to take the small wreckage of my life and put it back together like a tiny ship in a bottle to cast off into the sea, in hopes that whoever finds it will see how to rip out the rotten roots of what killed him, what killed me, what's killing us all.

And ghosts must do again what gives them pain.

I rise from the grave of my long sleep, once again, and wander back to the places where the arrow took me out, straight through the neck.

Walk with me.

You see this wound? It's festered.

23

E leven months. That's the span of time that I knew C.D. For a teenager, eleven months in love is a whole eternity— it's being tossed into an ocean whose floor is miles below when you can't yet swim.

Those months began with a boy who brought me sodas, who visited me at work, who stole a ring I said I liked, who worried about me as the cold fall air moved in, offering his jacket, instructing me to keep it. A boy who called and swore he wasn't like other boys, wasn't like his cousin, Jason—"a man whore," he said. A boy who said I was the most beautiful girl he'd ever seen and that what was done to me with the video was cruel, promising never to be cruel to me. A boy who begged me to say I love him. A boy who showed up on my doorstep with his cousin late nights asking me to hang out, telling me I was beautiful with no makeup and my oversized t-shirt as pajamas. A boy who asked me to go out with him in front of his friends, whose friends urged, "Say yes! He talks about you all the time! It's annoying."

My favorite memory of C.D. is from those exhilarating moments before you know that your beloved loves you back, when the love is just beginning to brew those tiny bubbles of water in a watched pot, when you're so new to the idea of being loved that it's as if you've just been pushed out of an airplane and have to pray that the parachute of love is going to inflate above your head before you collide with earth.

I'd been spending time with C.D., his cousin Jason, his best friend Logan, and some of their other friends. C.D. lived with his grandmother

47

in the trailer park by my house. His cousin lived there too. I never knew why C.D. lived with his grandmother—the only thing C.D. ever told me about his mother is that I looked like her. His father lived in Florida—C.D. only said he was an abusive addict and he hated him.

One day, while we were walking home, I asked C.D. to walk me to my house. We parted from his friends and walked down my street. When we got there, I said I wasn't ready to leave him. He told me to walk him to the end of my street towards his house. We walked. We got there and decided that he should walk me back. We walked. We got to my door and decided that I should walk him to the end of my street. We walked. We walked and we walked. Every time we'd get to the end, I'd turn to him, look up, and he'd say, "Don't look at me like that. I can't resist." I'd ask him to give me a hug. We'd embrace a long time. I'd tell him I can't let go. He'd pick me up and start to carry me. We'd decide to walk again, just one more time. When we finally parted, he held my waist, looked into my face, and gave me the gentlest kiss.

C.D., Jason, and Logan smoked weed daily. Having been raised in the era of The War on Drugs, I thought weed was a stone's throw from a life of crime.

But I was curious. I told C.D. that I needed to try everything so I could write about it, so C.D. and Logan taught Loralee and I how to smoke. We thought getting high meant that we'd have the sensation of flying; we were disappointed when that didn't happen, but the boys were amused by our stoned confusion and our cravings for snacks.

When C.D. and I were able to be alone—when my mom left the house for a few hours—I lit candles, turned on my blacklight, and put on some R&B music. Neon posters glowed on every wall and my ceiling was covered in fluorescent stars. We made out for hours. I laid my head on his chest and heard his heartbeat. C.D. wanted to have sex, but he "didn't want to do anything that made me uncomfortable." No boy had ever given me the option of feeling comfortable. We kissed and touched until our lips were numb and raw.

We loved each other with the electroshock madness of kids with attachment wounds.

It didn't last long.

24

It took only weeks for C.D. to beg me to tell him I loved him.
In months, he became the boy of my dreams.

When C.D. loved me, I loved him more.

He looked at me in a trance, said, "I hope I never hurt you."
"You wouldn't!"

Of course he would.
It was in his nature.

He was a boy, so to a girl he was a god.

He dumped me, said I was obsessive, said I broke his heart, said he hated me.

When C.D. hated me, I hated myself more.

25

C.D. may have hated me, but he saw me almost daily: I refused to give up my friendships with his cousin and best friend. C.D.'s cousin, Jason, was just as attractive, but more bold in his flirtations. Jason had the ego and charisma of a young Justin Bieber, flirting coyly with a sharp-witted humor towards every girl. C.D. always questioned: "Are you sure you don't like my cousin more than me?" After we broke up, I flirted obnoxiously in front of C.D.

My world was the building of a cyclone that would see me rip through decades, turning over foundations without looking back. The winds were just stirring; the dry leaves whirled around my body, crunched and caught in my hair. I was at the center, anchored by the buried traumas taking root: I heard and saw little else.

If I'd been more aware, maybe I could've realized what was happening to C.D. The signs are in my journals, but I processed nothing. I'd recreated C.D. I made him into the perfect boy whose perfection was polluted by a proximity to imperfect me. I stirred a hatred for myself to a boil through loving him. In the hologram of perfection that I projected onto him, I masked all of his open wounds.

C.D. changed rapidly—his style flipped from a hip-hop influence to the skater culture that was adding a new texture to the 90s. He started wearing beanie hats, a hemp necklace with Jimi Hendrix, and skater t-shirts. His best friend, Logan, whose beauty rivaled all the heartthrobs, was the poster child of skater culture—chill, angst-laced apathy, stoned from morning until night. C.D. began to match Logan exactly.

Then C.D. dropped out of school and began going to the alternative school for troubled youth. This baffled me: C.D. seemed perfectly capable of high school.

Then he began to get mean. He brooded and lashed out, judging us for doing things he didn't find fun or talking about things that didn't matter. I'd have moments of laughter with him, only for him to follow it with an insult.

Months earlier, C.D. and Jason had come to my door at night. I stood outside shivering in my pajamas as they told me that their grandma died. C.D. found her body. "Did you cry?" I asked C.D.

"When I was alone."

One day, the boys were playing basketball in a driveway. I saw C.D. sneak off into a shed. I followed.

He looked at me with a weary, uninterested acknowledgment. "Want one?" He offered a cigarette.

"No."

He lit his, squinting. "So, what's up, Anne?"

"Not much." We stood in awkward silence. "Take off your hat. I love your hair."

"No."

"Please, C.D. I'll climb over all this stuff to get to you to pull it off."

"Do it," he dared. I climbed over a lawn mower and a pile of rakes to get to the wheelbarrow he sat inside and pulled off the beanie.

"C.D., why don't you come back to school?"

"Because it sucks."

"Why?"

"Because it does."

"Let me see your hands."

"Why are you asking that?"

"Somebody told me I should see your hands."

C.D. was silent.

"Please," I pleaded. He held them out. I gently rubbed them, dizzy to be touching him, steadying myself for what I held.

"Why do you have cuts and burns?"

He pulled his hands away and put one hand on my back, rubbing up and down, as if I was the one who needed comfort.

51

"Don't worry about it. I just get mad sometimes."

I didn't worry about it.

For decades, the fact that I didn't worry about it would enter my head like a spontaneous tornado and I'd be sucked into its vacuum, a piece of debris from a wreck.

26

But this is a story about girls. Boys hold them in their palms like something illegal, light them like firecrackers, send them barreling through the night sky. If only we could have seen ourselves the way people saw us—hypnotic, dangerous, aflame. We only felt our burning from the inside out.

Girls deemed sluts in childhood might as well be the same as pups tossed into an illegal fighting ring. We had no agency of our own: whenever a boy plucked us up by the neck, we went limp. We did what they wanted. We sometimes barked but never bit—we knew better. They'd trained us to learn the rules, identify our enemy, injure, take every kill shot—the blood sport of girlhood.

Boys would ask us about each other: "She's a hoe, don't you think? Don't you think you're smarter? Do you really trust her?"

I defended my girlfriends—a sense of sisterhood meant survival to me. I now know that sisterhood is more than survival—it's sacred.

But for boys, what use is the sacred when the profane belongs to you?

I started hearing things that Loralee said—that she thought I was ugly, fat, boring, slutty. I didn't believe them.

Then Loralee started offering C.D. a ride home from school. I rode the bus home alone, jealousy coursing.

Then C.D. told me she had a secret: she'd had sex with my ex who'd cheated on me.

I knew it was true. It was in the realm of what the boys who used us would do. Many times, I'd been called and propositioned by boys Loralee was talking to. One boy would show up at my house on a moped and ask to take me around the neighborhood. I hopped on the back as he zoomed us out to the country by some railroad tracks, stopped, asked me to sit in front of him, felt up my shirt, and kissed my neck. I protested, but the next time he showed up, I flung myself on the back of that moped again. Anything was better than home. Every grope from a boy felt like I might be lovable, like I might exist.

I was no saint and neither was Loralee—that's why we were friends. We were girls with no boundaries, no roadmaps for love, no education on consent, which is to say we were caged, and like caged girls are trained to do, we turned on each other—clawed and foaming at the mouths.

I stopped talking to Loralee. Soon, just like Dee, she stopped coming to school, transferred schools, and graduated from a different high school.

What does this world do to girls to turn our love into a dogfight that we walk away from scarred and limping?

27

Even after the video, I'd been lured by Grayson's flirtations. I had sex with him once—then he stopped speaking to me. Miguel and I had sex three times, but I hated him. In my journals, I say I've "mostly forgotten the details."

Then I found myself at a party where Miguel was present. He locked eyes in a way that told me I needed to get out quickly. I wandered outside to talk to people. Miguel followed. I moved away. He moved closer. I squirmed until he eventually had me pressed up against the door of a garage. He opened the door; I tumbled inside. He pressed his back against the door so I couldn't leave.

In my journal, I mention this casually: *"Miguel tried to rape me in a garage and I was scared out of my wits. I really thought he was going to make me do something until Chad knocked on the door and he pulled his pants up and let me out."*

That's all I say. I don't revise my previous judgments about the girl accusing him of rape.

28

But something new started to come out of me: rage.

My mother's hatred of me felt pure and deep for as long as I've had memory. I watched my sister often get hugged and kissed; my mother always said outright she favored her. She was abusive to us both, but I triggered her vitriol more. I had no memory of her touching me with any tenderness whatsoever, only anger. I felt I didn't even have a chance to *become* an individual before my mother told me everything about me was wrong.

When I was young, I did everything to meet her standards, but no matter how well I obeyed rules, performed in school, or praised her, the goalpost for lovability kept moving. I believed my father loved me, but he ignored her abuses, no matter how bad it got or how I screamed for help. And he never gave me any physical or emotional affection either. But because he didn't beat me as often and seemed more reasonable than her, I thought maybe he loved me a little. At least, I needed to believe that to survive.

By teen years, I was no longer helplessly taking my mother's beatings, but pulling her hair, clawing her face, kicking her stomach. One day, my mother was choking me, and I snapped: my mind struck a brand new note.

Kill her.

I wrestled her off me and ran to the kitchen and grabbed a knife. Red-faced and heaving, I transformed into a different person. I had no fear. I had only a boiling tar pit of anger in my belly burning me alive—I needed to drown her in it.

"Don't fucking touch me." I held the knife, and, in that moment, I knew I'd do it. I'd stab her and I'd not stop stabbing until she died.

I could see the surprise and fear in her eyes—she didn't move. My dad, who'd been ignoring us, slowly approached and removed the knife from my hand, commanding me to my room. My sister followed; we locked the door behind us.

My twelve year old sister was like my surrogate mother. I sobbed on my bed. She tried to pat my back.

"Don't touch me!" I snapped. "I don't want anyone to touch me!"

I wailed this refrain into my pillow repeatedly.

"Okay, Annie. I won't," she said tenderly, "I won't touch you."

I cried until I was too tired to expel anymore pain; my sister sat through it. I finally asked, "Would you love me even if I killed someone?"

"Yes," she didn't hesitate, "I know you'd have good reason."

I remember this moment as the first time that love felt tangible: the tar in my stomach stopped bubbling.

29

It was the summer of 1998, and another young woman was recorded against her will, but this one was paraded in front of the world.

Monica Lewinsky was a 22 year old intern who worked in the White House under Bill Clinton. That summer, audio recordings of calls were released in which Lewinsky privately confided details about her affair with the most powerful 49 year old man in the world.

The Clinton-Lewinsky scandal fit perfectly into America's rabid obsession with clamping a young woman in the jaws of Puritanical hypocrisy and shaking her vigorously until she's a limp pest at our feet.

The scandal was made more compelling for its tawdry details: this didn't resemble a passionate love affair, but an insidious power imbalance in which an older, powerful man commanded a young, naive subordinate to bow to his sexual whims. The nighttime talk show hosts were a circus of slut jokes about semen stains. The president, who was diverting blame onto the woman thrust into the spotlight, was going to be impeached.

I didn't see a parallel between myself and Monica. My vision was shaped by misogyny: self loathing was my guiding principle. I was years away from any exposure to feminist thought: the evil of her unbridled sexuality seemed unquestioned. She was even mocked for not being beautiful enough to desire. Slut shaming her was an anchor we all drowned by.

The last time I saw C.D., I'd gone over to Jason's, hoping C.D. would be there. C.D. answered, looking happy to see me. He asked me to sit with him. He pulled out cigarettes and handed me one. While C.D. and I had been civil, I never knew if he'd be cold or ignore me. This time, I saw something softer registering in his face; I perceived it to mean his feelings were returning.

The news chattered: "I did not have sexual relations with that woman." We'd been hearing that soundbite for months.

"Speaking of sluts, you aren't friends with Loralee anymore?"

"No," I said.

"That's good."

"Why good?"

"She was holding you back."

"People say we're just alike."

"Only if they're looking at your bodies."

I laughed. "What else do you look at?"

"You don't need to be around a girl with no ambition or talent."

When C.D. said that, it filled me up in a way that nothing else could.

"You're going to do big things," he said.

"You will too."

He looked at me with a subtle smile and took a drag from his cigarette.

"I'm moving soon," C.D. said.

"Jason says you're just visiting your dad."

"I'm not coming back."

"Because you hate school?"

"Because I hate everything."

"What about Logan?"

"We aren't friends anymore. You know what he said to me? He said he thinks it's okay for a man to suck another man's dick."

"You think he was trying to have sex with you?"

C.D. shrugged.

We smoked cigarettes until my curfew. As I stood, C.D. said, "What, I don't get a hug?"

He hugged me tight and long, kissed my forehead, reviving me— the world felt beautiful again. He said, "You're not what they say."

For many years, as I watched the massive shark jaw of misogyny rise from sea to shining sea like it did with Monica, I survived by replaying C.D.'s last words: *You're not what they say.*

30

My paternal grandparents lived on a lake and had a wicker basket full of seashells. I'd go through them with my grandfather; he taught me how the shells used to be homes for creatures. He held up a sand dollar, shook it next to my ear. I heard the faint rattle of its porcelain doves.

I took it in my hand, caressed its chalky exterior.

When I touched C.D.'s face in the casket, it had the texture of that sand dollar—stiff, coarse, hard to imagine alive. His face was slightly bloated. Only his thick, silky hair felt alive and familiar. I ran my hands through it. I bent myself over his corpse and sobbed. I felt relieved that he wasn't in a suit, that they put him in his favorite shirt, that they let him rest dressed as a child.

Jason stood in front of the casket with an exhausted look of shock. He wandered the funeral home hugging those who reached out as if he didn't fully register our presence. He picked up a ribbon on the casket that said "cousin," held it in a trance.

Logan also appeared shocked and didn't say anything. When I saw him standing behind me, I muttered his name through tears and leaned against his chest. His hug was a clenching. Eventually my legs gave out and I nearly collapsed, but Logan caught me, lifted me back up, continued to rub my back.

To write these memories is to dig the sand dollar of this grief out of the shore of my body, to hear porcelain doves rattle in the fragile skeleton that's left of my long-lost girlhood: C.D., Jason, Logan, Home.

61

31

LETTER TO A GHOST: C.D.
I loved you so much that I thought the world should've stopped for you. That's what I remember most about the grief: waking up, remembering you were dead, and feeling stunned that the sun still rose, that people were going about their lives, that the whole world wasn't weeping. My mind transformed into a cave in which only memories of your voice echoed through darkness. I wrote all I could remember in journals. It was the only part of you I had the power to keep alive.

I found out when Mandy called. She kept saying your name. "What? Say it!"

"He's dead. Overdosed."

I hung up and ran to my living room, grabbed the newspaper, turned to obituaries, and found your name. I threw the paper, fell to the ground, and screamed.

I screamed something bestial. I'd never experienced such pain.

For a time, I told myself it was an accident. The idea of suicide was too horrific to consider. The details I knew were that you went to your dad's in Florida. Your dad was a heroin addict being treated with methadone. You snuck out, took all of his methadone, came home late, and never woke up.

Jason said you didn't commit suicide, but he also thought it didn't make sense: you'd both been instructed lifelong never to touch those pills your fathers took. "Why would he take all of them?"

Over the years, details haunted. How often you needed to be high. Your grandmother's dead body. The alternative school. The cuts and burns. The Prozac. Ending your friendship with Logan. The gentle way you said goodbye. Giving your music collection away. The fact that you called Jason two days before you died and told him you were dropping out of school, never returning. The fact that you'd told me the same. The amount of trauma in you and Jason's lives.

Was it not trauma that brought us together as children? What else did we have in common but that? We hardly spoke of it, but we were just kids trying to grow up amidst poverty, addiction, and abuse.

What muzzle did it have on your pains that you couldn't speak, that you could only find escape in drugs and anger? We were raised in cages and we performed at the clap of the whips that trained us. Our traumas were barbed wire around our tongues.

I began to believe that you left us on purpose.

What that meant shaped me profoundly.

If you killed yourself, that meant that my love wasn't good enough to save you. If I'd been good enough, we wouldn't have broken up months before you died. I would've been able to make you happy.

I already had reason to hate myself: my parents laid the foundation, but your death cemented it—*I am unlovable.*

What does a girl do in a world that rejects her?

I ignited. I blazed wildfire through the years, left whole decades behind me as ash.

I don't blame you for the pain that served as my broken compass, steering me further into a disorienting forest that I ripped through as flame. I never blamed you. You were always my most sacred pain.

I mourned for over a year. I'd wake at night, curl into my pink blow up chair and cry until exhaustion took me out. Those nights, the thought first started to bloom, a tiny new bud in my brain: *Kill yourself.*

My mother read my journals. She said you were a useless person. She said you were most certainly in Hell. I wrote angry letters to God on your behalf.

I began to write suicide letters to my sister and friends, to take scissors and saw them against my wrists, to stop wearing my seatbelt. I started reading books about suicidal girls: *The Bell Jar; Girl, Interrupted; Prozac Nation.*

I found this in my old journals:

I started writing suicide notes again, but I had a dream that I received a card from C.D. that said, 'Don't stop.'

It was the same message you'd give me 24 years later.

There's a poem that reminds me of you. It's called "What the Living Do" by Marie Howe. The poem traces the monotony of life's daily annoyances, as the speaker addresses someone who died. At the end, the speaker sees her own reflection:

> "I catch a glimpse of myself in the window glass,
>> say, the window of the corner video store, and I'm
>> gripped by a cherishing so deep
>
> for my own blowing hair, chapped face, and unbuttoned coat
>> that I'm speechless:
> I am living. I remember you."

I am living. I remember you. It's what the living do.

When I look in the mirror and see my pain looking back at me, having resurrected this wound again, I see so clearly—

a cherishing so deep.

Beloved wounded child, first love, ghost: I remember you.

Sometimes, in remembering, we find ourselves.

32

A *memory: Jason, C.D., and Anne, eating McDonald's.*
C.D.: "Let's smoke a square."
Jason: "Let's go."
They start walking. C.D. points to a pretzel shop.
C.D.: "Sweet Annie's. Like you."
C.D. drapes his arm over Anne's shoulder.
C.D.: "Must be named after you."
Jason: "C.D., you're so corny."
They walk outside to a parking lot. There's a light dusting of snow on the ground. It's dark. C.D. and Jason each light a cigarette. Anne pulls out her compact.
C.D.: "She's putting on makeup like she needs it."
Anne: "I do."
C.D.: "You're beautiful without it."
C.D. leans in to whisper in Jason's ear.
Anne: "Don't tell secrets!"
Jason: "He's telling them about you!"
C.D.: "I just said you have a nice body."
Anne rolls her eyes.
Anne: "I'm so cold!"
C.D.: "You want my sweatshirt?"
Anne nods. C.D. hands Anne his cigarette. He takes off his shirt. Anne takes a drag of his cigarette. He hands it to her.
Anne: "No, I don't want it."
C.D.: "Why'd you let me take it off?"

65

Anne shrugs.

Jason: "Just take it, Anne!"

Anne: "I just wanted to see if you'd do it. I smoked some of your cigarette."

C.D. looks at Jason. Jason shrugs.

C.D.: "I have an idea—I'll hug you and then you'll be warm."

C.D. wraps his arms around Anne. He stands like that for an awkwardly long time. Anne exaggerates her shivering. Jason steps in and wraps his arms around them.

They all burst into laughter.

Let it end there. Let me stay. You stay too. Stay with these children. Let this be their story. Just three lively children without a care in the world except for how much they need to be in each other's orbit. There are millions of children like them right this moment. They've always existed. Children who think themselves bad, because something told them they were; children who are only mimicking badness, because how could they be bad? They're children. They don't know it yet, but these will be some of their greatest lessons about love in their lives.

Let us stay here when they think they have so much life ahead.

C.D. only had six months.

Let me stay here, in both of their arms.

Jason had only a couple years.

Let it end here.

The energy of pain can only be healed—it cannot be escaped. An overdose is a landmine, intending to destroy its own pain but only expelling it as shrapnel into the bystanders who walk away maimed with various injuries, some fatal.

Jason was maimed in the worst way.

I received this letter from Jason 13 years after C.D. died:

Anne,

  Hey sweetheart, how's everything? I hope my scribe finds you in the best of spirits.

  I've thought about you a lot over the years we've been apart. I always had a thing for you, probably still do a little bit. I never pursued anything because I knew how much C.D. loved you. We talked about you, so I backed off for my cousin/ brother. I miss that dude a lot.

  I remember hanging out at your house when your mom was gone. By the way, how's your family? A lot of stuff before I came to prison is a blur, probably because of all the drugs and alcohol I was using. I've never forgotten about you though.

  After C.D. died, I went downhill. I started hanging out with the people I grew up with when I was living on the South Side. I started gang banging and using drugs real heavy and everything spiraled out of control. I hated the world, I hated everybody, I hated myself. All that hate and anger turned to violence. I hurt a lot of people Anne. This is why I'm in prison now. I'm gonna keep this short, but this is what I did. After I got jumped by these guys at a party, I went and got my bangers and we went back to the house about 3 in the morning and I kicked the door down and beat two guys in the head with a folding lug wrench until I heard their heads mushing. My homeboy had to pull me off them. They're lucky I didn't take my gun because I wanted to. They were in the hospital for weeks. I'm lucky they didn't die.

  I told you my mother died, right? She had a massive heart attack. It was her fault. She was smoking a lot of crack and the doctor told her if she didn't stop she'd die. That hit me hard. It was even worse being in here and not being out there, you know? I bugged out.

  I don't know if I told you, but right before I called you, matter o' fact the day before I called you, I got out of the hole. I was in there for 5 months. The hole is the prison inside the prison. You're locked down 24 hours a day, 3 showers a week, no T.V., no recreation. Shit takes a toll on your mind.

  Anyway, the bitches broke my MP3 player, threw my food away, and took my shoes when they packed my property. I don't have money to replace that shit. I hustle for mine. I want to beat the shit out of that officer. These bitches are so disrespectful.

  Well, sweetheart, I just wanted to write you a little scribe letting you know I was thinking of you.

  Love,

   Jason

Don't let it end here.

Don't make me admit that when I looked directly at Jason's wound from C.D.'s death, it was too terrible to bear.

Don't make me admit that I should've seen it coming: Jason's dad was in prison. C.D.'s dad was in prison. We were raised in the quicksand of generational trauma—abandonment, abuse, poverty, addiction, violence, and incarceration raised us.

Don't make me ask you to confront what you know deep down too: that this system of brutality is designed to prey on the trauma of children like us—children with addictions and mental health issues, children with disabilities—that the system is one head of the monstrous Hydra that snaps its jaws on the necks of our most vulnerable.

We aren't an exceptional tragedy: we're an American story.

A howl of grief camouflaged as a man's rage is destined to break through silence eventually—murderous and terrifying.

I think of Jason all the time. I see us connected like two branches of the same tree of trauma. CD's death is the trunk that roots us and toxic masculinity is a rot that infects us. Jason's fate slithers up the side of the branch of my grief, coils, threatens to choke me out.

This is a story about ghosts.

33

Logan had only a few years left.

Whenever I see Jordan Catalano in *My So-Called Life*, I think of Logan's startling beauty— hemp choker necklaces, gauged earrings, beanies and silky hair, half-closed eyes that communicated an apathy that made girls ache. A blue-eyed smile alighting upon you and breaking his stoicism stirred a flurry of butterflies.

Yet Logan never chose any girl. Every beautiful girl flocked around him. Me too—I'd rush to his side when I saw him in the hallway, link my elbow with his, and walk. He'd smirk an amused smile, flattered. He'd usually invite me to smoke.

Logan had the prettiest girls at his beck and call, but he treated us all as friends. I wrote in my journal, "I don't think Logan likes girls. Not that he's gay, but that he's much more interested in weed and music."

I never spoke to Logan about his falling out with C.D. It went unsaid that he was grieving, regardless of what happened between them. At one point, Logan asked how I was handling everything. I said, "I don't sleep much. You?" He said, "I guess I'm okay."

Logan was notoriously hard to know. He was taciturn and mysterious, rebellious yet gentle, and often stoned and orbiting the moon.

C.D. died in the summer; by Thanksgiving, Logan and I were hanging out daily. He was picking me up in his car, taking me to the park, to his house, to the woods, some hidden place where we could park and smoke. In my grief, I wanted to be near people C.D. loved. For a time, our friendship became close, but it always felt like there was something simmering to a boil beneath the surface, too dangerous to touch.

One day he came over, put his arm around my waist, pulled me to him, and kissed me long and lingering. In my journal, I call it "insanity" and say "I never thought Logan liked girls. What is he doing with *me*?"

That fall, a young man name Matthew Shepard was approached by men at a bar and offered a ride home. They drove him to a remote rural area and proceeded to beat, torture, pistol whip, and rob him, tying him to a barbed wire fence and leaving him to die. Matthew Shepard was in a coma, covered in blood—only the marks of his tears left trails that gave a glimpse into the boy behind the battery. The witness who found him mistook him for a scarecrow. His injuries were deemed too severe for hospital intervention: he died days later, at 21 years old. He was HIV positive and gay. Candlelight vigils were held for him worldwide.

Do you ever think about all the boys who've paid the ultimate price for patriarchy? I catch them in my peripheries all the time. I'll wake in the middle of the night panicked and bump into their ghosts in the hallway as I go to the bathroom. They're so young.

I love them so much.

They had no idea how loved they were.

Six months after C.D. died, Logan got in a car accident and killed someone. Seven years after C.D. died, Logan died of a heroin overdose.

They had no idea how loved they were.

Logan and I would kiss for hours in his room. In my journal, I remark how he wanted to turn off the lights, how he'd peck kiss me rather than kiss passionately. We fizzled in a few month's time. I interpreted what happened as an expression of grief.

We lived in a world in which beautiful young boys were murdered for their sexuality, a world in which supporting gay rights could cause boys to lose their friends, a world in which boys couldn't speak about their pain without being seen as weak. The boys I loved suffered in silence, masking every pain with drugs or alcohol, building an arsenal of anger they'd eventually turn on themselves.

They had no idea how loved they were.
None of us did.

A memory: Anne and Logan in Logan's bed.
Logan: "I smell like cigarettes. I'm getting some gum."
He rolls over, grabs his jacket off the floor.
Anne: "I want some gum."
Logan: "I only have one piece. Are you cold?"
Logan unwraps the gum and starts chewing, laying down beside Anne.
Anne: "A little."
Logan: "I think you'll be warmer if you take off your pants."
Anne: "Really? Because I thought that was the opposite of how clothes worked."
Logan: "It's body heat. They teach it in Boy Scouts."
Anne: "Boy Scouts camp naked?"
Logan leans in towards Anne, kisses her, and drops his chewed gum in her mouth.
Anne: "Gross, Logan, take it back!"
Logan kisses Anne again, takes back the gum. He swallows it.
Anne: "You know gum takes seven years to digest?"
Logan: "Am I gonna die?"
Anne: "Uh huh."
Logan: "When?"
Anne: "Soon."
Logan: "Well, in that case, since I only have a short time left, let me just…."
They kiss.

Let me stay.
You stay too.
Stay with these children.
Let it end here.

It doesn't.
Logan's lifeless body, Jason's imprisoned body, C.D.'s lifeless body.
In the tree of our trauma, Logan's branch is struck by lightning, aflame.
The python chokes.

I black out.
This is a story about ghosts.

34

This is also a story about girls. The girls of color whose voices jingled through hallways, refusing to be muted; who moved their curves like dangerous weapons concealed beneath their clothes; who reached for me and I reached for them until we were a sturdy net, catching each other's bodies before they collide with the hardness of the world inherited.

Drea was my closest black girlfriend—she had large eyes with naturally long, perfectly curled lashes. She wore her hair braided. Like me, she had large breasts that kept boys circling hungrily. However, she'd generally freeze into a statue at their attempts to flirt; she intimidated people this way, staring blankly with indifferent eyes when they dared bother her.

One of Drea's trusted friends was a black boy named Beaux. Drea loved sitting next to him, erupting into laughter every few minutes. Beaux was one of those rare people who had so much charisma that everyone felt like they were his friend.

Beaux congregated with the popular crowd. But Beaux was a different kind of popular, the rare kind that can mingle into any social group. He had a bow-legged walk that he manipulated to look like an exaggerated cool strut, and he would meander from group to group, chatting it up, giving everyone nicknames, charming them with his signature chin rub and wink. He was the class clown, making teachers chuckle against their will.

Though he was no saint—he also engaged in the hardened, cruel toxic masculinity that indoctrinated us. I watched him fist fight more than once.

The Valentine's Day after C.D. died, I got a phone call at the clothing store. My manager summoned; Beaux was on the line.

"Hey, Anne. Drea's been telling me that you've been having a hard time. It's Valentine's Day, so I thought maybe Beaux Daddy should call and tell you not to be sad."

After that, Beaux and I chatted often, sometimes three-way calling with Drea. The two of them kept me going—but my private reality was dark. My eating disorder returned—when I wasn't starving myself, I was throwing up. It wasn't the fear of fat that motivated me, but the terror of living a life where I had no control. I kept the darkest passageways of my pain hidden and wandered them alone.

Eventually, like Drea, I was so comfortable talking to Beaux that I confided more.

"Anne," he said, "you shouldn't, like, get so wound up in death. I mean, yeah, you should be sad, but don't let it control you."

"Things at home are bad too. My parents are bad people."

"My stepdad's always drunk. He beats on my mom."

"Does he hit you?"

"I'm old enough to fight back."

"I fight with my mom too," I said.

"You have to think about other things."

"Like what?"

"Me!"

"Right. I forgot."

"How can you?"

I can't forget.

I can't forget what I discovered shortly after when Drea called me, sobbing.

"Beaux's dead. His stepdad stabbed him in his heart with a pocket knife."

35

Welcome. Come in. I didn't know we'd be here again. Sit. Are you thirsty? He's just in the other room. Ghosts don't go far. How do you like the place? Not much has changed. There isn't much time for renovations in a recurring nightmare. Do you hear him? In the other room?

That's a part of the nightmare—you can't.

But he's here, I promise. He lives here.

Which is why we have to run—we have to escape, like we did that night.

The car. Get in and go. I don't know where.

Drive until the sun goes down, until the street lights click on and blur your periphery like tunnels of neon light. Scream. Ask God why. No one's going to answer.

Pull into a church parking lot. Get into your backseat. Curl into yourself. Pray. It won't do anything for your pain but it'll give your pain something to do.

Ask God why everything you love dies. Ask God if you've really been such a bad girl, if you're really so impure and dirty and slutty and sinful that He treats you just like any other man, wringing your heart out like a dirty rag.

You need a mother.

Drive to the candle shop where she works. The pleasant scents will assault you with their optimism: there's no perfuming your rot. You walk into her work not as her daughter, but as the living dead. You cry out, "Mama."

She seems afraid. She ushers you into the back room and tells you to stop heaving. Finally you speak the name of the monster: grief. You tell her your friend was murdered by his father. You tell this to the woman who you've half believed would kill you too. You tell this to her because you have no other mother to tell.

"Is he black?"

Step away from her. It's not safe here.

"No." His corpse is in your mind, his hand on his wound. You want to put your hand over that heart, to tell it that it matters, that it shouldn't stop, can't stop, because you need it. "He was mixed," you lie.

He's here. This ghost. Say hello.

You lied about his race because you wanted your love for him, your grief, to matter.

Your mother's response: "A zit off the ass of the world."

Run as fast as you can. Out of that mall, out of that parking lot, out of that street, out of that city, out of this country, out of this rancid history, this raging furnace of hate.

Find your friends, your grieving friends. You walk in and slump onto the floor and sit in silence and don't move for the bell, shuffle reluctantly for the grief counselors, skip your classes, decide to go to Beaux's house.

You walk into his room and find your phone number next to his bed—maybe you were the last person he called. His mom tells you to take what you want. You take a rap he wrote—a sign of the poet in him that speaks to the poet in you. You stop at the stairs, look down, trip on your own feet.

His mom says, "We haven't cleaned the carpet yet."

Beaux's heart is a red stain beneath you.

He's here.

He's kneeling on the stairs, clutching his chest; he's dripping on your feet, looking up at you, stunned, "He cut me, Anne."

Do you see him?

He reaches for you. He pulls you down. You sink your knees into the blood stain and touch it.

You feel like you're dying too.

36

In 2014, Michael Brown, a black teenager, was shot six times by a white police officer—twice in the head—all in the front of his body, while on his knees with his hands in the air, prompting nationwide protests for racial justice.

Darren Wilson, the police officer who shot him, described Michael Brown's body in towering language, exaggerated and supernatural: "He looked like a possessed demon" and "I felt like I was a 5 year old holding onto Hulk Hogan."

In the white imagination of America, blackness has been framed as a thing to fear—there's an obsessive focus with the strength, power, and sexuality of black bodies that ensures that Americans will defend atrocious injustices, consistently adding grease to the already well oiled machine of racism.

When Beaux died, I thought I understood racism—it was blatant with my parents. I understood it as a character default, each individual's responsibility. Beaux's death taught me differently.

When I got a hold of the newspaper that reported Beaux's murder, I was speechless.

OCTOBER FIGHT SET SCENE FOR STABBING

Tragedy stalked the house at [address redacted] that night.

The teenager stood there, fists balled, an increasingly hostile man-child, recently running with a bad crowd, who regularly spewed threats and profanities at his parents.

The stepfather readied himself for confrontation. Forty years old and 25 lbs lighter than the boy he'd helped raise for the past decade, the man snarled that he was 'tired' and 'sick' of the teen's 'shit.'

A kitchen knife lay on a counter nearby. A folding pocket knife wasn't far away.

The 17 year old was almost begging to get cut. Then the man struck, quick as a flash, and the teen tasted blood.

[Stepfather's name redacted], 57, stabbed stepson Beaux to death inside their home.

The eerie preview to his death played out last December in Portage District Court, when [redacted] went on trial on a domestic violence charge for punching his stepson.

Beaux wasn't an excessively large boy. He wore glasses and a goofy grin at all times. The Beaux we knew wasn't a "man-child," but, indeed, a child, like the rest of us. The part about him recently running with a bad crowd was fiction.

And he wasn't "begging to be cut."

Only at the end of the article is it mentioned, in passing, that Beaux's stepfather had a history of domestic violence charges against Beaux, nor did it mention the slew of other times the police were called. There was no mention about how drunk he was. There was no mention that Beaux was protecting his mother.

In fact, there was no Beaux.

This writer delighted in the trauma that sucked us into a lifetime undertow. He described it as gore pornography, even going so far as to mention our friend tasting blood.

This was not truth or memorial—the newspaper took the death of a child, and they decided to kill him again.

It's one thing to have a beloved stolen in an act of senseless violence: it's another to have their memory defaced due to racism.

At first, I was convinced the reporter made an innocent error, that he simply needed more information. Students and parents wrote to the newspaper, but the reporter continued framing Beaux as a gang-banging menace. I decided to take action: I felt if he simply heard from some of Beaux's friends and looked at our faces, he'd know we weren't a bad crowd and that he was misrepresenting Beaux.

After sitting in a conference room pouring out our grief, we waited for the reporter to respond. He sighed, "I've been doing this for 20 years. When a black kid dies, he brought it on himself."

This sentence is when I first had to come to terms with the real face of America.

There were hundreds of people at Beaux's funeral: every seat was filled while people huddled in the aisles. Teachers from all grades wept over his coffin.

Drea lost her facade when we walked to Beaux's casket, elbows linked. She pulled away, threw her hands in the air, and wailed like I'd never heard anyone wail. "Ohhhhhh, don't let it be true! Ohhhhh, make it stop!"

If C.D.'s death had been an ax to my base, then Beaux's death was the blow that tipped me over. But something else emerged: it would be a defining part of the rest of my life—the commitment to not be silent, the understanding that I had to learn about racism.

I wrote an article for the school paper for Beaux. No longer could I pretend that the world of adults was knowing, logical, compassionate, or educated.

Nothing can ever erase what that journalist took from us. I can only imagine how many times and in how many places these wounds have festered.

Beaux died defending his mother from physical abuse. He died again because he couldn't defend himself against white supremacy.

This is a story about ghosts.

37

LETTER TO A GHOST: BEAUX
If you hadn't died, would I have ever seen it?
I didn't know it's in the air we've consumed.
Look at that smoke that carried you off.
I can see it now. Charcoal sky.
I can heal this in myself.
But how do I make others see we're suffocating?
We won't survive if we don't face it.
I fear who I'd have been had you not died.
Yours was the first battle in which I was drafted to fight, to speak,
to write the worthy story.
Your life mattered.
Black lives matter.

38.

Some of those 80s slashers had heroines driving their plots. Sometimes a girl died and still returned in the sequel, only to die again.

And ghosts must do again what gives them pain.

This is a place in the story in which I died.

I went to dark realms I can't speak of because I can't access them.

My mom spent all her time online. My job ended at nine. She'd make me wait until past midnight to pick me up. I'd hide behind a tree and stare up at the moon. I'd ask C.D. and Beaux to appear as apparitions: I'd see nothing, so I'd pray for a car accident, cancer, something to take me out. I prayed, *Just don't let me survive.*

But there was a sequel.

Miraculously, I was alive.

So was the thing that hunted me.

II

39

I brought home boxes from work and haphazardly started throwing things in. I left nearly everything behind.

My dad lounged on the couch watching TV. My mom was at work.

"Bye," I said to my dad.

"Where you moving?"

"Sam's parents."

He nodded.

"Okay, bye."

"Yep, bye."

I felt the hot, damp mouth of that house finally take its breath off my neck.

Sam was my boyfriend. In the span of a year, I'd fallen in love. I started waitressing at a restaurant that served cheap food that old people loved, and the blonde-haired, blue-eyed broil cook fell for me. Everything happened the way I thought relationships were supposed to happen: he asked me on dates, we waited months to have sex, he told me he loved me before we had sex, he showered me with gifts, he held my hand.

I thought I'd pulled off an impossible ruse.

I was loved, despite not being perfect.

Sam had the kind of family that has cookie baking contests with prizes for Christmas, the kind that had family get togethers with a gaggle of cousins, the kind that went to church every Sunday.

I'd grown close to Sam's parents—he barely knew mine. I confided about my home life. When I won the journalism award, they came to my awards ceremony to find me bruised: my mother had beaten me just before. Sam's parents decided I could move into their spare room.

I'd never have to worry about a cruel boy or my mother's fists again.

When I drove away, I took a final look. 14 years old, Cassie stared back from her bedroom window. I could see the contortions of pain on her face.

I never felt as much guilt as that moment.

I told myself that if I were in her position, I'd be happy for her freedom. Cassie had to understand: I'd done my time.

But I feared what she'd face the next four years alone.

For months, I couldn't sleep, waking in panicked sobs.

"My mother's a cannibal, eating her alive."

"Your sister again?" Sam yawned.

40

When Sam and I had sex, my body rejected him.

My vagina started to burn. Then itch. All I could think about was how dirty I was.

Our health class showed graphic pictures of genitals blooming with disease, so I started visiting Planned Parenthood. The undercurrent of many lessons was a warning against the promiscuous girl: when you slept with her, you slept with all the men she slept with.

I'd sit in class and look at Grayson with contempt for my desire that had allowed him to ruin my purity.

Sam was pure. His family was Christian. Sam had only been with one girl—but she was a virgin. As the itching became more intense, I worried about "polluting" him. I made an appointment for another screening.

Before the appointment, I watched an episode of a talk show that said, "If you haven't taken a mirror and looked at your vagina, you need to do that immediately."

I hadn't ever seen my vagina.

I didn't even touch my vagina.

I never orgasmed before Sam. When I told people this, they looked at me sideways. "Not even….on your own?"

After people started telling me that they'd orgasmed only using their hands, I tried to touch myself, only to gag and feel nauseous.

The diagrams in health class focus on fallopian tubes and uteruses or heavily diseased genitalia, and the media showed all aspects of a woman's naked body except her vagina. I didn't have access to pornography—these were pre-internet days—and I'd never experimented with girls.

I had no idea what a vagina was supposed to look like.

What I saw in the handheld mirror looked like someone had taken a knife, sliced my body open between my legs, and let my inner organs glisten on full display.

I entered Planned Parenthood with the heaviest shame: I was sure I'd be the worst they'd ever seen.

But they didn't recoil when they looked at me. In fact, the lady said I had a *beautiful* vagina.

I had a yeast infection.

They told me I may be allergic to semen or he may be cheating.

I had infections for over a year—I was convinced they happened as my karma, a reminder that I wasn't good enough, a secret I kept permanently between my legs.

Now I know my body was remembering things my mind couldn't to survive. I also know Sam was cheating—with men.

The girl raised by survival is different than the girl raised by love. The girl raised by survival tries to avoid the truth: that she needs kindness, desperately. She builds walls around her so she can cower in cold, dark corners in privacy, starved for affection, withering to bone.

Then she tries to infiltrate the world of the loved.

The girl raised by survival is raised by her loneliness and the wolves who run with her. But she wants to believe she's not a wolf—this isn't her pack. She wants to believe that as soon as she stumbles back to civilization they'll recognize her as one of theirs.

I wanted to belong, to be loved. I hoped I was so unlike my parents that I could leave, become lovable, and never look back.

But I did look back. Because the girl raised by survival never leaves those woods: she splits in two and listens to her former self howling from the abyss she fled.

41

Look back.

Stare at your childhood as a black pool of water in a well.

A vision will rise to the surface like a bloated corpse.

It glows and sharpens into focus like the answer rising from a Magic 8 Ball.

You're a child. You're no more than four.

There's a neighbor. She's older. Maybe seven.

She says she's going to show you her game. She tells you to take off your clothes and crawl under her bed.

She instructs you to let her listen to your heart, to open your mouth and let her peer inside, to spread your legs.

She touches you with her fingers. Then with her tongue.

Her door flings open and her mom screams, "What are you doing?"

She has a belt.

She reaches under the bed and starts swinging. You scurry towards the wall but she grabs you by the ankle and drags you.

She whips you with her full force of strength.

You've never been beaten by a stranger. It feels worse than your parents' beatings as the welts appear. There's a sting that touches your soul.

She says you're devil children.

You didn't know the game was bad—but you know you're bad.

You never touch it after.

The water in the well undulates. The image blurs, sinks back to black.

This is a story about ghosts.

42

We did it in his bedroom under covers while anime boomed combat sequences. We did it before and after dinner, before and after church. We did it on the kitchen table when home alone—we chuckled watching his brother eat there later.

We looked at Kama Sutra. We did it and we sometimes succeeded, sometimes failed. We did it and after we'd do it, he'd tell me other things he wanted to do. We did it and I started to love how I looked in a corset, how it would let my breasts spill out. We did it with a vibrator; I learned how to give myself orgasms. I'd wait for him to go to work so I could do it again.

We did it and took pictures. We did it and he said I was beautiful. We did it and he would write me letters that said we were doing it and he was loving it. We did it and I thought I was happy. No one had ever spent any time showing me how to do it, kissing me. It might as well have been my first time doing it.

We did it until his penis bled from chafing. We did it until I was so sore I needed days to recover. We never had willpower, so we did it again.

Once, we did it and he grabbed my head when I was going down on him and shoved it over and over until my mind walked out of my body and then he came in my mouth and I gagged and cried and he said we'd never do it that way again.

We did it after fights, after I got new clothes and modeled them, only for him to ask who I was trying to look good for. I'd tell him I thought I was ugly and fat and I only wanted to impress him, and he'd say that's bullshit, and I'd think I was losing everything and my mind would go black and then we'd yell and cry and do it until we slept.

We did it so much I hung out with my girlfriends less, with my sister less. We did it so much that when he proposed on Valentine's Day in his car with a ring inside a candy box, I believed in happiness.

We did it and he told me he loved my body so much that he could never tire of doing it.

When he did tire, a leak in me started trickling—until something collapsed and I started to drown.

That comes later. First, we got married.

43

November 2001: two months earlier, 9/11. I was in a college math class when someone ran in, "America's under attack!" I drove to the small house Sam and I purchased with visions of the apocalypse in my head. We watched the towers fall for weeks.

With war, every civilian casualty made me think of C.D. and Beaux. I'd imagine how many people loved the dead and how many of them hurt the way I hurt and how many of them were permanently marred by grief. I committed to learning about the contentious history that spawned 9/11. This curiosity made me feel outcast.

Sam didn't care to talk about what I was learning ever. By the time we got married, it should've been clear that Sam loved my body only. I kept thinking if I succeeded, if I maintained perfect grades and became a writer, he'd be proud. I had English professors who I latched onto who patiently guided my reading and encouraged me to go to graduate school.

One of those professors taught me feminism: I dove into everything I could read. It flipped my world upside down. I talked to Sam about the idea of equals in a relationship. He treated me as if I'd suddenly sprouted a repulsive second head.

His world was video games, anime, action movies. He got a surround sound system so his video games would make the house vibrate. He'd zone out for days. I'd sit in the spare room writing.

I planned the wedding alone. Sam had no interest. I wanted us to write our vows, but Sam said he couldn't think of any. I found some for us to memorize. Sam said he'd try. I asked the pastor to cut "obey your husband" from the ceremony, and the pastor argued that I wasn't understanding it correctly: I was to obey my husband, *but my husband was to obey God*. I wondered why I needed some middle man to God, why my husband—whose papers I wrote for him just so he could pass classes—was somehow better suited to the divine.

On the wedding day, I floated through the motions. Someone did my hair, a bridesmaid did my makeup, two bridesmaids buttoned the dress up my spine as I sucked in and stared at the mirror, expressionless. Everyone said I was beautiful.

That was what mattered: would I be beautiful enough?

Would I be beautiful enough forever?

Would I be beautiful enough to be loved?

Beauty was the only thing that moved men: they loved nothing else about me.

I walked down the aisle on the arm of my father, who said nothing to me. Sam didn't know the vows. I squirmed uncomfortably as he stared blankly after I recited mine. I thought, *He doesn't even love you enough to memorize a few generic lines*.

At the reception, I found myself looking in the mirror in a daze.

"You're a married woman," Drea said, who'd helped me navigate the toilet with my gown, a strapless satin dress with rhinestones across the chest and layers of tulle.

A voice in my head said, *You'll be a divorced woman too*.

Sam got so drunk that he blacked out. I slept alone.

44

I finally muster the courage to ask my mom to take me to the gynecologist under her insurance. Since I'm married, it's acceptable to need reproductive health care: I have a hypothesis that my infections recur because I go to a free clinic.

My mom takes me to her gynecologist: I'm shocked he's a man. Not only a man, an *old* man. I feel cornered like a trembling cat at the vet.

I try to tell myself he has the wisdom to fix me, but when I spread my legs, something happens.

He barely says more than a terse hello, then he sits in front of my stirrups and begins to jam cold instruments into my body with no warning.

At Planned Parenthood, they walked me through the process in a gentle, reassuring manner.

When he scrapes my cervix, he's so rough that I have a terrible cramp.

It's then that I levitate out of my body.

It's as if I float to the ceiling. I can't feel a thing. My ears click off into the serenity of nothingness.

Suddenly, I'm jarred back into my body as the gynecologist shoves two fingers up my rectum. No one at Planned Parenthood had ever done this. The shock of it causes me to cry out.

After, I'm alone to put my clothes on. I sit up fast, reeling from the pain. I feel like I'm going to throw up. I know I'll vomit on the floor if I don't hurry, so I throw my clothes on backwards and reach for the door.

Before I make it, I fall.

I faint.

When I open my eyes, there's only blackness. My first thought is that I'm blind, but after a few disorienting moments, I realize I hit the light switch when I fell.

I open the door. A nurse is in the hallway, "Excuse me, I think I'm going to...."

She catches me before my body hits the floor again.

My ears ring and I lose hearing.

We'd like to think that the pain we survive heals as our body heals from pain. We'd like to think we can forget the fist that caused the bruise, the blade that carved the gash. We'd like to think that survival itself is the trophy, evidence of the win.

But the body never forgets. It may wipe out your memory to protect you. It may dial up your anxiety to prepare for the next onslaught. It may develop seemingly supernatural abilities like walking your soul straight out of your body, as if your body is just a ball chain you drag around.

The body fights itself into exhaustion against the shadow of each threat; illnesses bloom with the ease of algae in a swamp.

Whatever you can't recall, your body has the film negative buried somewhere in the folds of your flesh, and your body has to cope when it's unearthed, held to the lamp to reveal your truth: there's darkness where there once was light.

This is a story about ghosts.

45

Early in our relationship, Sam reassured constantly: anytime I was insecure, he said I was beautiful. Anytime I was angry, he said I was beautiful. Anytime I was worried, he said I was beautiful.

Sam wasn't a man to express emotions. Asking him to talk about emotions was a frustrating game, a maze with no way out. Emotionally, he was a robot programed with only a few phrases.

None of his reassurances about beauty filled the leak inside me. I went on birth control and gained ten pounds. At 135 lbs, I felt like a failure: my doctor told me my target weight was 100 lbs. Weight loss became another entity in our relationship, a house guest with a voracious appetite.

I joined Weight Watchers. If I ate too many "points" that day, I went to bed guilty and worthless. If I didn't eat my full points that day, I felt hopeful but hungry. We could no longer enjoy dinners out or desserts. I tried to deprive my body into obedience, into lovability.

In my journals, I worry I've trapped him in a marriage under false pretenses: a beauty I can't possibly upkeep.

Beauty was a tightrope I walked across high-rise buildings, anticipating the terror of a single misstep.

I was always waiting for the fall, so I was armed: I brought the cold combat I'd learned growing up with my mother to my marriage. Whenever a whiff of discord filled the air and Sam said something to hurt me, I'd lash out and seek to carve valleys of insecurities. I'd remind him that all his love letters had not a single mark of punctuation, that he was a zombie who played video games all day.

I'd been trained to be vicious my whole life.

As time went on, it was clear that Sam and I didn't like each other. Sam began to mock my writing: he'd lapse into an impersonation of me that was meant to sound like a mentally handicapped person.

When he wanted to cut deep, he knew which wound to reopen: he told me that I was only quiet when I was stuffing my face with food.

One day, we planned a boat trip with another couple. Sam was inexplicably moody. As I drove, Sam turned on music. I said, "You play this to death." We were at a stop sign. Sam said nothing as he opened his door and walked out, heading home.

I drove back and confronted Sam in our garage, "What's wrong with you?

"Fuck off," he said.

Frustrated, I took my keys and launched them his direction. They didn't land near him, but Sam snapped.

He launched at me with his full force, grabbed me by the shoulders and slammed me against the metal bars along the wall of the garage. I collapsed with the ease of a rag doll and couldn't get up. As I tried to stand, he lifted me and slammed me against the wall again.

He lapsed into his disabled voice, "I'm Anne. I'm a bitch and I got what was coming."

"I never thought you'd hit me," I said, in a haze of shock.

I had the gnarliest bruise—it trailed from my ribcage to my armpit all the way down to my wrist. Sam's repressed rage was an explosion of fireworks all over my body. It took over a month to heal.

There was no hiding it in my uniform. Customers and coworkers continually pressed me. When I told them I fell, they looked at me with the gravest concern, like they knew my husband did it. Cassie, the only person I told the truth to, was adamant: leave him.

I didn't. I believed what Sam said: I deserved it. I didn't belong in the world of the lovable.

Even now, I want to flip the narrative and reassure that Sam was a good man. Sam *is* a good man. Somewhere, Sam is with his second wife and his kids being a beloved, good dad.

But this is also the truth: that wasn't the last time Sam hit me.

I didn't know any other way of love but this.

One day, I had the flu. From bed, I called out, "Can you bring another blanket?"

Sam barged through the door and punched me in the face so my glasses flew off. He said, "Do you ever shut the fuck up?"

The more toxic my relationship got, the more weight I gained—135 turned to 185, and each time a physical altercation happened, suicidal ideation descended.

An anxious form of bulimia returned. I didn't throw up every meal, but if I had a meal that was enjoyable, I'd sneak away to the bathroom. I felt purged and pure. Fatness is always aligned with immorality and irresponsibility; I felt I was taming the beast of my hunger in a good way, like a drug addict who needs to barf so as not to overdose.

After three years, Sam started withholding sex. We were just roommates with a long list of gripes.

How could we have known we built a home on a bed of quicksand?

46

But this is a story about girls. Sisters.

People talk about virgins and they talk about petals unfurling like tongues.

People talk about girls as if blooms are an option.

Cassie grew into a teenager and started wilting.

Pictures from those years reveal a pale, thin girl, shadows under her eyes. She looked like one of her idols: Fiona Apple. She listened to the saddest music, all by girls who oozed rebellion.

Cassie started failing her classes. One of her teachers told her that she'd be "the smartest homeless person." She talked about dropping out. I urged her to go to the alternative school. Cassie seemed to be on a path I was familiar with, one in which the people I loved couldn't be saved.

As the wars in Iraq and Afghanistan began, Cassie and I no longer blindly believed our parents, who reveled in war, especially if those who the country attacked weren't white. Our father had been in the Air Force. He didn't talk much about it, but I had my theories: the Air Force was a root that led to our father's conservatism, his racism, his inability to express emotions except for the explosive anger that erupted in fights.

My English professors were protesting every weekend. By this time, I'd read all the classics about war that brought me to the same conclusion: it's barbaric. I asked my professors if my sister and I could join.

Every weekend, armed with our signs, "Drop Bush Not Bombs," I brought her. The turnout was lackluster: our opinion wasn't popular, especially in those early days of the wars that would drag on for two decades and trillions of dollars. I started to see nationalism as a pernicious virus that infected people around me. These people had no questions about the war, no curiosity about history, no desire to understand foreign policy—they needed only their sense of superiority through some arbitrary sense of belonging. Some people need so desperately to feel better than others; nationalism grants that illusion. I could easily see how something like the Holocaust happened.

Many protestors were people who'd protested Vietnam, people who understood America in a different context. They peppered speeches with the contradictions of American foreign policy: *What about Nicaragua? Cuba? Palestine?* Protesting taught me I had much to learn.

One day, I dropped Cassie off, and she called me later: our father had asked where she was. He responded by beating her worse than ever. She had bruises all over.

"I'm coming to get you," I said, "You're not going back."

My parents had become more authoritarian, refusing to take her to driver's education, forcing her to walk everywhere. It wasn't unusual for my husband or I to be driving and find her walking along the side of a busy road.

My sister's teacher called Child Protective Services. It was the third time they'd been called. I told the case worker I was capable of taking her.

Sam and I discovered soon after that she had an eating disorder. I felt I was failing, that I wouldn't be able to save my sister just as I hadn't saved C.D.

If I couldn't save who I loved, I surely couldn't save myself.

The shadow of that fell on me frequently.

I'd like to tell you I saved her and watched her bloom.

But Cassie and I were two girls raised on survival who hadn't learned a thing about love. Cassie latched onto a boy who was also raised on survival and she began repeating the cycle. I'd already been repeating it. When she and I were together, we could quickly lapse into the only thing we knew—the toxic forms of communication our parents used. Then we'd apologize, cry over our childhood.

We were beginning to know something was wrong.

But we were young, poor, alone, dependent on each other. We had no resources; we didn't know where to begin. As loved-starved girls, we sought to stop the leaks of our psyche with men. Cassie spent more time with her boyfriend; they had blowup fights. She moved in with him.

We tried to bury our traumas, but our traumas refused to be buried. Our hearts were active volcanoes, erupting.

This is a story about girls.

I never said they were good girls.

47

Then one day I collapsed.

All was normal. Then it wasn't.

I was leaving my Physiological Psychology class, which I found hard. I was double majoring in Psychology and English; normally, I found psychology so riveting I could ace any test. But with this class, I had to study. I was still acing my tests, but I felt like a fraud: I didn't understand a thing, but I had the highest grade in the class because I was so good at memorizing my notes. That night, my professor approached and asked if I'd like to be her TA. I told her I'd already been asked to be a TA. This was true, but the real truth was that I was overcome with shame—I'd fooled these smart people into thinking I was smart and normal, like them, but I could never be normal.

I sat in my car, watched rain slither down the windshield. I turned on the radio. A Billy Joel song came on:

"*Slow down, you crazy child.*

You're so ambitious for a juvenile.

But if you're so smart, then tell me why are you still so afraid?"

I put my head against the steering wheel and screamed.

When Sam got home, I was on the couch in fetal position in a towel. I wasn't crying, but I stared out the window despondently at a terror I couldn't describe.

Sam rushed to me. "What is it?"

"I don't know," I said, which was the disorienting truth.

"What happened?"

"I was in my car and I heard a song, and I...."

"A song?"

"Yes, a sad song."

"What's making you sad?"

"I think something is wrong with me."

"You're just having a mood," he assured.

I'd descended into a well, and his voice was an echo from above. As I pushed him away, the last sliver of light and sky above the well sealed off.

It was only me and whatever darkness was hunting me.

48

The sun came into my room and mocked me. I stayed in bed as long as possible, closing the curtains.

At some point between my exposure to feminism and my appetite for literature about depressed women, I fell in love with Sylvia Plath, the poet known for ending her life by putting her head in an oven, abandoning her two children and her unfaithful husband. Her macabre death in 1963 ignited a feminist wildfire her voice rose from, making her one of America's most enduring classic poets, bestowed a Pulitzer after death.

The Bell Jar, her semi-autobiographical novel about her suicide attempt and electric shock treatments at a mental institution felt like the closest I found to making sense of my life.

The protagonist, Esther Greenwood, is assaulted by a man at a dance. Upon meeting him, she knows he's "a woman-hater." She observes: "Marco's small, flickering smile reminded me of a snake I'd teased in the Bronx Zoo. When I tapped my finger on the stout cage glass, the snake had opened its clockwork jaws and seemed to smile. Then it struck and struck and struck at the invisible pane until I moved off."

This truth wasn't my truth, I thought—it's not what happened to me. Why should it strike me as if I had no invisible pane to protect me from the fang?

After her attempted rape, Esther goes home, opens her closet, and drapes all of her clothes out the window, watching stoically as their "batlike shadows" fall onto the streets. She likens it to scattering a loved one's ashes. The next day, she leaves the dried blood on her face and moves through the city, ignoring people's stares.

My pain sunk to unreachable depths: a cavernous ocean floor filled with creatures unseen, until Plath's aching moan of a whale song reached it. I read all of Plath's work.

I felt like I'd taken a hit of a drug that wiped the pain away as if it were only dust on my body.

What was astounding about Plath was she allowed herself to be angry. I'd never thought that a woman could be angry. I was so consumed with trying to be pleasant, likable, beautiful.

Plath ripped off the veneers, revealing the rotted fangs of what was feeding on me—patriarchy. Her poems were a hexing and a conjuring.

Plath's work gave me permission to rage, and, while suffocating in my own bell jar of depression, I began to write. Poems poured out of my pain like vomit that instantly makes you feel better.

I was thinking about graduate school. I'd planned to study fiction. I told my sister, "My mind isn't working lately. Everything's in fragments and images."

She read with casual interest, "Well, you're not a fiction writer. You're a poet."

You're a poet—the words were a lighthouse illuminating the tempest of my body.

You'll be saved. Land is near.

As I drove through the same gray streets, past the same fast food places, the same strip malls, the same corporate restaurants, the same dead and impersonal monotony of suburbs, I felt claustrophobia pressing in on me, a shrinking room. I had to travel. Plath studied at University of Cambridge, so I went to the study abroad office and met with a counselor.

"But I/have a self to recover, a queen./Is she dead, is she sleeping?/Where has she been,/with her lion-red body, her wings of glass?"
-Sylvia Plath, "Stings"

49

From the tears at the airport to the paralyzing culture shock upon landing, studying at Cambridge was about learning to stand alone.

I fell in love with the lilt of the accents of every man. Once I'd mastered navigating London and underground subways and quaint little villages in York without street signs, I ached for a life of experiences.

I woke one weekend, and, without the slightest idea of how I'd get there, decided to visit Plath's grave.

I took a bus, a train, a taxi with a scary driver. I took a pitstop at the Bronte's house, strolling along the foggy moors, I took hilly pathways in the rain, slipping down their slopes with the rolling patchwork quilt of the quiet English countryside spread around me. I took a steam train that didn't have passengers, only cargo: the conductor felt sorry for how lost I was. I took directions from strangers until finally I stumbled into a bar. Before I could say anything, a man said, "You looking for Sylvia Plath?"

"How'd you know?"

"It's the only reason foreigners come here." He gave detailed instructions.

I read a letter at her grave, overcome with emotion as if I was grieving a mother I never had.

I told her how badly I wanted to write with a power like hers.

There was one thing I wanted more than that, something I could barely choke out.

I want to heal.

I rocked back and forth repeating this mantra.

When I returned home, I started to look at the streets as if they were the bindings of a straight jacket.

I'd hoped England would make me run back to my husband, but the wound of our marriage only got more infected until I knew I'd have to cut off the limb that plagued me.

Another girl at work married young like me. She had a baby and was ready to leave her husband. We decided we'd do it together.

50

Another complicating factor was my desire: most the staff at the restaurant were young and good looking: we spent so much time together that we bonded like family, and we also fell madly in love all the time.

I had a crush on several people after I left Sam. One of them, a server named Daryl, carried on such a heavy flirtation that I set my sights on rebound.

One night, as Daryl and I sat at a bar after work, I looked up to see Sam.

Daryl became combative: "Go the fuck home, you psycho stalker."

"You look like a slut," Sam said.

"I'm hanging out with my friends."

"Then why are your tits out?"

"I want to feel attractive," I shrugged.

"You look like a whore."

"If I'm such a whore, go home."

Suddenly, Daryl was by my side, shoving Sam and yelling. The bouncers were quick to grab them.

In the parking lot, Daryl rushed Sam and they began to fight.

As Sam and Daryl rolled on the concrete, it was shocking and I was afraid. Sam was so enmeshed with my life that seeing him hurt felt like I was hurting myself.

Yet, there was something else too. A surge of electricity. An eruption of heat. A brass tongue of desire clanging between my legs. A question, as intruding as a quivering falsetto, a clock striking midnight:

What was this chaos?

What was this violence?

Was this love?

After several people worked to break them up, I stood between them in the parking lot, unsure where to go. "Come with me," Daryl said, "Don't give this crazy fuck any more of your life." I looked at Sam, my eyes full of apology. I got in the car with Daryl.

I tried to sleep with Daryl that night, but he shirked my advances. I was practically begging, starving for touch: "I just got in a fight with your *husband*," he said.

The next morning, I went to face Sam. He was bruised and drinking. I'd never lied to him; I didn't plan on starting. I sat on our bed and nervously admitted that Daryl rejected me. Sam stood at the foot of the bed, his face red, his breathing labored.

Then he exploded.

Without a word, he tore a piece of wood off the end of the bed as if it were made of cardboard, then he swung it above my head at the light fixture. I scrambled off the bed as shards of glass rained on me. I scurried to the spare room and locked the door.

Within seconds, I watched as Sam's entire leg came through the door as he kicked it. He reached in, unlocked the door, and charged at me. I ducked and ran to the living room where he proceeded to smash our wedding photos, then plucked them out of the glass and tore them up, screaming that I was a whore. I ran to my car and sped off.

Sam called later to tell me that the rest of my belongings were on the front lawn.

My roommate consoled me with a housewarming party. We bought lacy lingerie that we planned to wear as tops with jeans. I was so hungry to be sexually desired again.

My roommate bartended and the liquor flowed as people mingled. I was glued to Daryl. Every couple hours, my roommate would ask me to take the tip jar to my room for safekeeping.

I was doing that when something hit me from behind and knocked me to the ground.

It happened so fast I could barely make sense of it. I tried to stand and found myself flat on my back again, my ex-husband towering me. I had no idea how he found out about the party.

"What the fuck are you wearing?" I tried to stand and he struck my face, knocking me to the bed.

Someone yelled, "This guy's beating a girl!"

Four men charged after Sam. Sam ran up the stairs and out the door, and the men followed, tackling him and beating him mercilessly as he curled into a ball. I watched from the front doorstep, begging them to stop. Every blow to Sam felt like it was a blow to me. Finally, they backed off. Sam struggled to stand and hobbled into his car. He took off, immediately swerving and hitting another parked car before speeding off.

The party dispersed—the jovial mood vanished. Daryl gave me a hug and a sympathetic look.

"Stay with me tonight," I pleaded. Every cell of my skin was a gasping open mouth, begging to be kissed. He nodded apologetically.

Years later, I found out that Daryl was gay when he came out on social media. Back then, his rejection and Sam's fists and my loneliness only reinforced what I was sure had always been true. I was unlovable.

As revenge, Sam took my credit card and charged $25,000. He knew we couldn't afford lawyers, so the debt was mine.

In a matter of weeks, Sam started dating.

That's when I really broke.

51

Christmas alone. My roommate was having a hookup. My husband was dating someone new. Bush won re-election. I'd taken a second job in addition to full-time college: I was a client care technician at a drug and alcohol rehabilitation facility. I worked overnights and weekends.

I was a mess.

I knew I needed therapy, but I had no health insurance, so I listened to my body and what it told me I needed.

The broken girl's body has its own language. It never stops begging.

I spotted him outside the gym where AA meetings were held—a client who'd been in the program weeks earlier. His name was Ryder, a midwestern country boy to the bone: he didn't much care about whatever dingy clothes he threw on, his beat up baseball hat showed the wear of a man who got dirty, his large calloused hands told me I didn't have a clue the kind of things he could do. He'd flirted with me his whole stay, writing me poems and winking in the hallway as I did rounds. He chewed tobacco, chain smoked, and was battling an addiction to meth. He told stories about hunting—all the beasts he slayed.

I had a beast in me that needed slaying—meaner than the pike with their full set of teeth, their ability to make a grown man exclaim, *Look at this monster.*

Isn't she something?

Sleeping with clients was forbidden and even dangerous for their sobriety. I thought about that.

I thought about it as I boldly walked outside where Ryder was smoking and said, "Come into the office." I thought about it as he sat there, and I felt myself becoming aroused. I thought about it when I blurted, "You wanna come over tonight?" I thought about it as I watched his face register what I'd asked before simply saying, "Yeah."

Then I let the thought pass.

When I kneeled in front of him, he said, "You have the hungriest eyes I've ever seen."

When I mounted him, he said, "You look like you want trouble."

There's something wild about a man who goes to battle with nature. There's something predatory about a broken girl.

His cock was thunderclap and I was storm. His hands wrestled with my writhing until I fell still into the percussion of his thrusts: we crashed like cymbals. He'd move into kiss me and pull away and I'd call him a tease, then he'd fuck me hard until my body fell slack and whisper in my ear, "Am I a tease now, darlin?" I begged for more, harder—I wanted him to fuck me bestial, fuck the demons out of me, fuck my broken parts whole, fuck me to death.

We clawed at each other's skin, his hip bones battered me until bruises of blue and purple flowers bloomed on my thighs. We marked each other with our teeth, we collapsed onto each other in exhaustion, until my hunger stirred again and I undulated like a serpent along his body, waiting for his weapon to rise against me and split me in two, sever my head clean off.

When we'd finally fucked the wildness out of us into the early morning, as the sun rose and it was time to get ready for work, he took a drag from his cigarette and said, "Feel better?"

The shower stung as it hissed against my scratches. I struggled to walk, his sex a ghost lingering between my thighs.

I delighted in every ache.

Yes, I thought, *I feel better now.*

Until the next night, when desire ran through me again like a wolf's moonlight howl. There'd never be enough flesh to fill me.

52

They're animals clawing at each other.
No.
She's an animal; he's a hunter.
No.
Sometimes she opens her eyes during sex and he's a wolf.
It doesn't matter the shape of the predator—she wants him to win.

Disembowel her.
Rip it out of her guts.
This hunger.
This anger.
This fear.

53

In the early 2000s, the drama-comedy *Sex and the City* lit a fuse in young women. The show was refreshing for its frank examination of women's sex lives: the idea that women could desire sex felt like a secret only whispered in girl talk, and the show centered on how four successful New York City women girl-talked relentlessly about their string of affairs. The winds of the third wave feminist movement were stirring, and the eye of the storm was sexual liberation.

We wanted to erase the stigma of the slut, to wear the shame not with the archaic scarlet A, but with pink tutu skirts and the confident click of heels.

It was common to ask, "Which one are you?" There was Charlotte, the traditional anti-feminist, who longed for financial security through a man, children, and the princess fairy tale. There was Miranda, the jaded feminist who consistently suggested that love couldn't exist in a sexist world. There was Samantha, the unabashed slut who had sex with complete emotional detachment like a man. And there was the lead, Carrie, the everywoman: a little messy in all aspects of life, listening to her friends' views in equal regard, documenting their lives and perspectives in her column.

There's plenty to critique in the show—most prominently, the unbearable whiteness of it and class issues. It treated gay men as comedic accessories, even as it was revolutionary in including gay men in its narrative. I couldn't see this at the time. Thankfully, I had some professors who challenged me to read different books and go deeper into my feminist studies. My English professor, the reason for my interest in feminism to begin with, urged me to think about racial issues. My philosophy professor enjoyed my participation in class debates, regarding me silently with a smirk on his face when I went to battle with the rest of the class. One day he handed me a book, *Women in the Non-Western World*. I held it and said, "Oh, this will be good for me. Most of my feminist readings are so…."

"White," he said.

I often think of these professors—white men—who became scholars in more overtly racist and sexist times, who were doing the ground work for change at a community college. I hold a deep reverence for them. Their ideas were no where near popular, but they committed to having us consider them.

They changed my life. They taught that real wisdom came from listening to all experiences and struggles. They also gave me something that was lacking in my childhood: nurturing.

"Which are you?" Ryder asked, as I curled in his armpit, watching the show post-sex.

"Samantha."

"It's all sex with you, huh?"

"I also have a large dash of Miranda. I don't believe in love."

"Everybody believes in love."

"Love is temporary insanity."

"Are you using me, darlin'?"

"Don't act like you aren't playing the same game," I teased.

"I don't play games."

"No?" I said, reaching for him under the blanket.

At my touch, he stood, picked me up, carried me to the bedroom, and tossed me onto the bed. "You're insatiable," he said, putting the condom on.

Ryder became an every other day event: we had marathon sex that lasted through the night. We'd spend whole days together, our sex punctuated by moments of rest, television, and him fixing random things around the house.

I reveled in this new type of relationship: it was full of all the markings of love, but without any of its traps.

114

Ryder took out my trash, fixed my broken appliances, came up behind me and put his arms around me and kissed my neck, took showers with me and soaped my body, told me I was sexy. But we didn't say I love you. I didn't tell him anything about my pains. There was no emotional vulnerability but a blast of endorphins. We barely slept. I started being late for work because as he'd try to get dressed, I'd kiss him, his six foot frame towering over me, and he'd say, "You're gonna get it."

I'd be flat on my back in seconds, relishing his stamina.

On the days I wasn't with Ryder, I lapsed into anxiety. I'd write in my journals that he must be with other women. I'd fret over my husband's new girlfriend and what they were doing, how she eclipsed me. I'd find myself having panic attacks in bed, shivering with cold sweats.

But when he fucked me, my shackles shattered.

One day, I picked up Ryder and he seemed somber. "I used," he confessed.

"Meth?"

He nodded.

"Why?"

"It's your fault," he said.

I rolled my eyes. "How?"

"I really started using the minute I started you."

"Like sex is your drug?" I laughed.

His eyes were as stoic as stone, "Like it's not yours?"

I'd slipped on some ice at school and twisted my ankle. The next day, I woke with it swollen to the size of a softball. I went to the bathtub and tried to soak it. Ryder woke and came to the door.

"Damn kid," he said, "you really hurt yourself. I can wrap it for you at my house." As he held it gently, examining it from each angle, I let the thought of loving Ryder cross my mind.

But he'd voted for Bush, he didn't read books, he wasn't a feminist, and he was a country boy. He was everything I sought to escape, even as I consumed him furiously.

He wrapped my ankle, "What would you do without me?"

"Find another one."

He laughed, "Yeah, you're going places. You don't need a tumbleweed like me."

"Wanna know where I'm going?" I asked.

115

"Where?"

"Boston." The dream had been brewing ever since England. Boston was where Sylvia Plath had lived. I'd started looking at graduate schools.

"A city girl, huh?"

54

At a bar playing pool with Ryder, he pulled me onto his lap and told his friend I was his nurse in rehab.

"I remember you talking about her," he replied.

"What'd he say?"

"You're in a bar full of mirrors and you need to ask what he said?"

What I saw when I looked in the mirror was a fat girl, a desperate girl, a slutty girl, a wicked girl, a cold girl, a lonely girl, crooked-teeth girl, round-face girl, cellulite girl, thin-haired girl.

What I saw was a million reasons men could choose to abandon me.

I recently dug up pictures from this time; they startled me.

Breasts spilling out like a porn star in a pink lingerie top with jeans. Hand on my hip, my body curving like a serpent making its way to swallow a mouse. Blonde hair styled to painstaking perfection. My tan skin aglow despite heavy makeup.

My sexuality and my insecurity were two sides of the same coin, but I wore my sexuality inside out, projecting it like glaring lights to protect my insecurity from being discovered.

After the bar, I went to Ryder's and rode him on the couch in his living room. He took my face in both hands and said, "It's weird, huh? How you're just trying to have fun and then you fall into a relationship?"

"A what?"

"I enjoy my time with you."

"Me too. Naked."

"I like you naked or not."

"You don't even know me."

After he finished, I got up to put on my clothes.

"Got what you came for?" Ryder said.

"Didn't you?"

"I want to cuddle."

I let him spoon me until I heard him snoring. Then I slipped out in the middle of the night.

Soon after, Ryder disappeared but returned with all new clothes and a new haircut. He said he'd gone back to his ex-wife.

I looked for a new fix to keep the pain at bay.

I didn't need to look far.

There's a pit of them, slithering, coiling.

55

In slasher films, half naked girls wake in the night and go looking for the noise that stirred them.

Everyone laughs as they stupidly stumble *towards* the monster—up the stairs, down into basements—trapping themselves repeatedly until they end in a fountain of blood.

Who'd do that? We laugh. *No one in their right mind would do that.*

No one in their right mind.

56

Y ou're home alone writing an essay for your Asian Literature course when you're startled by the doorbell, followed by sharp knocks and a man's voice, "Police!"

You scurry to the door, open it, wide-eyed.

"Do you know this man?"

Peyton, the new man from rehab you've been sleeping with, is behind them. His eyes are half closed in a daze; he averts eye contact.

"Yes, he's my, um…" You hesitate. You've been having sex with him for a month, but you don't know what to call him. The word "boyfriend" tumbles out of your mouth like a broken tooth.

"Ma'am, he crashed your car at an intersection. Your car has been towed and has some serious damage. He's stated that he had a seizure. He's refusing hospital care."

"Yeah, he doesn't have insurance."

The officers nod. Your ears begin to ring as they talk you through the details of getting your car back. You nod your head perfunctorily until they leave. Peyton slinks in the house like a dog who knows it's been bad.

"What the fuck, Peyton!"

His responses are a beat behind normal. He slurs words, "I had a seizure."

"Since when do you have seizures?"

"I'm epileptic!"

"Since when?"

"Since always! You don't know me well!"

"I didn't even know you took my car! I thought you were upstairs! You have to ask!"

"What am I, your child?"

"No, but that's my car! You wrecked my car!"

"Well, what the fuck am I supposed to do while you write your papers? You took me from rehab."

"I didn't take you from rehab—you left. I never wanted you to leave. All you needed to do was keep a fucking secret. But you had to blab in group therapy that you were fucking me, then you had to run off with no where to go. Now I lost my job, lost my car, and have a roommate I have to feed and cart around that I didn't ask for!"

"I'm looking for a job!"

"I didn't sign up for this. I didn't sign up for a relationship. I can't believe you crashed my fucking car."

"Fixable," he slurs.

"And expensive!"

"I'm not your prisoner! What do you want me to fucking do?"

"I want you to not fucking steal my car so I can write my fucking papers in peace and graduate fucking college and get the fuck away from everyone in this fucking trash town."

"Okay, I see how it is."

"Did you really have a seizure or did you use?"

"I'm clean!"

"Why are you slurring your words?"

"I probably have a concussion."

"If you have epilepsy, where's your medication? Why haven't you mentioned it?"

"I'm off my meds obviously. For someone so focused on your studies, you really aren't that smart."

"Show me your arms." He holds them out. Clean. But you know the tricks of addicts, finding veins in the webs of their hands and feet to hide track marks, "Show me your hands."

"Go finish your paper."

You reach for his hand. He jerks away from you. "Show me," you demand.

121

You see something flash in his eyes—an alertness returns to them as he fixes them on you, grabbing your wrist before you can grab his arm. He squeezes hard, begins to twist.

"Let me go!"

He clings to it, twisting it behind your back and pressing his body up against you from behind. He's shoving you into your bedroom and you're helpless because your wrist throbs. He's six foot four with the bulging, veiny muscles of a man who does steroids. He does do steroids, but you haven't realized this yet.

"Stop Peyton!"

You begin to cry. He doesn't release you. He doesn't speak. He's shoving you towards the bed. You keep crying out, but he acts like he doesn't hear you as he pushes you onto the bed, face first. For a moment, you're free of his grasp. You hold onto your wrist and try to get up but he's already straddling your legs and has you pinned down.

"Get off me!"

He has your dress up to your waist and he rips off your flimsy lace panties. You start to scream louder. No one's home. He grabs a hold of the back of your neck and shoves your face into the pillow. You can't breathe.

You panic and let your body go limp as a barter to him: you won't fight, you'll choose air.

You can hear him undoing his belt buckle. Your tears pool into the pillow around your eyes and you let out a pathetic moan, hoping he'll let you up, hoping he won't accidentally kill you. As soon as he enters from behind, he releases your neck and you lift your head gasping, so focused on air that you don't even feel him, so he does it harder.

You turn to look and he's a wolf.

Then it happens.

Something rumbles in your belly like the first tremors of an earthquake.

Then it travels down.

A fissure.

A faultline.

It travels farther, faster, through your center, through your uterus, through your clit, until it explodes.

He feels it happening and hears you moaning and he comes too.

122

You feel limp and half conscious. You curl into fetal position as he rolls off you. Like a hit of morphine, the orgasm has taken you out. You can't keep your eyes open. You fall asleep. Neither of you say a word.

When you wake, you call the company that towed your car, sit down at your desk, finish the paper you'll get an A on.

This is a story about ghosts.

57

You'd parked your car outside the motel where Peyton was staying since he'd gotten a job. You weren't dating: you'd made it clear it was just sex. You'd decided to grab something from the vending machine. A car pulled up, drove alongside. You'd ignored it, then finally glanced over. A man peered. "How much?" He'd whispered.

When you got to Peyton's room, you'd slammed the door. "This man just thought I was a prostitute! Do I look like a prostitute?"

"You look like a blonde at a motel who he hoped was a prostitute. That's the kind of people who stay here."

You were dressed in your secretary clothes: once a week, you'd been working as the administrative assistant at the restaurant. You'd thought you looked professional. Fear ran down your spine like a zipper coming undone, as if they could see beyond the clothes, as if they could tell you were really just a slut.

No. You were a college girl. You were a secretary. You were a writer. You were better than where you came from.

That's how you'd wanted your clothes to lie.

You'd glanced at the TV: two people were having sex underwater, a halo of hair around their heads. "Do you ever stop watching porn?"

You'd seen that he was hard under his khakis, that he was rubbing himself.

"You have a problem," you'd said.

You'd been having so much sex that you both started counting how many times you had sex a night. The record was 13. You were swollen, chafed. You'd talked about having some time to heal. He was in pain too. But on days when he dropped you off at work then took your car to work, he'd kiss you goodbye with his fingers prying between your legs, and you'd quickly start unbuttoning your pants, mounting him. You'd fucked him from countertops to graveyards. You'd been in pain, and worse, you hated him.

"Come to bed," he said.

You'd taken off your clothes. You'd crawled into bed.

He'd seemed different. This time, you hadn't asked to see his hand. Instead, you'd held it in yours as if you meant to be tender, as if you were going to pull it to your breast. You'd seen the track marks. You'd said, "I knew it."

You jump out of bed. You scramble for your clothes. You know there's no time to waste: if you know the truth, you need to run.

He snatches your keys off the counter before you can.

You charge and scratch him, screaming, "Liar! Drug addict!"

He has you by the waist and he drags you kicking into the bathroom. He turns on the shower and throws you in the tub. You land on your back. You're momentarily disoriented.

You turn into a wet rag doll under that water. He struggles to pull you up to stand, to prop you against the wall. He's getting on his knees in front of you, putting one of your thighs on his shoulder. You say no and you really mean no, because you really want it to stop: you don't want to have sex with him ever again.

Then you feel his tongue and the sky cracks wide open and swallows you whole.

You hadn't been able to even stand afterwards. You collapsed like a marionette when he let you go, didn't you?

You did.

58

Noah, the general manager at the restaurant, came strolling into the office on Mondays with a cigarette dangling from his mouth; he'd chain smoke until the staff started trickling in. As his secretary, I'd do payroll and inventory with him alone for hours. I'd worked for Noah for a few months. The manager before him warned: "He comes off as a tyrant."

Noah's management style was to strike terror in the heart of staff—belittling for mistakes, stewing and giving the cold shoulder when he was pissed, chucking ketchup bottles at the wall after he skulked into the office to vent his frustrations.

Noah terrified me as much as everyone, but—much to my bewilderment—Noah liked me. Sometimes it seemed I was the only one Noah liked. The face he wore to the staff had servers visibly shaking to ask for a simple task. To me, he joked and laughed frequently in his deep-throated chuckle. His stoic face softened to kindness when I approached. I was his favorite, and I didn't know why.

"Are you two fucking?" This question was frequently asked.

"He's old enough to be my dad!" I'd retort.

One day, as we did inventory, I told Noah I needed to pick up doubles all week.

"Just don't go on overtime," he said. "Why do you need so many shifts?"

"I don't have any money. Like at all."

"Why?"

"You'll think less of me."

"I could never think less of you," he assured.

"I was fucking an addict and he stole my debit card from my wallet and emptied out my checking and savings account completely," I replied. I was sure if Noah knew the real me, he'd hate me as much as he hated everyone. Noah's life philosophy was that most people were worthless idiots. I was always trying to mask the fact that I, too, was worthless.

"I never imagined that was the kind of man you'd be with."

"Well, I'm not *with* him."

"I should hope not."

"When you're in a famine, you can't be picky about what you eat."

"I think you can afford to be somewhat picky."

"Well, I'm done with addicts."

"I was thinking about making you a shift supervisor."

I'd never considered climbing the restaurant ranks: there were so many older, long-term employees vying for that.

"You'd have to stop fraternizing," he warned.

"Of course," I nodded, though I knew I'd take my friendships underground.

My relationship to Noah was much like my relationships to any figures of authority: I obsessed over doing tasks perfectly, I hungered for praise and mentorship, I wished to show my intelligence and talent and not let them see what really resided behind all that—chaos. I felt that, at any moment, the facade could crack and expose the slut I held hostage in my ribcage.

After banishing Peyton, I began going to free therapy with student therapists at my college. I learned I was repeating the cycle of abuse from my parents and how to manage conflict without going into defense mechanisms from childhood.

One day, my therapist brought a bear and told me to yell as if it was my mother. I looked at the bear's sappy button eyes and said, "I can't."

"Try," she urged.

"That's not my mom."

"Try to imagine it is."

"If that was really my mom, then what I'd do is kill her."

The therapist sat silent and put the bear down.

Another therapist was harsher. From the first session, she identified I was the problem in my marriage. "The problem," she said, "is that you're only a half-person. You can't even get a sentence out without erupting into tears."

She has no idea, I thought, *how lucky I am to still have half of myself in tact.*

Peyton started to stalk me—showing up at my job, at my doorstep late at night. I'd keep my doors locked and refuse to answer as he left messages telling me he had Hepatitis and I should get tested, desperate ploys. I did get tested and I felt dirty for needing to.

I graduated college, Summa Cum Laude, 4.0 GPA. I desperately clung to achievement as a raft that could save me.

Noah began to randomly give gifts. I'd come to work to find a $50 Barnes & Noble gift card at my desk or a book I wanted. He'd leave notes on my to-do list, lightly touch my arm or wink.

Love for him began to swallow me like a black hole.

He'd sometimes snap, "Stop touching your hair. I hate insecure women," and that would fall on me like a sledgehammer; I could feel my buried shame, a massive monstrosity, an algae-covered shipwreck in the sea from some forgotten war.

59

He was my boss.
He loved Charles Bukowski.
His favorite book was *Lolita*.

He said He felt like an old romantic like Humbert Humbert.

He bought me books, first edition hardcovers.

He gave me raises.

He took me out to breakfast for my evaluations and paid.

He didn't take other employees to breakfast.

He was my boss, but He was also my father.

He couldn't express emotion, would revert to jokes when things got serious.

He made me CDs of His favorite music.

He drove me to corporate meetings blasting U2, Sting, Jamiroquai, Maxwell. He sang saccharine love songs at the top of his lungs with a jarring emotional conviction starkly opposite to His regular demeanor.

His love of sappy music made me see Him as a man who desperately wanted to be loved.

I wanted to love Him. I wanted His love. He was my father. He was my God.

He gave me smoldering stares from across the restaurant.

The servers said they were happy when I came on shift because that meant He'd smile.

He let me know that if I fraternized, I'd lose His respect.

He let me know that he meant that with a piercing stare, one that cut to the gut.

He talked badly about my friends, framing them as too dumb or too promiscuous.

When I made an error, He was explosively angry. I hated myself for being hated by Him.

He was my boss. He was my father.

I began to live a double life to please Him.

When He heard I'd carved pumpkins with a server, His wrath fell on me, first with the cold shoulder, then by raising His voice and asking why I'd risk my job to hang out with "that fucking fairy."

For Christmas, He bought the managers books about leadership. He gave me a personal gift privately.

He was my father. He was my God.

He loved Charles Bukowski.

His favorite book was *Lolita*.

He said He felt like an old romantic like Humbert Humbert.

I read Lolita because I wanted to know Him better.

I was shocked to realize that Lolita was only 12, that Humbert Humbert was a predator.

He was my God.

I read Bukowski because he gifted me his books. I watched the movie *Barfly*, also a gift.

I hated that he loved Bukowski, a vapid writer whose fame centered entirely on being a fucked-up, alcoholic, crude man who demanded his inadequacy be viewed as genius.

I told him I loved Bukowski—it wasn't a lie because I loved Him.

He was my God.

He'd prank me by telling me that He was quitting. He'd let the news sink in, watch my eyes fill with tears, then His eyes would sparkle; His deep rolling laughter crawled up my spine as he confessed His deceit. He'd be jovial after.

A couple times, He kissed me on the forehead and I'd think about that for weeks.

He told me He had no self confidence.

He told me He hated pictures because He hated to look at Himself.

He told me He hated his family and that everything He did for them was out of obligation.

He told me He was terrified of public speaking. I praised Him, told Him how much I believed He was better than everyone else.

He tanked at public speaking, shaking and tripping over His words.

Where was His pedestal?

Where was my God?

He left notes on my to do list to tell Him that He was wonderful. I told Him all day.

He talked about how hot the woman at the bank was. He said she was probably too young. "How young is too young?" He shrugged.

One day, He said I should feel lucky, because He was going to give me a piece of His soul.

It was a CD: songs that reminded him of his ex a decade ago. He printed out lyrics that made Him think of her and gave them to me.

I framed those lyrics, hung them over my bed.

He was my God.

He told me He was a powerful lover, that women never wanted to leave Him, that even though He had no love to give, they just wanted to change Him. "But when they're sick of me, they're *really* fucking sick of me," He said.

He said He only liked thin girls. He'd point out women's bodies who were thinner than me and say, "She's too chubby." I'd go home, weigh myself, cry.

He told me He never read women authors; I'd tell him that sounded misogynistic. "I'm not interested," He'd shrug.

He'd come into the office and turn up the music when "Landslide" by Fleetwood Mac came on, knowing I loved Stevie Nicks.

He sat in the office, head in his hands, some unspoken daily duress causing Him to ruminate, "Do you believe in God?"

He was my God.

I didn't tell him that.

He'd take away my shifts, leaving me to think I was being punished for an unknown reason. When I'd ask Him, He'd snap, storming off.

131

He'd come back hours later, say, "I'm just depressed." I'd open my heart like it had ornate, heavy church doors, heaving them ajar to welcome his confessions as he'd say, "I just thought there was more to life than this."

He never apologized for anything.

He was my father. He was my God.

He told me He hoped to get His ex back. He'd plot a grand gesture.

He told me He still kept tabs on her.

He told me she was perfect because she loved the same music as Him.

He was obsessed. He called it love.

When I asked how old she was, He replied, "10 years younger." I did the math and realized that she was around 30. I wished I was older so I could receive his love too.

It wasn't until later that I did the math to realize that she was 17 and he was nearly 30 when they dated.

He was my God.

He was a jealous God.

He demanded there be no other Gods before him.

He looked at my Myspace, went into a rage over pictures of me with people from work. He made me feel like I committed a crime by posing for pictures.

He was a vengeful god.

He made it clear that He'd cast me into Hell for the slightest transgression.

I was just a mortal girl, chock full of sin.

He loved Heath bars and Bit O'Honeys. When I brought them to cheer him, He almost seemed to love me for a moment.

He had a couple other employees he favored, but none of them had to constantly field questions.

I assured everyone that He'd never fuck me—I was too young, too fat.

I asked a server, "Why do you think He likes us but hates everyone else?"

"Because we had abusive parents," she responded bluntly.

He was my father.

He was my God.
His favorite book was *Lolita*.
He said he felt like an old romantic like Humbert Humbert.
Humbert Humbert was a predator.
Humbert Humbert groomed Lolita.

This is a story about ghosts.

60

But this is also a story about girls. Sisters.

This is a story about how sometimes your landscape shifts like a kaleidoscope and sometimes it shifts like a nuclear bomb.

This is a story about how, after my parents went years with no contact from Cassie and only minimal contact fueled by guilt from me, we showed up on their doorstep. Our father opened the door. I rushed to hug him. He trembled like a wet kitten, his voice strained, choking out his words, "I'm sorry us seeing each other had to be under such stupid circumstances."

In the living room, our father never seemed so broken. Ever the stoic man, we'd rarely seen him cry, so any expression of emotion struck like a brass bell.

"Why?" I blurted immediately.

He clutched his hands in his lap and looked at the floor. Our mother sat next to him silently. I glared at her.

That morning, I'd been woken with a call from police at 4:30 a.m. My mother was in the background screaming. She'd found my father unconscious in the garage with a shotgun next to him, both cars running. He'd tried to commit suicide.

When I rushed to the hospital, he refused me, so I drove to the college my sister attended, picked her up, and drove to confront him.

"It was your mother. I couldn't take it anymore. I always thought, in the back of my mind, that if things don't get better, I could always just…"

Our mother refused eye contact, wringing her hands.

Our father continued through sobs that made his voice sound so distorted it was as if a robot's voice emerged, "It turns out that killing yourself is a lot harder than I thought. Families are difficult. You don't get to choose them. You get stuck with people you may not like."

"You don't like us?" I asked.

"I can't speak about emotions without turning into this," he shrugged, "pathetic sap."

Cassie said, "Once you came into my room crying after a fight with mom. It really messed with me."

"I knew you loved me," I tried to soothe.

Cassie shot a look at me, "I didn't," she said firmly.

My mom looked at us with a bewildered expression, her voice rising to sound like a helpless child, "It wasn't all bad."

Cassie's posture jolted upright; she slammed her hand on her knee, "Really mom, it *was*. I'm not going to listen to you pretend that it wasn't."

Our father nodded, "The bad was so bad that it overshadowed anything else."

Our mother looked aghast, "I was abused!"

My sister and I often speculated on what sort of abuse shaped our mother. Sometimes during fights our mother would pull out stories of pastors who raped her or how badly her father beat her or how lonely she felt knowing she was adopted, but the stories always changed and always came when she was trying to manipulate us, so we never knew what was true. We were sure something happened, and that made me pity her in equal measure that I resented her, ensuring that I'd send emails on holidays, drop an occasional phone call.

"Anne and I were children of abuse too. We're dealing with it too."

"I don't think I'll ever have love because of you," I said. "I don't know if I'll ever be lovable."

Cassie put her hand on my knee.

"You should have stayed with him," my mom said. "In our generation, divorce wasn't an option."

"And look at you now!" I yelled.

"Look, I'm not going to do it again," our father said.

"Are you going to therapy?" I asked.

"They're making me go for a couple sessions, but I won't go beyond that."

"Why?"

"Because there's nothing fucking wrong with me," he snapped defensively.

I left the house feeling like an exposed nerve. Cassie looked at me in the car and said, "I can't have his blood on my hands."

This is a story about girls and their ghosts.

61

A memory. *Anne sits across from Noah at a booth. He's doing her evaluation the day after her father's suicide attempt.*

Noah: "I think you do an excellent job. I put that you meet standards on everything and that you excel at organization and dependability. You're still new to managing, so there's room to improve. You need to work on establishing your authority so people don't walk all over you."

Anne nods apologetically.

Anne: "I've worked with them so long they feel like family. I'm not very good with authority."

Noah: "Just, room for improvement."

Anne: "I want to do a good job for you."

Noah: "I appreciate that. I'm promoting you to assistant manager."

Anne: "I thought you were going to hire someone?"

Noah: "I changed my mind. No more serving for you. Just don't fraternize."

Anne nods.

Noah: "How's your dad?"

Anne: "He said it was because of my mom."

Noah: "Yikes."

Anne: "If my mom had done this, I don't think I'd care. I'd think it's a cry for attention. But it was my dad, so he meant it."

Noah: "If I had my choice, I'd never talk to my family again."

Anne nods. Noah grabs Anne's hand. He looks as if he cares.

Anne: "I should go home where I can have my breakdowns privately." *Anne laughs half heartedly.*

Noah: "I have something to get off my chest."

Anne: "What?"

Noah: "I've been fucking one of the servers."

Anne tenses.

Anne: "What?"

Noah: "For five months."

Anne: "What?"

Noah: "Yep!"

Anne sits silent, grief stricken. Noah grins like a teenage boy.

Noah: "Sooooo?"

Anne: "Why'd you tell me this?"

Noah: "I needed to tell someone."

Anne: "I don't want to know that."

Noah: "I just thought…"

Anne: "I don't want to know that."

Noah: "I feel like I've been lying to you."

Anne: "You're my boss. I prefer ignorance."

Noah: "I don't discuss things I'm passionate about with her like with you. I thought it was over the other week, but she called, wanted sex again."

Anne: "I really don't want to know this."

Noah: "I just need to talk to someone who understands me."

Anne: "Talk to her about your relationship."

Noah: "It's complicated."

Anne: "You just told me not to fraternize."

Noah: "Do as I say, not as I do."

Anne: "I'm on sensory overload. My dad just attempted suicide."

Noah: "I thought it'd make you happy to know me better."

Anne: "Maybe I'm just…I'm gonna go."

Noah: "You're just what?"

Anne looks down.

Anne: "Jealous."

Noah: "What?"

Anne: "I'll see you tomorrow."

It doesn't end here.

It doesn't end when both fathers revealed how easily they'd abandon.

But it should have.

62

First there was the new server—his neon polo shirt ironed to a crisp, his perfectly manicured hair, his smooth skin, toasted to deep tan, emulating the coiffed styles of boy bands. He left Valentines on my desk that Noah found and threw angrily in the garbage. Late at night, after the clubs closed, he'd call and I'd let his waxed chest collide against me until my coarseness was polished.

There was the broil cook, his boyish charm retreating from my flirtatious advances, until one night I was too drunk to drive home and my friends were fighting for my keys. He intervened: *She can come home with me.* He bashed against my bones until my joints felt like they were coming unlocked.

There was the other broil cook, who wore handkerchiefs on his head and a mischievous grin, who stormed in the office, demanded: *Why do you keep giving me those eyes?* I'd schedule him to close the restaurant, make him screwdrivers at the bar. He was sauced when I told him I wanted him to take me home. He said I was a tornado, that I come sweeping through and make doors fly off hinges, leaving men bare and small. I said thank you, left in the night.

There was my friend, Bryan, a server who'd take me out for wings and tequila and talk about philosophy, feminism, literature. He believed in unconditional love. We loved each other until he snapped like a rubber band, confessing that he couldn't stop thinking about me, even though he had a girlfriend. As soon as he entered me, I knew he couldn't possibly love me and everything changed.

140

There was his roommate, who gave me winks as we played drinking games, who slammed me against the wall after I came out of the bathroom and kissed me, asking me to come to his car. I let him take me in the backseat like a baboon. I must have looked like one when his girlfriend woke, came outside, and opened the car door on us. I gathered my clothes in the parking lot as I watched him chase after her car. She hit him and he toppled over the hood. I got in my car and drove home, grateful to escape the wrath I deserved.

There were men at clubs whose names I've forgotten, whose faces I couldn't pick out in a line-up, whose shadows pored into my void but evaporated when the sun rose.

There was me, wounded and untamed with pure instinct coursing through my veins. There was me loving my boss, pretending to be domesticated: sitting, begging, obeying, staying.

There was me and there was a void and I mounted everything I desired but conquered nothing, let them fill me but walked away with nothing. There was me and this hunger and what satiated it was nothing. There was me and there was fear and there was the moon that made a mournful howl escape my throat into nothingness.

There was me and there was fear and there was the pull to flee, to cast off my fur and walk upright, to wear skin again.

63

After I got into graduate school at Emerson College, after I saw the escape shoot manifest in front of my eyes, after I told Noah that it'd be my last summer at the restaurant, he did something uncharacteristic: he stood up and pulled me into an embrace.

Then I dreamed about it.

First, I dreamed the embrace had more weight, as if touch could replace words unsaid.

Then I dreamed I slowly peeled each arm off me like I was flaying my own skin. I spread them outward, pressed them against the wall, and stared at his openness until he draped his head. I took a spike and plunged it through one wrist, then another. I stripped off his clothes and observed what I'd created. I said, *There. You're finally known to me and finally dead to me.*

I washed his blood off of me in a river and pledged that whoever comes next, I'll come clean to.

Cassie had decided to move to Boston with me. I had no money saved and no idea how one uproots an entire life. But with my sister, I felt magic was possible.

"You know how you get that feeling that if you leave now, you'll be able to save the experience as something you cherish, but if you stay, things will soon go very sour?" Cassie asked.

"I started feeling it's going sour long ago."

"It's so obvious we were abused," Cassie said.

142

64

When I was harboring a love for my boss, I couldn't imagine what it was that made him value me, what prompted the gifts, promotions, confided secrets. My whole self worth was mirrored against the image I'd created of him: this towering, perfect giant.

All I could see of myself next to him was what I lacked.

Now I can look back and see my allure—in targeting me, Noah had the opportunity to go from a man to a god.

He could have a young, kind girl without her being the wiser that he didn't deserve her. Because some girls hate themselves.

When I finally slept with Noah, it was as if the planets flung out of orbit, as if he was a star and I was a moon and he collided with me and I evaporated like dust.

I'd convinced myself it was all my doing—I wanted it; he had sex with me out of pity and friendship; I should be grateful; I could die happy if only he touched me.

Noah announced at a meeting a new requirement to do "manager bonding" events. He had an event planned for all the managers, but I would have to close the restaurant, so he and I would have bonding time separately.

Our bonding happened a few days later: he invited me to his apartment for drinks. He kept my beer glass full. Romantic candles were lit; Maxwell played on his stereo. I didn't think he was trying to seduce me. I eagerly drank everything offered in hopes that I'd be drunk enough to excuse anything.

As we both started slurring words, he pulled out the futon, "I guess you're staying the night!" I fell back, disoriented for such good luck.

I was the one who nestled my body next to his. I was the one who put my arm across his stomach. I was the one who moved my face into the crook of his neck, let my breath strum against his pulse. I was the one who put my lips in line with his, who stared at him in the dark with the wide-eyed adoration of a little girl.

When he kissed me, I was the one who was sunk into him like a black hole.

When he fucked me, he'd hold me close and say, "You felt so good." He never said he loved me.

Here was a man who had his own apartment, who used coasters for beer mugs, who arranged his music alphabetically, who finished college, who chose masculine patterned sheets, who paid off his loans, who ran sales reports. Here was a man who didn't have kids, who'd never been in a real relationship, who bemoaned how needy and emotional women were, who could never find one perfect enough.

Here was a man.

Here was a god.

After sex, he'd sometimes say, "I just thought I'd be more than a restaurant manager."

"But you *are* more," I'd say.

It was a lie. But I didn't know it.

I was the one full of potential, containing multitudes I'd not even begun to examine. It would take years of growing up, of growing away from the young, worshipful shell of me in his arms before I realized that.

When men I cared for had sex with me, I'd have a period of feeling high, then I'd begin to feel bitter, as if sex was proof they didn't care at all, that they'd discard me the way every man did.

Bryan, the server who cheated on his girlfriend with me, was the rare soul everyone liked.

I loved that boy.

I felt entirely unworthy of him.

One day, while sitting in the office with several staff, I mentioned I hadn't dated since my divorce, that I'd "slept with some losers, nobody important."

Bryan looked at me, stood up, and walked out of the office.

Later, I told Bryan how I felt. "How can you say I'm your friend, how can you say you love me, only to make me the other woman? The one who can be discarded? I feel like you knew that I never say no to sex, and you knew I'd never betray you."

"You're this incredible woman that any man would be lucky to have. I'm really afraid that when you go to grad school, you'll realize how average the rest of us are."

"I've always put you on a pedestal."

"And I fell off. But that was *love*, Anne."

Was it? Was it?

65

JOURNAL ENTRY
7-2-2006

I'm in front of C.D.'s grave for what I expect will be the last time.

He embodies everything I've learned about our temporariness in this world and in each other's lives.

He is proof that I can kill everything I love and survive.

C.D. is what I know of grief and loss, C.D. is what I know of loving and letting go. C.D.'s death is the wind that propelled me to where I'm going. It fueled my dreams with the fiercest convictions, the deepest knowledge of pain.

All I wanted then, all I wanted ever, was love, was to know love and be held inside of love and to live this life secure in that. Now I know love in all its varied shades and I know that it's fleeting; yet there's nothing worse to let go of.

At the cemetery, it's beautiful and the sun is shining and the wind is cooling and I'm leaving soon. It's beautiful and I'm leaving.

People and places and passions run through my head and I want to cry but every fiber of my being is telling me I have nothing to cry for.

Boston isn't going to be an answer to my wildest dreams. Emerson could be disenchanting, I could fail as a writer, I could be lonely and maybe love will turn into pure memory. Maybe a man will never penetrate me more than the depth of recent occurrences and maybe not even that. I don't look at this as the solution, but I know it's the answer.

I felt a surge of something just now lying atop his grave.

I want to carry all that I've loved and left inside me the way I carry C.D. The lovers, the friends, my boss, and all the moments where I've felt a hint of the

146

essence of what I continue to subsist for—I want you to all lay down now. I want you to rest in peace.

C.D., I'll never be able to thank you. For the knowledge, the eye I've turned to the soul and the world, the strength, the failure, everything.

Here in the midst of death, I feel so alive and I'm getting ready to walk away with nothing. I pray that what I love and what I leave will not only forgive me, but remember.

III

66

Sometimes in those slasher movies, the heroine doesn't die—she conquers.

But the monster still comes back.

The story starts all over.

A different time, a different cast, a different setting.

And ghosts must do again what gives them pain.

67

Say it went well. Say she packed a few boxes and a blow up mattress into the back of a rented F-150 and watched the small life of the midwest disappear in her rearview as the sleek Boston skyline mushroomed over the Charles River in front of her. Say the buildings lit up like the earth fastening itself to the constellations.

Say the way the Hynes Convention Center's mirrored architecture reflected the oldest church in the city meant something to her about herself that she couldn't quite articulate.

Say that saying goodbye to everyone she loved was like carving pearls of tumors out of your intestines one by one. Say she cried every night for her boss, who sometimes sent an email or a package, but most often didn't.

Say that swallowing back love like vomit turns you to stone when you wish to be salt, washed away by the next rain. Say that there's nothing worse than feeling as muted and invisible as stone.

Say that she started smoking, sitting on her balcony and looking at the moon and opening her own heart in her hands to find a bursting pomegranate, overflowing with seeds of memories of men who couldn't love her. Say her desire was so red it stained her hands and everything she touched.

Say she kept flying back for a year, for just one more hit.

Say he never asked about her new life. Say she wanted to make him proud, to grow up to be good enough, but he never asked how she was growing.

Say it took her a long time to realize that he didn't want her to grow. He didn't look at her as a growing thing.

Say that in escaping, she might as well have walked through the tiny door to Wonderland, that her new friends were Cheshire Cats and Mad Hatters. Say that everything was neon, electric, and possible.

Say she got a job as a waitress at a fancy seafood restaurant in the heart of Boston's theater district. Say she loved her professors and books and the other poets. Say she immediately made friends and was woven into the tapestry of the lives of people who take big risks, make big moves, have big dreams, and have little fear.

Say half the waitstaff she worked with were gay, beautiful, and safe.

Say love rooted itself immediately, and deep.

Say the cocaine bumps that staff did in the bathrooms on keys became normal, that sitting on a subway car that caught on fire was just another day.

Say when she chanted, *Love that dirty water* at a Red Sox game, she meant it.

Say she meant it.

Say she'd never said the word love and meant it more.

Say that.

Say love.

Say home.

Say she never wanted to leave.

But say her old self didn't die and neither did her demons.

Say that's all over now.

Say it anyway.

68

It was late 2006 when I moved to Boston, and America had a rabid obsession: Britney Spears.

She was everywhere: MTV's entire business model seemed to rest on her smile and hip gyrations. Her cooing baby voice was so distinctly intoxicating that every song became an earworm. Reporters asked repeatedly: *Are you a virgin?*

In 2006, Britney was a young mother, so America frothed at the mouth, bearing the truth of how sick our cultural misogyny: even feminists abandoned her.

Pictures surfaced of her escaping paparazzi while driving with her son in her lap, more pictures surfaced of her trying to walk through a swarm of over 300 men with cameras, pregnant with her second son, as she almost dropped her son on the concrete. Then they swarmed the window to the cafe where she sat alone, weeping. Soon, she lost custody. Paparazzi struck gold when they hunted her to find her shaving her head. They followed her until she jumped out of her car, bald-headed and armed with an umbrella, releasing all her rage.

She committed the cardinal sin of self harm for women: she ruined her beauty.

The photographers, the magazine owners, the bloggers, and the late night talk show hosts mocking her got rich. There was a dark and thriving economy centered entirely on exploiting the mental health of Britney Spears.

It was the beginning of her Blackout era, in which she released her best album while the world collectively held their breath, wondering if this was the day she'd kill herself.

I, too, was descending into my own era, and my days were punctuated with Britney. I'd wake up in my shitty, expensive apartment, open my laptop, and go to blogs to view the paparazzi videos: Britney was generally trying to go to a store, and she'd be in a terrible wig, her acne on display behind some big sunglasses, speaking gibberish in a faux British accent that had everyone speculating what drugs she used. Before I went to bed, I repeated the ritual—I checked on Britney and felt afraid.

Cassie and I got jobs at a restaurant that boasted of celebrity diners. Cassie was a host and I was a server. In walking into this restaurant that was a city block long and two stories high with a labyrinth wine cellar—its waterfall cascading from the ceiling down the center staircase and its glass walls covered in ocean water views—I couldn't imagine I was good enough to work for such important people.

I felt similarly out of place with the staff—a group of people so stunningly beautiful and charismatic that they all seemed a chance discovery away from fame. We wore black slacks, black button up shirts with collars, and a long black apron. If we had an important event, we'd don a maroon tie.

A Friday night could easily have 30-40 servers; I was used to restaurants that operated with 4-8 servers a night. The energy and bustle was electric and chaotic—the young staff seemed to choreograph hefting large trays of dirty dishes, flamboyantly opening expensive bottles of wine, and shamelessly flirting with off-colored jokes with the ease of circus jugglers. Those first few days training, I wanted to disappear.

Until I met the most beautiful man I'd ever seen.

He walked into the locker room and locked eyes as if he recognized me, "Hiiiiiiiiiiiiiiiii!"

I felt flustered, thinking he must have mistaken me for someone. It was like he walked right out of a Calvin Klien ad—he was half Mexican with bright green eyes and jet black hair, tall and muscular. His dark chest hair peaked out of the top of his button up shirt and his wide, perfect smile nearly knocked the wind out of me.

"Hello," I said awkwardly.

"Oh my god, are you new? I'm Chris!"

"I just moved here from Michigan. I'm Anne."

"You're adorable!" He exclaimed. His exuberance hit like a tornado.

Just a few days later, he was friend requesting me on MySpace and sending me my first ever text, "Hi sexy," it said, "Do you like Britney?"

"I looooooooooove Britney," I replied.

"We're soulmates!"

Chris was gay, and that was a relief. I was able to relax about his intimidating beauty and absorb the adoration he showered. Soon, Chris and I were texting or AIM chatting morning until night and frequenting Club Cafe, Avalon, and Machine—popular gay bars.

Whenever Britney came on, we'd look at each other in wide-eyed excitement and scream at the top of our lungs. I thought, *Finally, a man I can be myself with*.

Chris was studying Linguistics—he loved languages, traveling, and corny jokes. He punctuated everything he said with a contagious jingle of laughter. Everybody wanted to be near him.

He introduced me to his friend, an equally beautiful Cuban American named Omar who was studying literature. Omar and Chris were night and day different—where Chris was exuberant, Omar was tempered and pensive. Where Chris was chaotic, Omar was responsible. Where Chris was loud and impulsive, Omar was quiet, excessively polite, and mild mannered—it was as if he belonged to another century, as if he walked the earth in the time of the British romantics whose poetry he adored.

Where Chris and Omar were the same was that they were unbelievably hot. Everywhere they went, lust followed.

Omar had been best friends with celebrity blogger Perez Hilton growing up in Miami, and they were still close, so Omar introduced me. I was starstruck, saying little. Perez Hilton was such an integral part of my life, and I could only think of him in terms of his proximity to the stars. Omar told me about him being bullied for his sexuality and his weight as a kid. I didn't think about how perniciously toxic bullying could be when it's projected, or how my viewing of his blog contributed to the endless torment of Britney Spears.

It's not because I didn't care about Britney. Chris and I loved her as if she was our friend. We spent hours on the phone fretting; we could get so worked up worrying about her. It was as if we were watching the demise of Marilyn Monroe.

What I don't think I realized was how much in lockstep I was with her. Sometimes I would shiver in a moment of recognition of her in a photo, her eyeliner smeared down her cheeks and her hair cascading in front of her face as a fluster of grease and tangles, her short dress and her parted legs and the photographers that shoved in to get a glimpse of her, and I'd be so thankful no one was following me as I was throwing back Long Islands and huffing poppers and dancing slutty and taking strange men home and laughing with Chris and never sleeping and waking up with gaps of my memory gone and avoiding all my problems.

The go-go dancer in the cage stared as fluorescent lights danced along his abs.

Inside me, I could hear something rattle, hiss.

The yawn of misogyny swallowed Britney in its fang. She became the seductive serpent everyone feared as a result.

So did I.

69

3 a.m.: my cell rang. I was doing my usual: chain smoking and staring at the moon, anxiety running through me like the quiet buzz of electronics. It was Chris.

Chris burst into a show tunes persona, singing Christina Aguilera, "Ain't no other Anne, that can stand, up next to you! Ain't no other Anne, on the planet, does what you do! You're the kinda Anne, a girl finds, in a blue moon. Aint no other Anne, it's true! Ain't no other Anne but you!"

"Do your thang honey!" I adored the way Chris embraced all things camp. When we went dancing, Chris was the life of the party. When "Ring the Alarm" came on by Beyonce, his eyes would light up and he'd start looking around, telling the people next to him, "Hold me back! Hold me back!" Then he'd launch into an impersonation of Beyonce's music video, jumping and lunging at me or Omar as if he was about to attack his cheating lover. When Britney's "I'm a Slave 4 U" came on, he'd transform into the full gyrating belly dancer choreography of her VMA performance.

With Chris, I could love what I loved with unabashed joy in ways I couldn't with others.

"I missed you tonight! Omar and I are so obsessed! We talk about you all. the. time." He was going a mile a minute, still buzzing from partying.

"The feeling's mutual."

156

"Tonight we went out and I saw this really hot guy who I wanted to go home with, but he didn't pay me any attention. He had the ugliest fag hag too. P.S. I'm so glad you're my fag hag because you're hot."

"I'm no where near as hot as you."

"Bitch please. You look like a porcelain doll. You wanna come over tomorrow and snuggle? We can watch every Beyonce video ever made from Destiny's Child to today."

"If you weren't gay, you'd be my dream lover. Yes, I want to watch Beyonce all day."

"Dreaaaaaaam lover come rescue me!"

Despite my conservative parents' homophobia and the rampant homophobia that infects every school in America, I recognized camp culture as in line with things I'd always loved. It was about defying the status quo, being yourself unapologetically, chasing pleasure without shame, and rubbing it in everyone's judgmental faces.

The gay clubs in Boston became my Mecca. Soon, they were the only clubs I frequented. We had VIP cards and would stroll in without waiting in line.

Women were the minorities, and I reveled in that. Strange men would approach, "You have amazing breasts!" They'd often grab them without consent, but I was flattered. When I was at a gay club, I felt safe: I knew that the man grabbing me didn't want to have sex.

Often, men would look at Chris and Omar and say, "You have a wonderful hag!"

"We know!" they'd reply, pulling me into a hug.

"Why is it called 'fag hag?'" I asked Chris.

"It's usually an ugly girl who can't get a man so she hangs out with gay men that she wishes she could have sex with."

"That's what you think of me?"

"Of course not! My hags can have any man."

"I'm a hag?"

"It's a term of endearment."

I look back at photos of the three of us and I see three beautiful, happy people who love each other fiercely. But I was haunted by Chris and Omar's beauty.

I was told I was beautiful a hundred times a night, yet it never rooted. Light doesn't enter the cave of self loathing that broken girls survive in.

Despite that, I had a physical intimacy with Chris and Omar that filled a void. It wasn't unusual for me to sleep in the same bed with them after a drunken night or to curl up on the couch with them to spoon and watch television. We danced provocatively together at the club as if we were lovers. With Chris and Omar, I had it all with no threat of sex to ruin the love.

There was a go-go dancer that worked at all the clubs. He'd approach me in his neon g-string, abs stacked brick by brick, and whisper in my ear, "Do you want to come home with me?"

Chris and Omar were fiercely protective. Chris would come up to us and begin to dance, wresting me away from his grasp and shoving me to another part of the dance floor.

"He's gay for pay. Gay for pay means stay away!"

The more I was told to stay away, the more I felt pulled.

On top of that, my classes were stressful. I was taking a Teaching Freshmen Writing class that was competitive. Around 50 students took the course and only 5-6 would be hired as graduate instructors. I was waiting tables 50 hours a week. Noah wasn't answering emails.

The less I heard from him, the more I felt as hollow as a rainstick: desire coursed through me like little seeds that roll over each other to make the sound of an ocean crash.

We didn't know the name of the go-go dancer. Sometimes he said it was Carlos. Sometimes he said it was Pedro. We came up with another nickname for him based on what we saw of his dancing: The M.C., short for "Monster Cock."

One night, the M.C. groped my breast. Omar saw and the smile slid off his face. He grabbed him by the arm, "Are you attracted to her?"

"Always," he said.

"You do anything to her, I'll kill you."

The M.C. nodded and walked away. Later, as we were hailing a cab, the M.C. approached again, "I'll give you a ride home."

Omar grabbed my wrist, "No."

"Omar!" I protested.

"No. He's low class."

158

The next week, Omar didn't come out. Chris was much more likely to support my bad choices, so when the M.C. came to dance and ask why I didn't come home with him, I hoped I'd be able to sneak away.

But Chris walked up to the M.C. and shoved him as hard as he could. The M.C. shoved Chris back, and Chris said, "You think you're good enough for her? You're not."

Later, he was back, whispering in my ear that it was time to go home. Chris yanked my arm so hard that I almost fell.

"Chris! Why?"

"Bitch please. I probably just saved you from AIDS."

But there was no stopping me when I was unraveling. To satiate my desire, I decided to take another server home from work and try cocaine for the first time.

I drank more too—to the point where I'd get sloppy. One night, as Omar was helping me leave after the bouncers kicked me out, the M.C. smacked me on the ass, "What a drunk hag."

"I'm worried about you," Omar said, "You don't know your limits."

After partying, I'd go home and watch Britney unravel on the blogs. The fear I felt for her inched up my spine until I realized it was really for myself.

Then it happened.

I snapped like whip.

First, I got a package from Noah: it caused me to book a flight to see him. When I went to the restaurant, he hugged me and was friendly. He told me I looked good. He told me to call him. He told me we'd have a drink.

I called twice. He never answered.

Then Chris and Omar broke the news that they were moving to New York City after the summer.

Then Cassie got into Amherst College on a full ride. She, too, would be leaving. I'd be stuck with rent alone.

When a girl who believes she is unlovable loves others, love practically fills her lungs and drowns her outright.

I did what I always did when I felt people I loved leaving: I scanned every room to find the snake.

When the M.C. smiled, I saw what his teeth could do.

I rattled.

So did he.

The speakers blared Rihanna's "Please Don't Stop the Music."

We desire what we think we deserve.

This is a story about ghosts.

70

Every horror story has a death.
And ghosts must do again what gives them pain.

71

JOURNAL ENTRY
7-2-07

Chris leaves soon. We had a big hurrah. What a mess.

I saw the M.C. in the bathroom. He came up before I had my first drink. He smacked my ass, asked how I was. Omar came and put his arm around me, which really pissed him off. He said, "You're so rude. Can't you see I'm talking to her?"

Omar said calmly, "Yes, I'm rude and I pride myself on it. You're not talking to her anymore."

The M.C. said, "You ever been cussed out?"

"I don't think I'd care if I was, so you can just leave." He left and then Omar was stern, "Don't talk to him. He's trash."

I think Omar made the M.C. so mad that he tried harder. He practically stalked me on the dance floor. Omar would catch it and pull us to another area. Then he caught me giving him a flirty look. He goes to Chris, "That's it! I'm done with her! She'll never listen." I hate to have Omar think badly of me.

I got drunk, stumbling. The M.C. offered me a ride. I said yes. I was so drunk I had no idea how to get home. We drove forever. He kept telling me how dumb I was. Finally, I recognized where we were. But I made a mistake and walked up to the porch of the house next door. It took me a few minutes before I realized I wasn't home.

When I got to my porch, I realized that Chris had my keys. I went to Cassie's window. She jumped out of bed.

"What the fuck? I fucking hate you, bitch."

She let us in.

We got inside and the M.C. insulted me repeatedly for my mess. Earlier in the night, he called me chunky. When I got mad, he said, "It's a compliment."

As much as he scares me, he also intrigues me. I just want to know his story. He gave me a couple hits of coke so my heart was racing. With the alcohol, the room was spinning.

He's from El Salvador. Came here when he was 8. Lived in Charleston. Was in a gang by the time he was 10. Saw people die. Saw his best friend die. Beat people up. Never killed anybody. Played all sorts of sports to get the body he has. Became a personal trainer and a dancer. He believes in love and monogamy. He doesn't like girls who sleep around, so a lot of times he just goes home with girls to see if he can do it and then leaves. He said, "In El Salvador, girls are shy. Nice girls." He seemed comfortable talking to me because he threw his leg over my leg. At one point, he petted my hair and said, "What do you want?"

"A girl lets a guy take her home—you know what she wants."

He took my head and shoved it down. He kept telling me to put it all the way in. I really had to control my gag reflex. He was rough.

It's been two days now and once I got to this part I felt unable to write more. But I have to get it out.

He got up and turned me over. He took off my pants. He put on a condom. We started to have sex.

I don't know what was wrong with me. How drunk I was or why the room was spinning. It hurt only for a moment and lasted only for a moment before he pulled out and put it in my ass.

I tried to pull away, but he was fast, forceful. I was surprised how quickly it happened. I said no over and over. I suddenly felt like a child. So humiliated. I begged him to stop. It hurt so bad and he was pounding away. It was degrading. Finally I put my head in the pillow and sobbed. He stopped.

I immediately turned over so he wouldn't get me again. He looked at me, slowly took off the condom, and said, "I don't know why you're stopping." I said it hurt. I asked him why he did that. He said, "Pussy gets tired sometimes."

I laid on the bed, shirt down to my waist, no pants. I closed my eyes. He asked if I was okay. I said I was fine, but he should leave. He stood for a minute. I kept my eyes closed. He asked if I was sure I was okay. I said yes. He asked how I could sleep with the coke. I said I wasn't really tired; I just wanted him to be gone when I opened my eyes. He said, "Well, I'll see you around. Be a good girl." I said I wasn't going to Avalon anymore. He said, "I'm sure I'll see you. But I might not talk

163

to you. Sometimes I don't talk to girls I sleep with." I said whatever. I kept my eyes closed. He said, "Remember not to tell." I nodded. He stood in my doorway. He said, "Hey, look at me." I opened my eyes. "I respect you," he said. I said okay and closed my eyes again. He left.

I was bleeding. I couldn't go to the bathroom. I felt like I should hate him and I couldn't understand why I didn't. I know he violated me, but I am a dumb girl that takes insults and still craves that physical thing. He didn't even kiss me. It was just this vulgar thing that I'd prefer to live without.

The last thing he said, the one nice thing he's ever said, what was that? Was he perceptive enough to realize that I'm actually a smart girl aside from the mess I am? Or is it what I feared? He's more manipulative than he looks, and as he looked at me and asked if I was okay, he realized that I was not okay and that maybe later I'd get that word into my head—rape—and he could be in trouble. So he told me he respected me and it worked.

Today I wandered like a ghost. I broke down in my sister's room. I said I just didn't know what was wrong with me, why I'd let this happen.

I wasn't threatened. I wasn't attacked. It wasn't a stranger, even though I don't know his name. I had consented to have sex with him. I wasn't hit and I didn't fight very hard—mostly cause I knew I wouldn't win. So, was I raped? And if I was, what does that mean? I knew I was in a dangerous situation. Everyone said to stay away. Yet, I invited him in.

I guess in the textbook sense I was raped because I said no, but in the psychological sense—did I invite this? Did I let myself get raped? Was there still a part of me that wanted to please a man, even if that's what it took? Why wasn't I more mad at him? Why did his respect for me ring in my head? Why did it feel like that was exactly what I needed to hear?

Today I had flashbacks. I wasn't normal. Whenever a part of the incident came into my head, I'd jam my iPod further into my ear. I could visualize his face perfectly. He looked crazy. Then I'd visualize him dancing. He looked hot. I didn't want to light my cigarette with a lighter because I had an image of him lighting my cig for me, so I used matches. I feel really depressed.

And I'm depressed over Chris. He moved today. I was determined to have a great time, make it all about him. So many people showed up for him. It was like a movie, dancing on the stage and laughing, all of us together one last time, all of us so young, beautiful, happy. Chris met a boy and went home with him. We said goodbye. We were all quiet. Omar said Chris was like a bird we had to set free, but he'd fly back. "You know," Omar said gently, "as much as you love Chris, he loves you too. You don't give yourself enough credit."

Now he's gone. And that's just the way life is.

I wandered today wondering what I'm supposed to do. How to act now. People ask if I'm okay. I say, I'm fine. Because I am, right? I'm alive. I'm walking. I'm breathing. I got up. I cleaned my room. Life keeps going. I feel it should be different. But I suppose resilience is better.

Maybe I need some counseling.

I got the teaching job.

72

I walked into the restaurant. We served in teams; my partner was setting up our section.

"Hey A.C.!" he said.

"Hey."

He stopped in his tracks and grabbed my arm.

"What?" I said.

"You had sex."

I squirmed until I was free of his grasp. "No, I didn't," I lied, ducking him by heading to the break room.

I'd met Cal the day I was hired; he latched onto me immediately. We both said that we felt a weird flash of recognition upon meeting. Seeing his face for the first time filled me with calm.

We were inseparable. The managers made us partners because we were both new, but soon our closeness and our teamwork made our work partnership permanent. If we ever walked into a shift and were assigned another partner, we beelined to management to complain. We had the same work schedule, and even though we spent so much time together at work, we spent more time together after, having drinks at a bar on Boylston Street. My earliest memories of Boston are of walking through wind tunnels amongst the skyscrapers after work with Cal.

Cal was tall, handsome, confident. He was a pianist studying at Berklee College of Music. Girls and gay men on staff drooled over him; he was jovial and flirtatious. People often came up to me asking what it was like to date him. I'd explain he had a girlfriend—a beautiful violinist

166

—we were just friends. Cal got a kick out of feeding the rumors by calling me his wife and flirting openly.

There was something else about my friendship with Cal, something weird: he had a strange psychic sense about me. One day, while walking home, Cal looked at me and said, "Don't fall." Then I promptly tripped on my own feet and fell flat on my face.

"How'd you know I'd fall?"

"I have no idea," he laughed.

One thing Cal could predict with stunning accuracy was when I'd had sex, which I never wanted to tell him; he felt like my big brother. I chalked up his knowing to a glow I might have.

But this time there was no glow: I looked haggard.

Cal followed as I shoved my purse in a locker. "Who was it? The go-go dancer? The sauté cook? Someone new?"

"I didn't have sex, Cal," I said flatly.

"Look at me," he said. I glanced at him and he searched my face. I looked away quickly in fear that he'd see every dirty detail. "Yes, you did!"

I sighed, "Cal, I'm not in the best mood."

"What's wrong?"

"Nothing."

"Then tell me who you had sex with."

"No."

Cal dropped it for a moment and we set to work. But Cal kept bringing it up. "It was the go-go dancer?"

"Cal, stop."

After the tenth hour of work, as the restaurant was finally calming down from a dinner rush, I dropped a wine glass. Shattered wine glasses were a daily event at the restaurant, but when that glass broke, so did my ability to hold my composure.

Cal stood behind me and teased, "Good one, A.C."

I looked at him, put down my tray, and burst into tears. I ran to the dish room and out the back door to the smoking area. I let out full, body-heaving sobs.

Cal followed. Saying nothing, he pulled me to him and wrapped me in a hug. I cried on his chest uncontrollably.

"What happened?"

"I'm just depressed."

"Is this new or have you been depressed for some time?"

I shrugged.

"Is it Chris and Omar leaving? Your sister?"

"Everything," I sobbed.

"You've been going too fast. Too much work, too much partying, too much school."

I nodded.

"Let's get some food after work."

I looked up at Cal, embarrassed. "It's been a lot lately."

He continued to rub my back. "I know."

I looked at his face to search if he did know, *really* know, what I meant. He didn't.

He couldn't see what happened—what I'd brought on myself, being the desperate slut I was. He couldn't see the type of men a girl like me slept with or the humiliating ways they treated me. I couldn't let him ever see it.

In my mind, like Chris and Omar, Cal was so near perfection that I was unworthy. I thought his girlfriend was a goddess. She wasn't threatened by Cal's friendship with me, often joining us for drinks.

I needed the people I loved to not smell the stench of my truths.

This applied to Chris and Omar too. I tried to tell them both via AIM the next day. They both said what they had every right to say: we told you not to mess with him. I don't think either interpreted what I said as rape. I still didn't interpret it as rape myself.

I felt the trauma, but I didn't know if I had the right to my trauma because I deserved it.

So I buried it in the darkest cave of me, the excruciating hurt of it, how fiercely it reinforced what I'd believed since I was a child. I'm not the type of girl men love. If I love a man, like I loved Cal, Omar, and Chris, then I had to hide the truth of who I was, lest I lose them too.

In that cave, this is the truth that rooted—growing until it coursed through every vein and the trauma sat in my heart, a fat Buddha, an ancient tree, a long shadow.

If you want to know how I survived, I'll tell you.

I survived because when Omar's graduation came, Chris asked me to be his date. Chris showed up at my apartment in a striped collared shirt with dress pants and a bouquet of flowers.

"What are these for?"

"Mi amor," he said seductively, then burst into laughter. While I was putting the flowers in a vase, Chris plucked one of them off its stem and held it between his thumb and forefinger in my face. "Look, it's a snapdragon," he laughed. "I love these." He played with the flower so that it looked like a jaw opening and closing. "See, there's its tongue," he said, "Roar!"

He shoved it in my face and we fell on the bed onto our stomachs giggling and playing with the flower to make it look like a dragon. I wrote a poem called "Snapdragons." It was one of my first published poems and was nominated for a Pushcart Prize.

I survived because after Omar and Chris moved, I spent weekends in New York City. I sat with Omar in his beautiful space at NYU that had a perfect view of the New York skyline at night, reciting poems. Our favorite was Elizabeth Bishop's "Filling Station," with the surprise last line: "Somebody loves us all."

"Somebody loves us all," Omar cooed, wide eyes in wonderment.

I survived because I laid on my back with Chris in Central Park on sunny afternoons, chain smoking and gossiping. Chris pulled chunks of grass, held out his palms, and blew them in my face for the camera—a cloud of earth hovered in front of him like an aura—we giggled. We aimed to get the perfect laying-in-grass profile pictures for MySpace; we snapped pictures of each other, each staring at the camera with a look of pure adoration. We took pictures with the skyline behind us, and I marveled at the girl I saw: a girl whose dreams were coming true.

I survived because when Gay Pride rolled around, Chris and I were decked in feather boas dancing our hearts out in the streets. Glitter and rainbow confetti rained from the sky and the streets were transformed by parades of drag queens; every spectrum of queer occupied every corner of the street.

When I watched Chris dance—his joyful, authentic, unashamed, unapologetic self—I knew that every essence of his being was a revolution.

I survived because sometimes Chris and I sat outside and watched the dawn come with quiet reverence, having been up all night, and I knew that we both had some deep wounds, that we were people who patriarchy had tried to batter, shame, deny.

If you want to know how I survived, the answer is love.
The girl who thought she was unlovable was so very loved.

And even though love ran through her like a water balloon with a leak, she found men whose love was a tsunami that coursed through her like a white water rapids.

When I was a child, there was a scene in a *Forrest Gump* that impacted me. A little girl, having been molested by her stepfather, grabbed her friend's hand and ran into a sea of corn husks to escape. She fell on her knees in the dirt and prayed: "Dear God, Make me a bird so I can fly far, far away from here."
I had flown far, far away from the home that hurt me. I landed in Boston like a terrified, wounded child. It was as if Chris' inner child found me in that corn field—broken, praying. He grabbed me by the wrist and we ran further into the corn fields and into a magical place, where his inner child was so alive, full of laughter and wonderment about the majestic world around us and the adventures that await us on this playground of life.

If you want to know how I survived, the answer is love.
But, as Omar often quoted from Robert Hayden, *What did I know of love's austere and lonely offices?*

73

After the go-go dancer, I changed fundamentally, but I didn't realize I was transforming. It took a few more blows for the new me to emerge.

One drunken night, high on coke and watching the sunrise with Chris, he said mournfully, "I feel bad for my ex. He needs a green card, but he can't find someone to marry."

"I'll marry him," I shrugged.

Chris lit up, "Really?"

"Why not? I'm never going to marry anyone for real."

This led me to meet Pedro. Pedro exhibited much of Chris' traits: excessively loving, kind, funny, light-hearted, adoring, physically affectionate, stunningly beautiful. He was Brazilian and had a chiseled body with an adorable face. Early on, he was snuggling me the way Chris would, telling me he loved me. "Why do you love me?" I asked one day.

"I love you for the same reason I love Chris: you're both so beautiful, but you have no idea how beautiful you are."

"Why do you think gay men love me?" I asked Cal.

"I think they see you as vulnerable and wounded, but very, very loving. Maybe they admire you a little for your ease and need to love or your strength underneath it."

I hated that my need for love was so apparent.

On a weekend when Pedro visited, I saw the go-go dancer again. In a club bathroom, I stood in front of the mirror when suddenly his

171

image appeared over my shoulder. At gay clubs, men and women used the same restroom.

I stared at the face that bloomed in the mirror. He looked me up and down in the mirror, then whispered, "Fat slob."

The face that looked back at me in the mirror turned haggard.

Since my sister moved, I moved in with a co-worker. I needed help. Cal and Pedro both agreed to lend muscle.

When it was over, I took everyone out. I'd assumed Cal would take a cab and Pedro and I'd sleep in my bed. I was surprised when Cal said he was sleeping over. I told him he could have the futon.

Halfway asleep, I was shaken awake. Cal was at the side of my bed gripping my shoulders. "Have a drink with me." At this point, Cal and I'd been partners for a year. Whenever Cal asked me to do something, I said yes.

We went to the kitchen and had a bottle of wine. Cal was drunk and flirtatious. My relationship with Cal always had flirtation, but I never took the things he said seriously. I trusted that Cal would never cheat. I couldn't fathom a world in which he'd be attracted to me. I remained steely, determined not to let any of the flirtation sink me into a quicksand of longing I couldn't get out of. When the wine was gone, he asked me to lay on the futon.

I grabbed my teddy to have a barrier between us. He took off his shirt and pulled me close. I tentatively wrapped my arms around him. "What are you doing?" I asked.

"It feels good to hold you."

I laughed.

"I'm not being sarcastic," he said. "You hold a special place in my heart."

"Okay."

"You're cute," he said. I shook my head no. "Do you want to take off your shirt?"

I hesitated, but it was if I was physically incapable of saying no.

I took off my shirt. He quickly unfastened my bra and looked at me. Then he began to kiss me all over.

172

My tense body relaxed. I began to kiss his body back, his chest, his stomach, his neck, his ears. I made a move to kiss his lips. He abruptly moved away.

Immediately I thought of the go-go dancer. Cal refusing to kiss me touched a wound that was beginning to fester.

I was the girl who men wanted to fuck, but they didn't want to kiss.

I untangled myself from him, told him I was going to bed. I put on my shirt and went to the kitchen. When I turned around, Cal was there. He put his arms around me, pressed me against the wall, then took off my shirt again. He stared at me, earnestly, lustfully.

"Cal, you're drunk. You have a girlfriend." He was only wearing his boxers. I toyed with the elastic band along his stomach.

"I want to," he said. He pulled down his boxers and I saw all of his desire.

"What are you doing? Go to bed. This didn't even happen." I went back to my room and fell asleep.

The next morning, Cal made jokes about being drunk and wondering why he had bite marks on his chest. I did my best to act as if nothing happened.

Soon after, I went out dancing with Pedro. After the club, we got wine and put on Britney's *Blackout* album and danced in my room. Pedro was sitting in my chair as I danced wildly, twirling and gyrating in front of him in a full performance. He looked at me with a smile, mesmerized. I acted as if I was giving him a lap dance and teased him as if I was about to kiss him. "You're afraid," he said.

"No, I'm not," I said, and kissed him full on the lips.

But he didn't stop. He stood, put his arms around me, and kissed me with full tongue, with a passion that felt real. I fell backwards onto my bed and he fell on top of me. Without words, soon we were both stripping off each other's clothes urgently, and before I could realize what I was doing, I was suddenly having passionate sex with my gay friend. We had sex all night, from the bed to the floor, over and over. As soon as it seemed that sleep and exhaustion were about to take us out, his desire would be roused again and we'd be clawing at each other.

"I hated when you left me for Cal. I was jealous. I think of you so much I wonder if I'm turning straight," he said as he was fucking me.

The next morning, I asked what happened. He shrugged, "Maybe I'm bi."

Guilt over Chris came to me like a fat rhino that sat on my chest. How could I sleep with his ex? If there was any man who had my devoted loyalty, it was Chris. My betrayal suffocated me.

Meanwhile, my relationship with Cal had fissures that trembled and threatened to ruin us. I couldn't trust him. I couldn't talk to him. I avoided him as much as I could. He felt the strain, trying to get me to talk, telling me he missed me, missed us. One night at the bar, we were chatting with friends when he suddenly turned to me and said, "I want to kiss you."

"Funny, you didn't before."

"Are you coming home with me?" I nodded.

Again, Cal simply moved the line of what was acceptable to cross in a relationship: I left in the middle of the night, confused.

I'd never had sex with someone who knew me the ways Pedro and Cal knew me. I'd let my guard down to both, thinking them both safe: Cal had a girlfriend and Pedro was gay. I believed that this barrier allowed us to have an enduring love.

With men I slept with, I never told them about my past. I gave them only an outline—writer, teacher, server—but the rest of who I gave them was either who I thought they wanted or nothing at all. I was simply a seductress whose only purpose was sex—easy to cast off.

To have sexual intimacy with men who knew me left me profoundly exposed. I'd think, *Now they know all of me.*

And they don't want me either.

Cal stayed with his girlfriend, then informed me he was moving to Texas. Pedro got a boyfriend soon after: his calls stopped.

Both felt like devastating abandonment. It was nearly cemented fact—if they could sleep with me, after knowing all of me, and that still wasn't enough, then I wasn't enough.

Memories of the go-go dancer came in dreams and I woke with my body outlined on the sheets in sweat.

This is when I changed.

One day, after hearing a rumor that Cal hooked up with another server, I felt my heart harden. When it'd been only me that Cal cheated with, I was able to tell myself that there was something special. When I heard he'd been with someone else, I realized that I was to Cal what I was to any man: some whore. I gave Cal my bitterness in the form of the cold shoulder.

As I was waiting to check out, I looked up in astonishment to see Cal strolling towards me. He'd left the restaurant hours ago, and now he was all dressed up, as handsome as ever, "I need to talk to you."

"Why?" I said coldly.

"Anne, please."

I got up and walked with him to a table in the back of the restaurant.

"I know I haven't been good to you. I know I've yanked you around," he looked at me with an earnest expression that practically begged me to hear him. I didn't say anything. "You don't deserve it. I won't insult you by asking you for forgiveness. But I'm going through something. I can't really articulate it, but it's rough."

"Obviously," I said sardonically.

"Look, I don't care what anyone in this restaurant thinks of me. I will leave them and never think of them again. But I care what you think of me."

"Why does that matter?"

"It matters," he said emphatically. "Everything with us was real, except it shouldn't have happened because I'm messed up."

I looked intently at him, and his eyes were the nearest to begging I'd ever seen. "Okay," I said.

"Okay?"

"I care about you. That won't change."

He nodded, "Well, that's the best I deserve, I guess."

I didn't think the world could hurt me anymore. I no longer could even cry. "I'm just one of the undead now," I wrote in my journal.

A horror television show called *True Blood* came out on HBO. It was full of seductive vampires and sex. On one episode, the main character goes to a vampire bar for the first time and is disgusted by the humans who flock desperately, addicts who throw themselves lustfully at vampires who might kill them after fucking them. The vampire bartender replies, "Everybody who comes here wants to die. That's what we are: death."

175

I was one of those girls who'd stroll into a nest of vampires and let my desire pour into their mouths until my body matched my spirit.

I just needed to find the right vampire.

The one who'd drink me to death.

I didn't have to look far.

This is a story about ghosts.

74
JOURNAL EXCERPTS AS A MISTRESS

I've lived in a cloud, fed wholly by the memory of Brad's caresses—his dominance, persistence, laughter—this bubble will pop in a couple days.

***

I got a bottle of wine and chain smoked watching Sex and the City. By the time I realized he wasn't coming, I was puking in the toilet, too drunk to care.

***

I search for that something, that fix, like I'm ready to shoot up, that rush that makes you feel, for a moment, that your life is lived; then I can come down, feel inspired, filled with a new something.

***

He exaggerates about people's reaction to him. I don't know if that means anything.

***

He's too good for me and he knows it.

***

I slept through three alarms and missed work.

***

I cannot shake the feeling of deceit from him.

***

If only I could trust that he <u>loves me all the time</u>. I can't even trust that he loves me at all.

***

All I asked was to respond to texts. Why does he blatantly hurt me if he cares?

***

I don't understand the white lies, the push and pull. I don't trust him. But he's also the nicest guy in the world.

***

He comes back around: we fight, we make up. I'm head over heels again.

***

He makes me feel needy, cold, and bitchy. That's not who I am. He's bringing out the worst in me. Will I ever do what's good for me?

***

Maybe I need to open up more. I've never told him any of my feelings or my past. He doesn't even ask about me.

***

When's the last straw? When will you respect yourself enough to walk away?

***

He's impossible to be mad at—he's so adorably <u>nice</u>.

***

Maybe I'm crazy. Maybe this is all in my head.

***

He said he'll never leave me alone: he'll harass me until I break. It's not about me, or my feelings, or losing me, it's his stubborn assertion: 'I can have you. I will have you.' It's about his ego, not about me.

***

I think he just wants to know I'll always be there.

***

Sex lulls feel like surviving the Great Depression: you never know when you're gonna eat again, so you don't turn down food when it's offered.

***

I slept but awoke nauseous and sweaty. I think it's anxiety, but it's definitely him. I'm having physical withdrawal symptoms when he lets me down or lies.

***

Am I really in love? Can it be possible we're living the same feelings?

***

Tonight I thought I'd give him a dose of his own medicine. It only took 20 mins for him to jump to the conclusion I was with another man.

***

Why does he get so territorial over someone he makes no effort to see?

***

He said he loved me, begged and groveled. Can I accept my secondary place?

***

He told me I was always 'just his bitch.'

***

What am I doing? Something in me is dying. It's rotting. It's already dead. I can't bury it.

***

I came home, tormented as fuck, and broke out in hives.

179

***

He said his wife is a crazy bitch. He said it with such venom.

***

This sinking feeling comes to me whenever I think of a relationship. I feel like a dog reluctantly getting into its cage. But otherwise, I'm just scavenging—getting fucked by mutts, searching for shelter, starving, always starving.

***

My sister said, 'I'm afraid to ask what's been going on while I've been at school. Have you been staying away from Brad?'

'Not…really,' I tried to explain—all justifications crumbled in my mouth.

'You're the sweetest person I know. You deserve so much more.'

'He makes me happy sometimes.'

'You're repressing your sadness,' she said. 'I hate him. I could kill him.'

75

I started teaching. In the summer, my sister would return to Boston, working at the restaurant with me. In just a month, Cal was moving.

When I walked into the bar, Cal spotted me. He stood and gave me a lingering hug that revealed us as more than friends—it was a territorial hug.

Then he kissed me in front of everyone and whispered in my ear, "I know who it is."

I looked at him, incredulous; he didn't break his stare. "I am *very* smart," he said.

He'd been hounding me to tell him who I was sleeping with for weeks. "You don't know anything," I said, walking away.

He gently grabbed my wrist and pulled me back. "And I know why you don't want to tell me," he whispered in my ear. "Because this person is in a *very* serious relationship."

He looked at me, then looked across the room at Brad.

"Don't worry," he assured, "I don't judge."

Our connection always made me feel as if he could see my naked soul. I wonder if he saw the things I didn't know yet: that Brad would hurt me in unspeakable ways, that I was pregnant.

I was on birth control. I didn't always remember it. We used condoms, except for a few times when we were drunk and he just… didn't. I didn't insist: I wanted to please him.

After a whirlwind six month affair, I came out of the shower one day and noticed how tender my breasts were. I threw up in the sink.

I couldn't believe I'd made such a dumb mistake.

I hadn't even graduated—I had a thesis to write.

I considered Brad a friend. He was a tall, pale, skinny redhead, a lovable stoner, quick witted and jovial, the life of the party. Managers loved him, staff loved him, customers loved him.

I loved him.

God, how much I loved him.

For two years, we had a seemingly innocent flirtation. We were often on the best parties together with a team of other servers who catered to the most wealthy guests. Those of us who worked those shifts had a blast—we loved the money and the chaos.

When we first hooked up, Brad had recently gotten his long-term girlfriend pregnant and agreed to a shotgun wedding. As far as everyone at the restaurant knew, Brad was in an open marriage.

Brad was a career server—he was in his thirties; he'd been with the company for years, having dropped out of college after studying acting.

When he asked me to "come see the fireworks" at his apartment while his wife was visiting family with their newborn, I didn't think I was doing anything wrong.

Brad's sexuality pierced me like an anchor and sunk me into oblivion.

Because I lived with a coworker and Brad lived with his wife, we ended up getting creative with how we had sex. He'd tell me to meet him in a parking garage, on the roof of the restaurant, in a park late at night, at a playground, in the bathroom, in an elevator, in his car, at a casino. The sex was urgent, hurried, obsessive.

And I needed it.

When I say I needed it, I mean I *needed* it.

When I didn't have it, I'd start to feel crazy.

It was this major part of my life I couldn't speak of, so I started to crave it more just to prove it was real.

Orgasm was the only way my secret escaped.

Once I had to confront an abortion, I couldn't survive the secret without friends.

I had the abortion within weeks, taking one of my friends, Caitlyn. Brad didn't come and he didn't help pay. It was a painful, albeit short, procedure.

Soon after, Brad became less reliable. Texting less, asking to come over and standing me up, ignoring me at work, then going back to rooftop sex. The more unstable the affair became, the more I transformed.

I bought lingerie, took sexy photos, dyed my hair platinum, offered his every desire. I met him where he wanted, dressed in what he wanted. I greeted him in a corset and immediately dropped to my knees in the doorway. Sometimes, his first orgasm happened before I'd even taken him upstairs.

The more sex I had and the more unreliable he became, the less I ate, slept, functioned. Within months, I'd dropped 50 lbs.

But he was consistent enough that when we did have sex, it was the most explosive of my life. When things that were important to me happened, things I wanted to share with people—like the election of the first black president—he'd reach out via text, knowing it mattered to me.

When I finished my thesis, I won the Academy of American Poet's Prize and texted. He didn't reply, so I got sloppy drunk in celebration. When I stumbled off last train and was walking to my apartment, he jumped out from behind a tree. I flung myself in his arms, elated: life was perfect in that moment. I had my art, my friends, a man I loved.

I knew that what he had for me wasn't love, but it felt so *close*.

The thing that hung me up on Brad for so long was that he was so nice. Even when I caught him in a lie, when I expressed frustration for a broken promise, when I finally got the nerve to tell him that the affair was not healthy for me, he'd react with kindness. From time to time, he'd say something so hurtful it made my head spin, but I could never see those moments as authentically him.

Then I began to find out about the other women.

Then began the night sweats, the hives, the panic attacks that made me pass out. Then began the fights, my attempts to break free, the stalking, the love bombing, the trauma bonding. This went on for four and a half years.

And ghosts must do again what gives them pain.

76
TRAUMA BONDING WITH A COVERT NARCISSIST

This is a story about ghosts.
It's not a story I want to tell.
This is the story I'm ashamed of most.
I rarely speak about it well.

It's not a story I want to tell.
I dated a married man who cheated and lied.
I rarely speak about it well.
I had to bury it to survive.

I dated a married man who cheated and lied.
Call me mistress, call me slut, call me idiot.
I had to bury it to survive.
We fucked on a roof, on a playground, in a parking garage.

Call me mistress, call me slut, call me idiot.
Which is to say I didn't love myself at all.
We fucked on a roof, on a playground, in a parking garage.
We fucked behind a tree, in a van, in a bathroom.

Which is to say I didn't love myself at all.
He made it clear he didn't love me either.

We fucked behind a tree, in a van, in a bathroom.
He said it was sex and friendship.

He made it clear he didn't love me either.
Sometimes he ignored my texts for days.
He said it was sex and friendship.
Sometimes I sat alone, waiting.

Sometimes he ignored my texts for days.
Sometimes he told me to come out and left as soon as I arrived.
Sometimes I sat alone, waiting.
Sometimes I said I was tired of being treated like shit.

Sometimes he told me to come out and left as soon as I arrived.
Sometimes I would perform "chill mistress," like it didn't sting.
Sometimes I said I was tired of being treated like shit.
Sometimes I told him I was ready to end the fling.

Sometimes I would perform "chill mistress," like it didn't sting.
I was afraid of needing a love I didn't deserve.
Sometimes I told him I was ready to end the fling.
He always said no, no, no, no,—

I was afraid of needing a love I didn't deserve.
He took his wife on vacations, posted pictures of the family.
He always said no, no, no, no,—
He didn't love her. He was in it for his son.

He took his wife on vacations, posted pictures of the family.
I would collapse, cry, beg him to let me go.
He didn't love her. He was in it for his son.
He told me he had dirty desires.

I would collapse, cry, beg him to let me go.
He would send hundreds of texts, call until I shut my phone off.
He told me he had dirty desires.
He didn't say love.

He would send hundreds of texts, call until I shut my phone off.
He could never let go. That started to scare me.
He didn't say love.
I kicked the love I needed to a corner with my panties.

He could never let go. That started to scare me.
It started to fuck with my head.
I kicked the love I needed to a corner with my panties.
I believed he must love me more than anyone could.

It started to fuck with my head.
How could love be harassment? How could love be sex?
I believed he must love me more than anyone could:
No one had ever chased me like that.

How could love be harassment? How could love be sex?
When I discovered he was sleeping with other women,
no one had ever chased me like that.
He sent flowers, wrote letters, he *finally* said love.

When I discovered he was sleeping with other women,
I broke in pure shatter—glass erupting from a falsetto.
He sent flowers, wrote letters, he *finally* said love.
He said he was sorry, he was stupid, I was beautiful.

I broke in pure shatter—glass erupting from a falsetto.
I cried, I railed, I told him he was scum.
He said he was sorry, he was stupid, I was beautiful.
I'd bury all my needs and mount him.

I cried, I railed, I told him he was scum.
It didn't matter—I was more loyal to him than my own pain.
I'd bury all my needs and mount him.
He'd be good for a while. Then exactly the same.

It didn't matter—I was more loyal to him than my own pain.

Which is to say I didn't love myself at all.
He'd be good for a while. Then exactly the same.
I was too fat, too ugly, too needy, too much.

Which is to say I didn't love myself at all.
I accepted love's consolation prize: him.
I was too fat, too ugly, too needy, too much.
He told me I was sexy and no one made him come like me.

I accepted love's consolation prize: him.
I wore lingerie. I performed his fantasies.
He said I was sexy; no one made him come like me.
His come on my skin wrote the story of my worth.

I wore lingerie. I performed his fantasies.
He continued to cheat and publicly adore his wife.
His come on my skin wrote the story of my worth.
Our fights were punctuated with orgasms.

He continued to cheat and publicly adore his wife.
I started to break out in hives.
Our fights were punctuated with orgasms.
I said if he loved me, he'd leave her.

I started to break out in hives.
I lost 50 lbs., vomited if I didn't hear from him.
I said if he loved me, he'd leave her.
He didn't leave her. He couldn't leave her. He said it was his son.

I lost 50 lbs., vomited if I didn't hear from him.
Nights alone, my body trembled in cold sweats.
He didn't leave her. He couldn't leave her. He said it was his son.
He showed up at my gym, at my job, at my window.

Nights alone, my body trembled in cold sweats.
I was an addict; he was my drug—it felt so close to love.
He showed up at my gym, at my job, at my window.

The texts went from hundreds to thousands—nonstop.

I was an addict; he was my drug—it felt so close to love.
Eventually, I'd cave: I'm so needy, I'm so crazy, I'm so sorry.
The texts went from hundreds to thousands—nonstop.
What would you call that other than love?

Eventually, I'd cave: I'm so needy, I'm so crazy, I'm so sorry.
He could never let go. That started to scare me.
What would you call that other than love?
What do you call a girl raised in a hurricane of shame?

He could never let go. That started to scare me.
I never had a foundation to stand on.
What do you call a girl raised in a hurricane of shame?
Call me mistress, call me slut, call me idiot.

I never had a foundation to stand on.
One day, his wife found his emails.
Call me mistress, call me slut, call me idiot.
She took their son, snuck out in the middle of the night.

One day, his wife found his emails.
He lied and said he'd confessed.
She took their son, snuck out in the middle of the night.
All prayers answered, a miracle.

He lied and said he'd confessed.
I became the girl he posted pictures of.
All prayers answered, a miracle.
I had an insatiable hunger for this kind of love.

I became the girl he posted pictures of.
I became the girl he told his mistresses he didn't love.
I had an insatiable hunger for this kind of love.
It took me years to see he was incapable of love.

I became the girl he told his mistresses he didn't love.
It hit me like a stun gun—laid me out cold.
It took me years to see he was incapable of love.
He would send hundreds of texts, call until I shut my phone off.

It hit me like a stun gun—laid me out cold.
I cried, I railed, I told him he was scum.
He would send hundreds of texts, call until I shut my phone off.
He didn't leave. He couldn't leave. He said it was love.

I cried, I railed, I told him he was scum.
He made promises about how he'd change.
He didn't leave. He couldn't leave. He said it was love.
He'd be good for a while. Then exactly the same.

He made promises about how he'd change.
He'd fuck me with passion, several times a day.
He'd be good for a while. Then exactly the same.
He'd shower me with gifts and dreams. Then leave.

He'd fuck me with passion, several times a day.
I began to think it impossible for him to cheat.
He'd shower me with gifts and dreams. Then leave.
Fear's firefly madness entered my gut.

I began to think it impossible for him to cheat.
There was never a time he wasn't with at least one other.
Fear's firefly madness entered my gut:
I'd scour his social media, find the evidence I need.

There was never a time he wasn't with at least one other.
I was in an elaborate trap.
I'd scour his social media, find the evidence I need.
Even faced with the bare bones of his truth, he'd deny.

I was in an elaborate trap.
An escape room with disorienting puzzles.

Even faced with the bare bones of his truth, he'd deny.
Even faced with the bare bones of his truth, I'd pine.

An escape room with disorienting puzzles.
Call me mistress, call me slut, call me idiot.
Even faced with the bare bones of his truth, I'd pine.
He showed up at my gym, at my job, at my window.

Call me mistress, call me slut, call me idiot.
Call me dumb, dumb girl—it's no different than what I call myself.
He showed up at my gym, at my job, at my window.
He climbed my fire escape, cut out my screen with a pocketknife.

Call me dumb, dumb girl—it's no different than what I call myself.
He said I was perfect; he was a fucked up man.
He climbed my fire escape, cut out my screen with a pocketknife.
Eventually, I'd cave: I'm so needy, I'm so crazy, I'm so sorry.

He said I was perfect; he was a fucked up man.
He promised to get therapy and make me happy.
Eventually, I'd cave: I'm so needy, I'm so crazy, I'm so sorry.
He'd be good for a while. Then exactly the same.

He promised to get therapy and make me happy.
In therapy, he said he had to cheat because I was a nag.
He'd be good for a while. Then exactly the same.
When I found the next girl's texts, I raged.

In therapy, he said he had to cheat because I was a nag.
I broke in pure shatter—glass erupting from a falsetto.
When I found the next girl's texts, I raged.
He broke in pure manipulation—a child collapsing into tantrum.

I broke in pure shatter—glass erupting from a falsetto.
I told him he had to respect my needs.
He broke in pure manipulation—a child collapsing into tantrum.
He threw silverware and dishes in restaurants, begged on his knees.

I told him he had to respect my needs.
He showed up at my gym, at my job, at my window.
He threw silverware and dishes in restaurants, begged on his knees.
He said he'd never leave. I realized I should be afraid.

He showed up at my gym, at my job, at my window.
He climbed my fire escape, cut out my screen with a pocketknife.
He said he'd never leave. I realized I should be afraid.
He said if he couldn't have me, no one will.

He climbed my fire escape, cut out my screen with a pocketknife.
I punched him, called the police.
He said if he couldn't have me, no one will.
The police read me my Miranda rights because of his black eye.

I punched him, called the police.
I was terrified no one would believe me.
The police read me my Miranda rights because of his black eye.
It was me who seemed a lonely thing, jilted, out of mind.

I was terrified no one would believe me.
This is the story I'm ashamed of most.
It was me who seemed a lonely thing, jilted, out of mind.
This is a story about ghosts.

77

Sitting in court waiting for my restraining order case, I'd never felt so low.

I had a stack of papers in my lap, furiously trying to focus and give meaningful comments, terrified this relationship would spill over into my work and take everything I'd achieved.

I didn't tell anyone at work I was seeking a restraining order against my boyfriend. The shame I sat in was so deep that I worried it'd expose me.

Not writer. Not academic. Not professor.

2 years into the affair, after an already frustrating cycle I'd repeatedly tried to leave, Brad's wife found his emails. She left him a note that she knew about his mistress. Brad had been promising he was going to tell her. When she left, he seemed nearly catatonic. I asked why the affair would be a problem if their marriage was open. He said it was because he'd expressed feelings. This seemed plausible.

But when I went to console him, I found her letter: that's when I learned they'd never had an open marriage. Brad begrudgingly explained that they'd had an open relationship before they were married, but after the marriage it was supposed to be closed.

Another lie.

Later, I'd learn he was stalking his wife during this time, begging her back.

In the fantasy world he created, I was his everything after his wife left. In all the years we were together, there was never a time that we saw each other that we didn't have sex. Our hunger seemed insatiable. Even when I went to the ER with a kidney infection, he came over after, climbed into bed with me, and climbed on top of me.

I later found out that while I was in the ER, he was in bed with a coworker.

Sex was everything to Brad: he needed it many times a day.

Towards the end of our relationship, his father died of cancer. I rushed to him. When I got to his house, he seemed apathetic. Even at the funeral, he never cried.

The people he cheated with shared no common similarities other than they were people who'd fallen for his charm. He would cheat with people who were beautiful or ugly, in relationships or single, much younger or much older—they didn't need to have anything in common.

I first found out about his cheating via a dream: he was cheating with a mutual friend, yet I'd never seen flirtation between them. Furthermore, she was in a relationship. I woke, covered in hives. I felt completely out of my mind, but I texted him: "I know about you and her."

His immediate reply: "That only happened once, I swear."

I dropped my phone in shock.

Then came the cycle I'd come to know for years: flowers, gifts, tears, begging, crying, promises, adoration.

He'd show up at my house in the middle of the night, scream at my window. I thought, *No one has ever loved me like this. He can't let go. He must feel like I feel.*

After fights that lasted days, I'd cave.

In the years we were together, I slept with several people in hopes of moving on.

No one was him.

One time, after finding his messages to escorts, I went to the train after a shift. I saw a man jumping over the turnstile to avoid paying. I admired his revolt, smiled. He beelined to me and began to chat. He was a 19 year old foreign exchange student from Amsterdam.

We sat next to each other. He took my headphone out of my ear and said, "Slit your wrist music?"

When the train pulled to my stop, he said, "Can I make sex with you?"

193

I laughed.

"Did I say it wrong? How do you say, 'make sex?'"

"You should just kiss me."

I stood to get off the train and he pulled me to him and kissed me passionately.

I turned around to look at how people were reacting before we stepped off.

There sat Brad. He'd been sitting behind us the whole time, following me.

I stepped off, turned off my phone, and fucked that man all night.

But for all my attempts, I couldn't escape. His attempts to get me back would always convince me.

Nothing he did could ever turn my love into hate. When he wasn't abusing me, he was perfect.

His cheating magnified my every insecurity. I bought hair extensions when he cheated with girls with long hair. I bought lash extensions. I laid in tanning beds. I got wigs to use in bed so he'd feel like he was cheating. I bought loads of the most risqué lingerie. I sunk into eating a strict diet of 550 calories a day. When he cheated, it wasn't hard to eat nothing. He never told me I was fat, but as I deteriorated, he'd say, "You've lost weight." That was all it took to keep me starving.

I also tried to love him harder. For holidays, I spent thousands of dollars. I kept thinking if I loved him enough, maybe he wouldn't need to cheat.

We never fought about anything except his cheating and lies. If it weren't for that, we had the happiest relationship, full of laughter and passion.

Towards the end, I found flirty messages he'd sent to a new coworker. I reached out: she said she'd been dating Brad and considered him her boyfriend, that he'd warned her about his crazy ex.

It crushed me: Brad never said anything but praise. It was impossible to reconcile the hurtful ways he talked about me to other people when he said I was perfect.

The girl said Brad had followed her to the train, gotten on his knees, and begged and cried for her to believe him. All this time, he was also texting me. The girl suggested we confront him together.

When Brad saw us walk into the bar, his face fell.

We sat down and showed our texts.

He held his head in his hands as if his brain was about to detonate: I'd never seen him so wrecked. He admitted that yes, he lied, but he loved us.

We left him crying with his head on the table.

But I awoke later to a shadow at my window on my fire escape. He was using a key to cut my screen. The lock on my window didn't work—I could only afford an attic apartment in an old house. He easily slid the window up and slipped in.

I jumped out of bed and started screaming, but he was louder.

"She's a LIAR!" He yelled, "She's a crazy bitch! I can't believe she tried to make up those stories! I told her I loved you! I told her leave me alone! She's trying to separate us because she's jealous! Don't tell me I can't make this work! I know what I want!"

Tears were streaming down his face: it was the first time I'd seen real tears. He also became aggressive—he got in my face, threw stuff around my room, broke things.

"Do you not remember what just happened? You admitted everything."

He yelled petulantly, "I did not! And if you don't listen…"

It was my first threat from him.

It's easy to look at this story and say I was stupid, as this is all written with the knowledge that this man was abusive. But, at the time, this was disorienting. This was a man who was beloved by all. This was a man who I was friends with for years before I'd ever slept with. I was the only person who saw this side of him; when I tried to explain, I came out looking crazy, so his behavior made me feel crazy.

I'm also empathetic. When I saw him rage, what I was seeing was a severe mental break, a narcissistic collapse, a dangerous rage experienced by a person with Narcissistic Personality Disorder who's been unmasked and is triggered by fears of abandonment. I didn't know how to name it at the time, even with a psychology degree. I didn't register him as a narcissist, or even as a dangerous person, because his narcissism was covert and my understanding of it was limited. The man threatening me was so different than Brad that it was like Dr. Jekyll and Mr. Hyde.

It reminded me of how my husband acted when I left: I felt responsible. We began couple's therapy.

Months later, we were at dinner with friends when the ding of his phone hit the pit of my stomach like a gong: I knew it was a mistress. I asked him outside and demanded he give me his phone. I called the person. "Are you his crazy ex?" she said.

I knew I had to be done. I'd lost myself entirely. I'd lost sleep, I'd lost time to write, I'd lost my mental health, I'd lost joy in my job, I'd lost my self esteem, I'd lost inner peace—constantly worrying about what betrayal lurked in shadows.

I said I was done. He said he'd never leave me alone. He took my computer, knowing it had my writing, and dangled it out the window. I punched him in the face. He threw himself on the bed and I climbed on him and punched him three more times.

I told him I was calling the police. He ran out the door. He called my bluff and sat in my driveway texting. I called the police. They came and spoke to both of us and let him go.

After letting him go, an officer came to my door. I nearly fainted as he began to say, "You have the right to remain silent. Anything you say can be held against you…"

They questioned me, letting me know that he told them I'd assaulted him; they were trying to decide if I needed to be arrested. I burst into tears.

"Ma'am, why didn't you leave?"

The police called a judge, who decided it was self defense. I was granted a temporary restraining order that I had to go to court to extend.

In the meantime, breaking up with him was like quitting an addiction: that's not a simile. I experienced excruciating pain.

It was years before I learned about trauma bonding: whenever I experienced abuse from him, he was also the thing that comforted me, and he did so most often through love bombing, gifts, and sex. When he cheated, my body sought the drug to dull the pain, and that drug was sex with my abuser. It's no wonder I had such physical responses to his betrayals—hives, puking, disordered eating, panic attacks—because when he gave me positive reinforcement, my brain flooded with chemicals which I became dependent on.

Without him, I felt I'd die.

I sat on the train, layers of winter clothes, shivering uncontrollably. I woke with my sheets drenched in sweat. I couldn't eat, yet my weight seemed to balloon. I gained 70 lbs, which further crushed me. I felt powerless. There were nightmares, anxiety attacks, deep longing. I'd pray for him to finally realize how to love me in a healthy way.

Heading to work, my hands were shaking, but the train was too crowded to sit. A ringing started in my ears; then I felt hot, then everything went black.

I woke up sitting. A woman fanned me with a newspaper. A man held a cold bottle of water on the back of my neck. Another women knelt in front of me, "You want us to tell them to stop the train?"

"I'm fine, thank you," I said, humiliated.

I got through my lessons mechanically. My classes, normally filled with boisterous students and laughter, became quiet and tense. A student came to my office.

"I wanted to see if you're doing okay."

I knew I wasn't hiding my grief well, but I didn't want to be confronted with my failures. "I'm going through a hard time in my personal life," I said.

She reached into her bag and pulled out a teddy bear and a card and set them in front of me. "Stay strong, okay?"

When she walked out, I shut the door, put my head on my desk, and cried.

I thought that if my students knew who I really was, the dumb slut in an abusive relationship, they wouldn't love me.

The reason I thought they couldn't was because so many people incapable of loving me had already punctured my heart.

After a few months, I solved the problem of my addiction.

What's better than one vampire?

A whole nest of them.

IV

78

I'm a ghost.
My mind's a wasp cocoon that hangs above the doorway to hell.
A dusty antique lantern that dims on and off in gaslight.
And ghosts must do again what gives them pain.

79

Then I lost my sister.

Cassie expressed frustration at my stupidity with Brad: in trying to talk about it, I found myself without a shield against insults. I was stupid, shallow, sex-obsessed, naive. At college, she had a new boyfriend: he was kind, destined for greatness, she said. She stopped calling entirely. I stopped trying, because when I talked to her I felt bad about myself. Why didn't good men like me? To hear Cassie describe it, it seemed it was because she was simply better. She found men of caliber and depth because she was, herself, destined for greatness. I, unfortunately, was basic: no man of worth would be attracted. When I tried to defend myself, telling her I loved poetry and literature and had a rich creative life, she'd shrug out a reluctant, "uh-huh." The message was clear: you aren't a good writer or a smart person.

Cassie gave three other wounds: 1) She told me my poetry had always been bad. 2) She refused to read it, explaining that because she was now a poet too, sharing poetry would be competitive. I never felt a competition between my writer friends: I didn't like to think of art that way. I thought we all had something to share. 3) She dedicated her thesis to her boyfriend, even though I'd dedicated mine to her.

I also dedicated my first book to her, *Reluctant Mistress*.

My dream had come true.

Just one book, I'd always said.

I thought perhaps my writing accolades would bring my sister back, that she'd recognize my writing had grown. When I sent her a copy, she never said a word—not about the book itself, the poems, or the dedication. I thought she must've thought it terrible.

I started getting published regularly. My sister was also getting published. I bought every journal she was published in. I posted her poems on social media with pride: she never did the same. I was astounded by my sister's art. I began to tell anyone who complimented my poetry: "You should read my sister!"

We kept in touch in a distant way, with required birthday gifts or holidays, but we never recovered our relationship.

I made a choice to accept that love wasn't something in my cards.

I needed to accept sex as a consolation prize for the love I didn't deserve.

I uncoiled Brad from around my limbs, and I promptly jumped into a pit of snakes.

The first one to slither into my bed was a grad student teacher whose cubicle was next to mine. A couple months after my breakup, he overheard me on the phone. He popped his head in.

"I'm Dwayne," he said.

I knew who he was: I'd been avoiding him. Dwayne walked around telling female professors how sexy we were. One professor said, "It's like he's stuck in the 1950s and this is *Madmen*. He's obsessed with how we look. He seems to have no idea he's sexually harassing us, that we might not want the 'compliments,' that we might just want to get our work done."

However, Dwayne was magnetic: he was a young and handsome black man at a college that was notorious for its lack of diversity. He wore bow ties, something he later explained was to make him appear non-threatening. Dwayne had confidence: he let you know he was destined to be a star—in rap or poetry—most likely both.

"I'm sorry about your boyfriend. You need a distraction?"

"I'm good."

"I have season tickets to the ballet."

"How old are you?" I asked.

"26."

"Too young," I smiled, turned back to my papers, "I'm 32."

Then, a new proposal: "Who's doing your book launch party?"

I shrugged, "I didn't plan on having one."

"Let me organize it."

It was beyond the scope of generosity I'd received from a man. I bit that lure like a snapping turtle.

Dwayne threw me the best party. He rented a popular club, booked a live band, made beautiful flyers, sent email invites. He performed his rap alongside some friends.

It was a boisterous event—the bar was packed and he MC'd. Never had I felt so celebrated.

As the party dwindled, Dwayne was no where to be found. I was unsettled that I hadn't been able to properly thank him. I texted: he said he left to another bar. I was hurt he'd leave without saying anything, but I went after him.

I found him surrounded by friends who parted like a sea as I approached. There he stood, leaning casually against the bar with a smug smirk of accomplishment. I threw myself on him in a hug. He acted nonchalant: "Glad you liked it."

As the bar closed, I stood with Dwayne in an alley smoking. He gave me a seductive sideways glance. I couldn't help myself—I pressed my body into his, pinning him up against a brick wall, and kissed him.

In seconds, his hands were between my legs. I pulled away. He asked if I needed a ride home. We got into the back of his friend's car, where he played his music and I fawned. He kept grabbing my chin and pulling me in for kisses.

Once Dwayne had me, he dropped his former pretenses. He stopped saying the word "women" and replaced it with "bitches," referencing other women he was sleeping with. He started intermittently ignoring texts, making me wonder if he was losing interest or if I was simply too needy. He began to show his jealousy and temper.

One night, as we watched TV, he asked, "Who was the last person you slept with, Anne?"

"You," I said. "A month ago."

"It was like two weeks."

"Three and a half, but who's counting?"

He changed the subject, "So, I bought this bitch a stuffed animal, right? I'm trying to figure out if it's cheesy."

I stopped him, "Dwayne, do we have to do this? I don't want to hear about your other girls. It's fine that you don't want to sleep with me exclusively. I expect it. But do I have to hear about it?"

He got quiet, nodding slowly.

"What?" I said.

"Things are starting to make sense is all." He was cold; I couldn't understand why he was turning on me so quickly. "You say you can do friends with benefits, but I don't know what that means."

"I thought we were being friends," I said.

He raised his voice and started to yell, suddenly animated, "How can we be friends if you won't let me talk about my other bitches? We can be the best of best of friends, but I have to be able to talk about everything. There must be some reason why you won't let me. You're not willing to admit you caught feelings."

"I recently got out of a relationship where I was cheated on. I don't judge you—you're being honest—but it makes me feel worthless."

He took a deep breath and said, "Okay." Then he proceeded to ream me out. "Do NOT compare me to your other n*****s! I've had my heart broken! I've slept with one girl all year—you! I ain't no motherfucking womanizer!"

"I'm sorry. I'm not saying…"

"You can't let shit go. I know you still have feelings for your exes."

"You don't even know me."

"I know all I need to know."

I felt despised. I stood, apologized, and quietly left.

He texted immediately: "Your ego is too sensitive. You caught feelings."

"I have my issues. I own that. I'm sorry I pissed you off."

I never got a chance to share emotional intimacy, because it never felt safe. As a result, I shut my authentic self away in a casket.

I bought the raunchiest lingerie; I perfected my selfie angles and my seductive stare, dead-eyed, pliable as clay, ready to mold to whatever fantasy they needed. *It's just sex,* I thought. *It's just my body. There's nothing more that can happen to my body that hasn't already happened.* My body didn't need love, affection, or protection. It just needed to be touched—to pretend, for a moment, it was desirable.

To get that, I had to perform.

I had to learn how to charm the snake so it rose for the whistle of my breath, fangs out in disoriented hypnosis.

I tried to get them to undulate, but never strike.

I thought that by sheer will, I could make my body the antidote.

I ended up poisoned.

80

Dwayne would bite, leaving bruises that lasted days, awe-striking souvenirs. I hated watching them fade, thinking he was fading, his desire was fading.

With every thrust he marked his territory. He'd whisper in my ear, "When you touch yourself, I want you to think about this dick."

"Yes," I'd respond dutifully.

"No one else's," he'd command. When he'd declare ownership over me, a chill would run through me that pooled and pulsed between my legs.

"I always do," I whispered, feeling the orgasm cascading through me like an avalanche.

I wasn't thinking of him or anyone when I touched myself. I was starving: like a potbellied stray infected with worms, nothing could fill me and nothing that approached seemed kind.

When he wasn't fucking me, I looked for the next. I never said no —a master juggler.

When you're infected with this hunger, you'll take what you can get.

I told Dwayne not to come in my mouth, but he'd do it anyway.

Not only will you take what you can get, you'll be grateful.

81

But this is a story about the girls.

They're easy to look past when they get swallowed into the quicksand of a man's need for adoration.

After I broke up with Brad, a girl put a branch into the mud and hauled me out.

I met Sandra in poetry workshop: I'd write long fan letters on her poems. She had this ability to begin a poem in one spot and meander through a narrative that would land with a gut punch in an unexpected spot.

Soon, we were sitting next to each other, passing notes like it was middle school. Sandra would lust after our professor, scribbling haikus about his tight pants or his dad sweater.

To know Sandra is to know a firecracker—she's no wallflower. Sandra was vocal in her opinions, unafraid to challenge any pompous male know-it-all who thought they were the next Whitman. She also never took life seriously—she was always quick-witted, providing comedic relief when class got solemn.

Sandra loved attention, constantly dreamed of being famous, and viewed life as an exciting 1980s romance in which Patrick Swayze could sweep in at any moment, pull her from a corner, and heave her over his head and into his heart.

With Sandra, life felt like a perpetual adventure. Her confidence in her body, her talents, and her sexuality had a positive effect on me.

Even as I was broken, I couldn't help but feel joy and strength with Sandra. Her energy was contagious.

Just as I was leaving my long-term, older, career-server boyfriend, Sandra had recently dumped her long-term, older, career-bartender boyfriend. Albeit, Sandra's tale was more interesting: she'd met a scuba instructor in Mexico while vacationing with her boyfriend and fell in love, carrying on an emotional affair online until she dashed off to Mexico to be with him. It was the movie she'd always wanted, until he suddenly discarded her.

Sandra returned to Boston. Having seen my single status on Facebook, she texted, "What happened?"

She scooped me up like some stray pup and said, *Okay, you belong to me now.*

We had many differences, but there were also uncanny similarities: we both had narcissist mothers; we both had a tender and complicated affection for our fathers; we both had been writing since we were children; we both were outspoken and wrote our truths unapologetically; we both loved ghost stories, witches, and magic; and we both had a lifelong wild streak.

If you're paying attention to the story about the girls, then you may have noticed a pattern.

We both had sexual trauma. We both had lifelong cycles of parental and patriarchal abuse.

But we didn't dwell in darkness. When Sandra and I left our boyfriends, we had a new life motto.

No longer were we interested in trying to bend over backwards to the whims of men never satisfied: we were ready to dive head-first into our love affairs and explore the disorienting and dizzying mazes of whoever we wanted.

Men who slept with us felt insecure about our friendship. A repeated complaint was that our lovers didn't like us together, believed that we lured men to their destruction like some topless mermaids lounging on a rock waiting to sink a sailor like an anchor.

In the summer of 2013, Sandra proposed a girls trip to Puerto Rico: "We can lay on the beach, meet a bunch of men, have them tell us their life stories, and write a book of poems about them!"

That's exactly what we did. We chatted with bartenders, waiters, random men selling wares, tour guides, other tourists. We flirted shamelessly and dug into their life stories. "Are you married? How did you meet? How did you propose? Do you love her still? Do you cheat?" Any man who flirted had to face our questions like a firing squad.

During the day, we laid on the beach and passed a journal back and forth, alternating line by line as we reimagined these men as the lovers of a speaker who ditched her fiancé and ran off to Puerto Rico. Dwayne would text, giving me the rare compliments I longed for.

But this is a story about the girls, girls broken so young that they should come with parental advisory warnings. This is a story about girls who've already killed many versions of themselves, girls who have internalized landmines they tiptoe around, who threaten to take down any man in their radius by detonating. Girls whose sexualities balloon like mushroom clouds, provoking parents to leave firework displays of bruises on their bodies. Girls who are in awe of what their bodies will do to heal. Girls that promise to be each other's bridesmaids, dream of buttoning a wedding dress up each other's spine, which they know to be an ancient column of female ruin. Girls who shoplift boxes of platinum hair dye, knowing that the power they're allowed to have over men lies in what they can steal, how they can lure.

This is a story about girls that run off to Puerto Rico and ask the bartender where they can get cocaine, taking bumps off keys in the bathroom, strutting confidently into the kitchen to flirt with cooks. Girls who the staff don't kick out as they're shutting down, feeding them shots of tequila and tastes of their lips in drunken kisses. Girls who wear flirty summer dresses and make silly videos. Girls who erupt in girlish giggles. These are the girls—*those girls*—who get together and crack the world open like an egg, let it simmer on the heat of their longings.

We're the bad seeds: the ones whose parents forced us to enter adulthood as a one-winged bird. But we find each other—it's magnetic—we grow our own stitches, sew ourselves into one, and escape, soaring over the world, conjoined twins of trauma.

82

I stood at baggage claim after my trip in a sundress smoking a cigarette with Sandra. A car horn beeped. I hugged Sandra and ran towards Dwayne.

When Dwayne said he'd pick me up, something in me swelled to see him actually there. I had someone waiting for me, almost as if I mattered.

"Hiiiiiiiiii!" I said, hopping in the passenger's seat.

"I'm in a mood, Anne. Traffic's a bitch."

"Okay, grouchy!" I replied. "I got you a gift," I said, pulling out some lollipops. "I guess since you won't let me blow you, you can blow yourself."

Dwayne lit up—nothing like a gift to make his moods soften.

While on top of him in bed, I looked him in the eye and said, "Do you want to know how many dicks I sucked?"

His face fell. "How many," he said flatly.

I bent over and kissed him, "None," I said, "I only think of yours."

"Tell me you love it."

"I love it."

"Tell me you love this n***** dick," he said forcefully.

"Dwayne…"

He fucked me harder, raised his voice, "Tell me you love this n***** dick!"

"Dwayne, no."

"Say it!"

I shook my head, "I can't say that. I care about you."

He chuckled, "Then tell me I'm your black Jesus."

That night, Dwayne clutched me with the force that a child clutches its stuffed animal. While sleeping, he moaned, seemingly distressed.

In the morning, he said, "I kept dreaming the police were chasing me."

I paused before erupting into laughter. The idea of the police chasing Dwayne seemed absurd.

When I laughed, Dwayne laughed too. He could've corrected me, could've told me what it was like growing up in D.C., but he rarely spoke of that. Instead, we laughed. "You're safe," I said.

A few weeks later, I'd get an awakening. While driving, he froze to see police lights flashing in the rearview. Beads of sweat appeared on his forehead; his breathing became rushed.

"We're fine," I soothed. "It's probably a tail light or something."

The officer approached from my side. I fumbled to roll down the window. Dwayne asked if he could reach into his glove compartment. I understood later that Dwayne was trying to be cautious with his movements for fear of being shot.

As the officer looked over Dwayne's documents, he leaned in and whispered, "Do you know this man?"

"Of course," I said firmly.

I can't remember what the offense was that got us pulled over, but I remember that it was something so mundane that I could never imagine being pulled over for it. Dwayne breathed an audible sigh.

"Did you hear him? What was he trying to say? That you're my kidnapper?"

"Anne, you're white. To them, I'm not Dwayne the poet. To them, I'm just another n*****."

"But this is Boston!" I said, ignorantly.

"Ha," Dwayne said flatly.

A year earlier, I was having trouble sleeping, so I grabbed my laptop.

On the home screen, the soft smile of a young black boy greeted me. The headline read, "Unarmed black teen shot in Florida."

The headline alone was enough to sink me. I remember that moment distinctly, how I'd opened my computer and suddenly fell into despair.

I remembered Beaux and the racist media depictions. I remembered what I'd learned about Emmett Till—his open casket a picture of horror that compared to nothing else—and I thought this boy, this soft smile, this Trayvon Martin, looked like Emmett Till.

I began to face the full truths as the weeks went on, as white people argued, calling Martin a thug, posting pictures of him with grills as evidence for why his death didn't matter. In the moment of his death, Trayvon carried a packet of Skittles and ice tea. The man that killed him, George Zimmerman, was a self-designated "neighborhood watchman" who regularly called the police on black people.

Trayvon's death was as if Beaux had crawled out of the grave. The swiftness in which the media took a racist approach revealed that what happened to Beaux was not a one-off event.

It was America.

The monster of America projects its sins onto black children to preserve its false self: that we are a nation of freedom and equality, the best in the world.

Shortly after the incident with Dwayne, news broke that George Zimmerman was found not guilty.

I cried a lot that night: I cried for Trayvon, I cried for Beaux, I cried for Dwayne, I cried for myself, I cried for America.

I marched late into the night, crying out "Black Lives Matter." I found some people I knew and walked with them: they were black, and when they opened their arms to hug me, I cried on their shoulders like I didn't deserve their love. I felt a distinct acknowledgement of being a part of something big, of something history books couldn't ignore.

I had no idea how much I still had to learn, but I was committed. I started reading everything I could. I changed my syllabi to confront issues of racism. One night, after reading *The New Jim Crow* by Michelle Alexander, I said to Dwayne, "Did you know 1 in 3 black men go to prison in America?"

He grimaced, "Anne, I can't talk about race."

Wishing I'd considered Dwayne's racial trauma more carefully, I nodded and shut up. One thing I was learning was that being white meant I naturally had blind spots, and I had to take it upon myself to remedy them, but those blind spots were stinging people all the time without me even realizing what kind of weapons my blindness shielded.

This is a story about the ghosts this country makes of us through its disorienting reign of blood and terror, causing us to wander aimlessly as accomplices to hauntings.

And ghosts must do again what gives them pain.

83

I'll tell you what happens to a girl raised in a pit of snakes.

Covered in fang marks, drained of life, blood replaced by venom.

The poison settles in her belly like a steaming pit of tar she can feel all the time. When she's alone, thinking of them, she can hear it hiss.

Then she hisses.

Files her teeth back into blades.

Remembers the bite that made her.

Whenever she hears a rattle, she follows it, coiling with snake after snake.

They shed her like their own skin and walk away.

Then one day she picks up the discarded skin and tries it on.

It fits.

She descends into the snake pit in her costume, her dark knowledge, ready to bite back.

84

Dwayne became a predictable cycle. One moment, he'd be saying I was his muse or his poet hero who he wanted to be, the next he'd be fucking me like I made him feel powerful, and I'd perform the submissive femme fatale who worshipped him.

Then Dwayne would say something to hurt me, or he'd ghost for a few weeks and come back as if nothing happened, or he'd call and tell me about some new girl, careful to detail the things that made her better than me.

When I began to use Dwayne's tactics back on him—say, ignore his texts for a few hours—he'd become agitated, text more. If I continued, he'd fly into a rage with words that stung so badly I'd swear never to return.

Then I broke like a dry wishbone, clean in half. My emotions turned off.

I felt nothing for men.

I vowed to treat men exactly how they treated me.

It seemed that what men resented in me was my love: Dwayne always accused me of "catching feelings," even though I never told him I loved him, even though he asked if I loved him all the time, even though sometimes he was the one to say he loved me.

"I need more than one egg in my basket," I told Sandra on the phone.

"There's a new dating app," Sandra replied. "Tinder."

Sandra and I would laugh at men's profiles—holding a gun, sitting in their car, posing next to the dead carcass of some animal.

"Men are so unevolved. They're like, *Look at me, big man, I kill nature. I have car. I hate women. I here for sex. Roar.*"

"I know," Sandra said, "I love it."

Sandra and I were aflame and ready to burn down forests with our desire, but we were opposite about our feelings for men. We both attracted hyper-masculine, damaged, toxic men. Sandra could fall in love on nothing but a furtive glance. Any details they'd give, she'd immediately weave into her own life story like a perfect cocoon in which love would transform her miraculous. Every man was the opportunity for her own romance movie.

In contrast, I believed I'd be alone forever. The notion that a man would appreciate me seemed too fantastical to consider anymore.

While driving, Sandra and I saw the most beautiful man I'd ever seen: 6 foot 4 inches, Dominican, shirtless, beads of sweat glistening along his abs as he dug in dirt—a landscaper.

Sandra slammed on the breaks, laid her body into the horn. We rolled down our windows and catcalled.

His name was Santiago.

I thought he was just a garden snake.

It turned out he was a cobra.

For a time, my body was the flute to make him rise, writhe, ache, dance.

His hypnotic stare fixated on the ways my music made him undulate.

Then he struck.

This is a story about ghosts.

85

Santiago laid on his back, naked, staring at the ceiling. "Do you think you could ever fall in love with me?"

I bristled, my fear of manipulation in the question—the word love clinging like a burr. "No."

He propped on an elbow and leaned close, "You don't think I could wear you down?"

His muscles rippled in oceanic waves. When he looked me in the eyes, my vagina pulsed.

"No."

He leaned in, put his plump lips millimeters from mine, "Look at me," he said.

"I am."

He put his hands between my legs, "You don't think I could wear you down?"

I closed my eyes. "No."

"Open your eyes."

I did as told.

He climbed on top and fucked me so hard that I came in seconds. Every few thrusts, he asked if I loved him.

No, no, no, no.

86

When Santiago approached me on the street where I'd walked by him working, I marveled at how he was even more perfect close up: his face, baby smooth and clear; his lips, plump and perfect; his lashes, long and upturned. I couldn't find even a freckle.

"How old are you?"

"26, you?"

"29."

I was 32. He was 19.

By the time we both fessed up—me coming clean first—we'd already slept together; we shrugged the age difference off—there was no undoing what had been done.

One night we did coke and fucked all over the apartment and went outside at 4 a.m. to a playground and rocked on swings and talked about our childhoods and dreams. He talked about going to juvenile prison at 17 for assault.

I talked about the fact that some stars we looked at were already dead and their light was only the universe's memory—how could it be that things could light up your whole world like that even though they're dead?

Santiago loved to film me, wanted to make videos of me when we were fucking or not, send them to his friends and brag. He'd zoom on my face and ask if I loved it, if it was the best I ever had, if I was his.

I'd find Santiago going through my phone, going through pictures on my computer; he'd interrogate, "You slept with him?"

"That's my roommate. He's gay."

"Him?"

"A few times."

"Why do you still have it?"

"He's a friend."

"Why do you need to be friends with exes?"

"To have exes, I'd have to have boyfriends."

"I don't fuck with hoes."

"Aren't you sleeping with others? You stand me up half the nights you say you're coming."

"Not really."

Years later, I learned he fathered a child while we were sleeping together.

I was hypnotized by Santiago. We had nothing in common: I thought his intelligence was on par with a rattle. But I'd never say no to Santiago.

Often, the differences between Santiago and I were interesting, like a curious science experiment. I'd nod and listen, amused at how little he actually understood the world. Once, after going down on me, he said, "Doing that is going to make me have boobs."

My mind tried hard to compute, "What?"

"Man boobs—you ever seen 'em?"

"Yeah."

"When you see that, you know that guy eats too much pussy."

"How do you figure?"

"Because you're eating women's hormones."

"I'm pretty sure what you're saying isn't science."

"I don't trust science—I'm an *eyewitness*."

When we fucked, I felt the stress of the world leave my body. He'd waltz in, peel off his shirt, and drown me in abs. He'd follow me to the kitchen after sex and prop me on the counter and fuck me again.

Santiago was a new kind of high.

He worried that he couldn't last long, wasn't able to please me; I assured he was the best.

Yet, there was a darkness in Santiago I overlooked.

He'd not call for a month and come back as if nothing happened. He'd demand I get STI tests but refuse to do the same. He'd ask for money, ignore me for weeks when I said no.

I thought he was just a garden snake.

It turned out he was a cobra.

But before his venom paralyzed, it numbed like heroin.

We coiled for several years.

Dwayne came slithering back whenever I posted with Santiago. He'd woo with words about how maternal I felt, how he hoped "no one ever took advantage of that."

So I continued the cycle. I had the sense that whenever I was getting invested in someone new, Dwayne needed his ego massaged to prove I belonged to him.

It was like I was an old toy, and he wasn't looking to play with it, but he wasn't looking to share it either.

There were others too, because Dwayne and Santiago filled me and then left me feeling empty. There were the snakes I met on Tinder and fucked a few times. There were the times I went out with friends and ended up making out with a stranger on the dancefloor. There were the dorm rooms I woke up in. The friends or co-workers I casually fell into bed with.

The more I wore the skin of the snake, the more they all wanted to drain me. They projected whatever fantasy they wanted onto me.

I worked hard to be whatever the man that crashed into me seemed to need to wreck.

Deep down, they all wanted to wreck themselves, but I carried their wreckage.

By the summer of 2014, I was eager to get out of my body. "I'm more than this," I told Sandra, "I care about the world."

The dream infected me like a virus, as dreams do. "Palestine," I told Sandra, "I want to pay witness."

"You're not afraid?" Sandra asked.

"I'm enraged."

87

But this is a story about the girls.

Cassie and Anne.

What happened to them?

What happened is we went to war. We were soldiers hiding in a ditch through a rainy night, hyper-vigilant and armed, taking turns sleeping and standing guard.

Then I woke and looked over and a sniper had taken my sister out.

I endured the rest of the war alone, traumatized, missing her, always remembering the way the weight of her body felt against me, the way the weight of her blood in my veins makes my bones ache.

Throughout college, she'd stay with me during breaks. Then it dwindled to holidays. Then Christmas only. Then nothing. She didn't call, text, or email. I did, but I eventually stopped trying.

She never said a word about any of my books.

I didn't know what I needed to be good enough for her.

She met a man and married him. When we met, only a handful of times, he seemed nice, but not interested in getting to know me. With him, Cassie's whole personality changed: she no longer had a sense of humor. When I asked what happened, she said she'd adapted to him.

It felt like I revolted her. I asked repeatedly: will we ever be sisters again?

For fifteen years, she said yes.

But that wasn't her.

Remember?

She died in that ditch.

That was a ghost saying that.

This is a story about *ghosts*.

Sandra and I loved ghost stories. We loved to take day trips to Salem, hitting the witch shops and getting professional photos taken dressed as witches. We went on countless ghost tours, eager to hear a message on recorded tape, to watch dousing wires go wild in a graveyard.

We conjured magic everywhere: we looked for it in every crevice.

We forgot to look in our rib cages.

Sandra became more of a sister than my sister. When Christmas rolled around, we decided to jump on a plane to the Dominican Republic. "We're each other's family," we said.

Life with Sandra felt full of potential. She greeted every day as if a new plot twist could emerge at any moment. Sandra eagle-eyed every man to audition him in the role of her movie like the most adept casting director. In moments upon meeting, Sandra could spark a conversation and dig furiously towards the roots of men's stories like a dog digging up its favorite chew toy. She loved taking selfies with strangers and posting pictures of us in the arms of men.

When we rang in the new year on the beach, I watched the fireworks with Sandra in my blue sequin dress, euphoric.

"2014 is going to be OUR YEAR!" Sandra exclaimed.

We were sisters in the truest sense, yet, I still wondered—who was the sniper that took my real sister out?

88

I had a flight to Washington D.C. to embark on my peace delegation. I took a covert picture of the man sitting shirtless on the edge of my bed getting dressed—a Tinder date from the night before.

"Good luck in Afghanistan," he said.

"Palestine."

"Same difference."

"It's not actually."

He shrugged, walked out. I finished packing and waited for Dwayne to pick me up.

I'd immersed myself in reading. The more I read, the more I was shocked.

When our brains grow around certain untruths taught as children, about the black and white fantasy of pure good vs. pure evil instead of the nuanced reality, something beastly rises up to defend lies—a guard dog of our childhood bares its teeth and growls, denies truth any entry.

But I say this about Palestine with unapologetic, urgent, and firm conviction: what's happening is a human rights horror on a scale unimaginable unless you see it.

I don't know what I thought going there could do, other than I needed to look the monster in the face without fear.

I fell in love with *The Diary of Anne Frank* at 9 years old, which led to several years of a heartbreaking immersion in Holocaust literature. I asked my mother, "If it happened here, would we stand up?"

"I'm a good person," she said.

I promised myself I'd hold true to being a good person in action, not just in words.

During training, I partnered with a red-haired girl with a stylish bob, covered in tattoos. Her makeup was perfection and her aura had the ferocity of a wolf, defiant in every way.

Her name was Valerie; everyone called her V.

The leader asked a question: "What are you most afraid of?"

I thought for a moment, "I'm afraid of not having access to a bathroom for long periods of time."

She burst out laughing, "Me too! I could give a shit about a soldier—where's a damn toilet?"

"I'm afraid of peeing standing up."

"Or worse…"

"I can't even bear the thought!"

We laughed so hard that the other delegates thought we didn't take it seriously. We hushed conspiratorially and continued.

"I'm afraid of sweating off my makeup," she confessed.

"I'm so glad someone else here wears makeup," I said, "There's no way I'm going bare-faced anywhere."

"I'll be in full face daily," she nodded.

Just like that, I had another sister.

The thing you have to know about us is we genuinely had no fear. There's a reason for that, but we didn't know what it was.

If we feared anything, it was something inside us.

Something rattling our bones like bars, begging to be let out.

89

When I stepped foot in Palestine, I felt I'd been swallowed by a beast. I sat in its belly, looked at all it's consumed—I saw the way the world worked.

It wasn't pretty.

People don't believe me when I say this, but Palestine is my favorite place in the world.

From the way the Call to Prayer echoed through our days, to the elaborate and ancient mosques, synagogues, and the Church of Resurrection—a longing for God aches from every limestone brick in Palestine.

There was something divine in the wreckage of hate.

The prayer notes tucked into the crevices of the Wailing Wall made me think of the way we all cry out for some invisible strong-arm of love to steady us.

The graffiti of martyrs on the walls of refugee camps put ghosts on parade, forcing us to confront the defiant eyes of those swallowed.

The tanks, the weapons, and the tear gas raining from the sky upon unarmed children aren't what you'd think you'd find in the place of the divine.

But Palestine is the intersection of heaven and hell.

I thought I was visiting to help; I soon realized I was there to learn.

The apartheid wall, cutting through Palestinian villages, separating families, taking land and livelihood, forcing people into abject impoverishment; the checkpoints built as cattle shoots, standing in the hot sun for hours just to get to work; the black barrels on top of houses, collecting rain water in the dry heat to use for bathing or drinking; the separate roads and entrances and license plates that dictate the privileged versus the second class; the bulldozed homes with personal belongings scattered across the ground—no book could prepare for such brutality.

And no book could prepare for such hope in the face of it.

Palestinians lived vibrantly, inviting us into their homes with the most generous hospitality, telling us stories of war, torture, and imprisonment with the barest vulnerability and the strongest spirt of resistance. They danced Dabke, smoked hookah, and came up with acts of resistance that left me in awe at their creativity.

There was violent resistance too, as has happened in every history in which people were oppressed. Trauma breeds mental illness.

While we were there, three Jewish boys were kidnapped and later found killed. In retaliation, a 14 year old Palestinian boy was kidnapped from a mosque, taken to a field, made to drink gasoline, and set on fire. As a response, Israel launched Operation Protective Edge on Gaza— killing over 2,000 Palestinians, half of them children, in one of its deadliest attacks. The cycle of violence coiled and hissed and never stopped.

I'll never be able to write the pain of Palestine. Not a sentence I craft can address the commingling of despair and love that stirs in me for it.

There was a statue in Jenin of a Trojan horse, made entirely of scrap metal from cars after a bombing.

There was a woman who collected tear gas canisters, filled them with dirt and seeds, and made a garden.

There were teenagers with spray cans, decorating the apartheid wall with vibrant resistance art.

Everywhere I went, Palestinians showed me the deepest truth: when you are living in the belly of the beast, a hunger that knows only destruction, the most divine thing that'll bring you closer to God is to create.

They showed me the ways this all linked to a bigger history— from the Native American genocide and land theft, to the pilfering of African resources by Europe, to the slave catchers turned police in

225

America, to the Jewish Holocaust—Palestine was simply the modern day scapegoat of greed and fear.

Somewhere, some men were getting obnoxiously rich selling war machines and racial propaganda, no different than the plantation owners living in obscene wealth while torturing and raping to maintain their entitlement or the brutality of South African apartheid.

Colonization is not post: it's an active present. Genocide is alive and well, choking out indigenous populations through war machines, starvation, mental health deterioration, pollution, horrible living conditions, and countless other daily humiliations that slice through human after human like nicks of razor blades all over the psyche.

It changes kaleidoscopically over time, but it's made of the same parts.

In the Holocaust Museum, I walked through haunting exhibitions, relics, faces, and names of those swallowed by a similar beast. I couldn't make it through without breaking down into sobs. How to carry so much pain? How to carry so much senseless suffering?

If only we can understand the root of this sickness and address it.

The sickness that was birthed by colonialism, spread through patriarchal religions, peddled by the narcissistic madmen whose propaganda manipulated the masses. The sickness inherent in the very notion of power, the toxicity of a culture of shame, the horrifying misstep that humanity took when it began to believe that any one person is better than another. It infects us to our very cores, the damage plays out in our families and our misguided values and ignorance, our callous lack of empathy and violence, our blind support of politicians.

We are a sick world.

I cried many tears, but I belly-laughed in Palestine too. On top of a hill overlooking miles from Israel to Jordan, V and I mounted a teeter totter and let our inner children free, snapping photos in the air with the most giddy smiles.

We both loved a good selfie, feigned for strong, fragrant Arabic coffee first thing in the morning, and used humor to cope with pain.

When I came home, the true trauma began to sink in. I'd find myself standing at an intersection, frozen, and the landscape turned to Palestine and I saw some horror play out in front of me: it took me

226

moments to return to the world where people were hurriedly walking around the girl stupidly staring.

I expected people to be as hurt over Palestine as I was. I expected people to want to self educate, join the cause. I at least expected my friends to care.

I couldn't believe the extents of torture we'd invested in when we couldn't invest in healing our own communities and how unbothered people were when it came straight out of their paychecks. We're robbed to commit horrors, and the silence of that is the eeriest thing I've ever known.

In the summer of 2014, 18 year old Mike Brown was shot 12 times with his hands in the air when he'd committed no crime. That summer, Eric Garner, a black man selling homemade cigarettes was put in an illegal chokehold and killed on video. In the fall of 2014, 14 year old Tamir Rice was shot in a park playing with a toy gun. The officer murdered him in less than a second and a half.

I saw no difference between what I'd seen in Palestine and the racial reality of America. America was a colonized country that had systematically used violence as a means to control its colonized population, and the military industrial complex was made rich through this system of oppression. The more that oppressed people fought for rights, and even made gains, the more funding given to the police to militarize and use excessive force anytime citizens dare assert human rights.

I didn't hesitate to join the marches. In Boston, these marches were stunning in their scope; they'd only grow more so as the movement continued to gain followers. But those first protests—in which we shut down highways, protested in front of prisons, shut down the train, and surrounded police stations—were full of violence *on the part of police* in riot gear. The tear gas that rained on protestors took me right back to Palestine.

We did die ins and dance protests, marches and chants. We flooded the streets and shut the city down.

But what was hardest: I did it alone.

That Thanksgiving at Sandra's, one of Sandra's friends launched into complaining how selfish protestors were to shut down roads when people needed to get home.

I retorted that some people never got a chance to come home because of racism, and disrupting the lives of those who enabled it simply made it their problem too. So they had a choice: they could try to help us solve it or suffer an inconvenience.

I still don't care what people, especially white people, think about my investment in racial healing, but I did care that Sandra didn't defend me. I asked her to protest and she always casually declined, then would tell me not to be violent. I wanted to shake her awake: did she understand how violent this system was? Did she realize the racism inherent in assuming that the protestors were the violent ones and not the police? None of us had the power of U.S. military grade weapons to have some kind of violent standoff.

Many people seemed cowardly, apathetic, or outright racist. It was an alienating experience.

But I had my students.

Many students had honest and painful conversations about race in my classrooms, tears shed from all races—they were young and idealistic enough to believe in change. They'd ask me to escort them to protests, often admitting how scared they were. I'd come full circle, from student protestor to professor mentor.

The truth of America is that its freedoms were not granted to us by white, male colonizers or any president: they were fought for by courageous people who didn't make history books or whose histories have been intentionally erased, paid for in blood.

To honor freedom meant to honor the spirit of courage to believe in something better. As Cornell West said, "Justice is what love looks like in public." Palestine taught me that kind of love.

I learned it from the whispers of its ghosts.

90

But this is a story about the girls.

I'd lost my sister, but I had substitutes.

Sandra, V. My new roommate, Caitlyn.

Caitlyn and I had worked together at the restaurant; she came with me for my abortion. Only months after meeting, her sister died in a drunk driving accident.

This tragedy made me have a tender spot for Caitlyn. Grief over C.D., Logan, and Beaux was still readily accessible to me.

Caitlyn always received signs from her sister: sunflowers. She had psychic readings that gave specific details, in which her sister assured her that she was proud, she was okay, she was sorry, and she needed Caitlyn to heal.

This is a story about girls and their ghosts.

This is the story about what happens when they pour all their love into ghosts and leave no love for themselves.

Have you ever seen girls in a love drought? Have you ever seen the way the sun blisters their skin, the way they burn so deeply that even standing too close hurts them? Have you seen what happens when they thirst so desperately they lose their voices? Have you seen the mad, wild woman crawling in the desert, having visions of hellfire and apocalypse, hair matted and skin cracking? Have you ever seen the full moon shift a girl into beast?

Caitlyn and I watched each other do this.

Caitlyn's ghosts anchored her to alcohol.

When Caitlyn moved in, I was aware she was struggling with alcoholism. It was something she was able to hide from friends, and maybe even herself, for several years—everyone at the restaurant drank themselves to blackout or bad choices.

Eventually, Caitlyn confessed, as her addiction began to affect all aspects of her life.

I was worried, but I was determined to remain by her side. I knew Caitlyn to her core; she was always full of laughter, eager to watch absurdly goofy YouTube videos and quote them incessantly. She was pensive, philosophical, and deeply spiritual. She was the friend that people turned to for comfort. It always felt like she was wise beyond her years, as if she'd lived many lifetimes.

Even so, her hauntings were out of her control.

More often that not, I came home and Caitlyn was intoxicated. I could always tell immediately, even though she tried to act alert.

It wasn't only her slurred speech: it was that Caitlyn wasn't there anymore. She'd been replaced by someone angry.

She never lashed out at me, but stories I told seemed to make her upset. She'd be outraged about something and then go into a tirade about that subject. Often, the anger was justified—it was only the volume of it, the passion of it, that I didn't recognize as Caitlyn.

I felt more alone living with her than I did living alone.

A couple times I woke to police knocking on our door. They'd found Caitlyn walking in the road aimlessly. I'd thank them and apologize while Caitlyn cussed them out.

Addiction was as close to possession as anything I'd seen.

While doing laundry, I put Caitlyn's clothes in the dryer and was surprised to find something heavy wrapped in her wet clothing: an empty wine bottle.

When I brought the bottle upstairs and told her I found it in the washing machine, a look of shame came over her face that reminded me of a child, readying themselves for punishment for breaking a rule. I immediately regretted telling her.

But my ghosts anchored me too, and I was oblivious to the shackles.

Sometimes while I chanted "Black Lives Matter," I'd think about the black men who'd been in my bed. I'd think about how I loved them so much—even knowing that my lovers treated me like something expendable, something to hurt for sport, a rabbit clawing off its own leg in a trap.

Still, I knew, instinctively, that much of the pain they heaped onto me came from a culture that heaped so much pain onto them.

But Dwayne and Santiago were broken records. They'd have sex urgently—often aggressively and sometimes violently—then they'd put me back in timeout, stay away for days, weeks, months.

I wanted to be the lover they said they wanted: the girl with no feelings. So I didn't react to their abuses. I readily forgave whenever they returned. It seemed that made them angry too. I couldn't win. They wanted me to chase and be monogamous, but if I did either of those things, I was deemed as "catching feelings." But if I pursued other lovers, they became possessive.

My ghosts chained me to my bed, turned me temptress, drained me of my blood, filled me with venom and semen, covered me with fang marks that wouldn't heal, fed from the same wounds repeatedly.

I was getting ready for a Tinder date. I had hair extensions, false lashes, makeup to perfection. He wasn't even single.

He said I made him orgasm "like a fire hydrant." It almost made me feel I had worth.

Caitlyn knocked on my door. She'd been crying.

"What is it?" I asked, fastening my earrings.

"I'm moving out."

"Like, right now?"

"Like right now."

"Are you serious?"

"I don't have rent money. I drank it."

"But it's due in two days!"

"I know, and I'm sorry. I'm going to long-term treatment."

I sat in silence with my head spinning. I couldn't argue that she needed rehab, and I wanted her to heal, but it felt as if the ground was swallowing me. I kept getting abandoned by roommates with little warning. Every year the bills went up; every year I never got any kind of raises at any of my underpaying teaching jobs.

"Are you coming back?"

"I don't think so."

This is a story about girls and their addictions.

This is a story about ghosts.

91

nne's changing out of lingerie. Santiago approaches behind, wraps his arms around her, gropes her breasts.

Santiago: "Whenever I'm with you, I go home and look at your pics and get horny. Then I miss you and have to come back. I've stuck around a long time with you."

Anne: "That's weird because you're almost never here."

Santiago: "I try to get over you."

Anne laughs and puts on a bra. Santiago wraps his arms around her and they look at each other in the mirror.

Santiago: "You're a really down chick. I could never stay mad at you. I can tell you're just a really good person. You make everything fun. You're so easy to talk to you and you don't get jealous. And you're hot. You can have any man. Whenever I leave, I think, 'She'll find someone else soon.'"

92

Most horror stories have several deaths.
And ghosts must do again what gives them pain.

93

JOURNAL ENTRY
1-15-15

This is a hard entry to write. Maybe the hardest ever.

I've done nothing but sleep. I'm dead to the world.

The truth is, I don't know what to say, because I don't know what the truth is.

Santiago called. He wanted to come over with his cousin. My instincts were all saying no. I said, "There's not an expectation that I'm going to have sex with you both, right?" He said, "You don't trust me?" I said, "I trust YOU. I don't know him." He said, "We just wanna chill." I said ok.

They came by around midnight. They brought Hennessy, weed, coke. His cousin was kind of attractive. He had loads more personality than Santiago. Santiago was practically mute. We were drinking, dancing, doing lines. I started to feel comfortable. I even started to think—maybe I'll have a threesome?

Then things start to get blurry. I remember Santiago pushing me into the bathroom and pushing me to my knees and saying "Suck my dick." I did, briefly. I remember him doing it again in the kitchen and being like, "Cous, watch!" And me stopping and getting up, not wanting to be seen like that. I remember thinking I just wanted to go in the room and have sex discretely, but both Santiago and his cousin (I

235

don't even know his name) grabbed my ass and looked at me like I was food. I remember being in my room, and Santiago saying, "Come get this, cous!"

Then he was taking off my pants, fucking me from behind, and I didn't say no. I remember thinking, "Ok, now you've had a threesome." I remember them switching places, and I still don't think I said no. Then it was suddenly morning and I didn't remember how night passed. Then I remember wanting it all to stop.

I was feeling sick and feeling like this thing, like the garish porn stars, not human. I was SO THIRSTY. I started saying I wanted to stop. Santiago brought me water. I went to put on my pants and Santiago grabbed me, ripped my shirt off and ruined it, and took off my bra. I fought him, but he's huge. He got it and he lifted me and threw me on the bed and told me to suck. I felt all the flaws of my body exposed. I felt fat and worthless. I didn't even try to cover myself because it was too late. They had all of me. I was theirs to mock and use.

I remember his cousin telling Santiago to stop and he was "doing too much." I remember Santiago getting behind me but he wasn't hard. I put on a sweatshirt. Santiago took the sweatshirt off and kept trying to get me to suck his dick, but it was soft. His cousin got behind me and put it in my ass. I said no a million times but Santiago pushed my head down, made me keep going. Finally, I got away and ran to the bathroom. His cousin came and bent me over the sink. He tried to fuck me but I fought him off. I kept saying I wanted Santiago.

He left, I went to pee and they both came in as I was on the toilet naked and laughed. I felt humiliated and they both carried me to the room and his cousin fucked me again. For a while, Santiago just sat on my radiator staring into space. I called his name and he wouldn't look at me. His cousin said, "Dude, you need to talk to her. This bitch just wants Santiago, Santiago." He didn't respond. I looked him the eye and said, "You're not into me anymore?" He sat stoic, didn't show any sort of reaction. I was looking for the Santiago who was sweet and he wasn't there.

His cousin said, "I gave you free coke."

I said, "And I fucked both of you! Leave me alone!"

Both of them were mad. His cousin said, "She needs to talk to you. You have a history."

Santiago said, "I don't talk to that bitch."

I picked about 15 condoms off my floor. I kept finding more and feeling disgusted.

I told Sandra and V I felt like I was raped.

I also feel I wasn't raped, I'm just stupid, I'm a slut, and I feel humiliated. There were moments they definitely violated and harmed me, but I brought it on myself.

I told Santiago we should call it quits. He texted, "Feeling some type of way?"

I told him I wasn't mad but I think we should move on.

He said, "lol. No one put a gun to your head."

That's the end. That's all he said and all I have in me to say about it.

V

"*Dying*
is an art, like everything else.
I do it exceptionally well.

I do it so it feels like hell."

—"Lady Lazarus," Sylvia Plath

94

You're on a boat with V in South Africa. You'd just visited Robben Island, where Nelson Mandela had been imprisoned. You'd suggested a trip to learn more about the history of apartheid. You'd thought that understanding methods of resistance could help you understand how to better support equality movements.

"Are those penguins?" You'd asked V.

A man behind you answered, "Those are definitely birds, sweetheart."

You turned and found a tour guide. He introduced himself as "Shopping Bag Drizzy."

"What does that mean?" You'd asked.

"The poor man's Drake."

If you squinted, and lowered your expectations, he could look a little like Drake.

He'd told you he liked that your toes matched your dress: he wanted to talk about 2Pac, race, revolution.

At dinner, V submerged into an all-out war. She was furiously texting, outraged that her girlfriend wanted to go to a club.

This was her normal behavior. She'd comb through years of social media, on alert for any sign of disloyalty. When V's partners weren't with her, she wanted them alone, pining.

Once, V met a nurse—she quit her job and lived off of her financially. When you'd suggested she may be moving fast, V said she no longer could be friends with you; she went cold shoulder for months. You were so grateful when she returned and agreed you could visit and

239

meet her partner. V immediately suggested you get matching tattoos—an olive branch on your neck for Palestine, a symbol of forgiveness.

Olive trees take hundreds of years to grow: you have to have patience that they'll nourish someday. You have to have faith peace will come.

You'd said to V, "We have to be friends forever if we do this."

You'd offered up the back of your neck and got branded with V, got branded with the only kind of love you believed in—the love between girls at war with a world that sought to snuff them out—got branded with your insatiable hunger to be loved in a way that didn't hurt.

You'd tried to talk to V about her jealousy: "We all have a past. I have men who mean nothing now, even if I tell stories about them. You can't expect all your partners to have never loved anyone before. It doesn't mean they don't love you."

V lashed out, "Shut the fuck up, Anne."

"But I think you'll be happier if…"

"Shut the FUCK. UP."

You knew better than to say anything when V was in a mood. So V had gone to the hotel after dinner, got on Facetime, and railed at her girlfriend.

What could you do?

You texted the tour guide.

The weather was gorgeous, the landscape was lush and enchanting, the stars were glowing pin pricks of magic, the wine smelled of honeysuckle and butter, the laughter was a percussion that drove out all pain.

You were alive. You were in Africa.

What could you do?

You wanted to eclipse the violences done against your body with other men's hands.

What could you do?

You took off your shirt and kissed him.

You grabbed a condom from your purse, pulled him to a tree, pulled down his pants, put the condom on, and bent over in front of him like an animal.

Who are you to deny what you are?

240

At 5 a.m., you crawled into bed with V. You got a text from the tour guide: "You're the woman I want for my wife."

For days, he texted incessantly. You had to block him. He reached out to your friends on social media.

You'd bemoaned to V, "What is it with men? When they fuck me, I can tell I'm no more than a sex doll. They love their own hand more than they love me. They want me to have no feelings and no personality, and they treat me like I'm gum on the bottom of their shoe. But when I do exactly what men want—go dead inside and give them my body— they lose their mind and act exactly the way that they always accuse of women: clingy, obsessive, and irrational. Can you imagine if I sent texts like this? They'd crucify me."

"That's why I don't fuck men," V laughed.

"Did you work things out with your girlfriend?"

"I think I'm going to break up with her."

"You said this was the one!"

"Sometimes it scares me how easily I can cut anyone off."

Sometimes that scared you about V too.

95

Then the 2016 election.

I plummeted into a cold truth.

It'd be better if I wasn't alive.

I laid in bed with a man who I thought was perfect—a Harvard grad student who only wanted to have sex as "casual monogamous" who ghosted me regularly. Watching clips of the inauguration on my phone, I turned to him, "I'm going celibate."

I didn't have sex again for six years.

I didn't write in my journal again for three years.

This is a story about ghosts.

96

LAST ENTRY
4-10-17

I went to Ireland to learn about The Troubles. I got sick immediately when I came home. I had strep throat, then a cold virus, then an ear infection, then boils on my head, an achy body, fatigue, fever, dizzy spells. Work's been impossible.

In the midst of being sick, I plummeted:

How disgusting I am. How ugly I am. How fat I am. How much I've aged. How boring I am. How tired I am.

And worse:

Do I want to live anymore? Isn't this world terrible? I can't fix people's hate. Why do I care? Why do I have compassion for a world full of terrible people? This species doesn't want love.

I've been alone so long. I'm past the age where love is possible. No one I've loved loved me back. I don't have any energy to love anymore. I can't even shower on my days off.

My life is pointless. I don't want to interact with people.

I hate that my sister abandoned me. I thought she never would.

The nightmares and PTSD are never-ending.

Sandra and her apathy is like a knife in my back I can't reach and yank out. All she talks about is men and sex.

I have my students but work is so overwhelming and a few can drag me under easily with hate.

Is it worth it to live for writing? I get feedback that I'm good but am I good enough to <u>live for it?</u> I have confidence that my ideas are genuine, but not my craft.

Do I believe in God? It's the hardest question of my life.

I've felt premonitions before and thought: something is telling me this. And it came true.

Often my writing felt like it came from elsewhere.

Often I've had such strokes of luck, that my gratitude to something outside me was unshakable.

Often I've traveled and seen things and divine blessings felt undeniable.

But what God would let people be born into suffering? What can I make of that?

I keep begging, God make me lovable.

I've worked so hard to cultivate a person who is lovable. But I'm so easy for people to betray.

I feel lost and beat down. I feel lonely. I'm resentful. I feel abandoned.

I'm trying hard to stay tethered.

97

When the #MeToo movement swept social media, it seemed the culture was catching up to something I already knew. But I wanted no part in the conversation.

No one is hated more than a person who endures violence and has the audacity to speak about it.

I'd buried my rapes under the dirt of self blame. I knew I wasn't the perfect rape victim, so I could never speak.

Something changed after an article came out exposing comedian Aziz Ansari. What struck me was there was no rape—the woman was uncomfortable for being pushed into giving oral sex. I called Sandra to parse its allegations: this seemed like every date we ever had. They feel entitled to sexual pleasure like you owe them something; they're pushy, whiny, and oblivious to your discomfort. To us, this was normal.

"Her line is at what she says no to," I said to Sandra, dumbfounded, "I never considered that my line could be at no."

In my mind, my line for abuse was at physical attack. I didn't realize my emotional pain mattered. I started to feel resentment going all the way back to childhood.

Then I got the flu. The flu turned into two months of pneumonia.

Then a mystery illness took root and I sunk for over a year: I was defecating blood; my intestines felt like a pack of wolves were tearing at them; I was leaving class to vomit; I was fatigued with severe body aches.

I was becoming a ghost.

When I landed in the ER, they ran some tests that confirmed I had a bacterial infection that usually only affects old people. I was given antibiotics, but they didn't work.

Then the college I worked for merged with a larger university and laid off all its faculty.

Then I lost Sandra.

My rape was a wedge between us I never spoke of. I no longer wanted to talk about men. Ultimately, her devotion to dangerous men felt like a burn victim standing next to a bonfire.

One day I started to cry about how much pain my body was in.

Sandra replied that maybe we needed a break.

That rusty knife to the chest: *You're not lovable. When you're at your lowest, the people you love most won't be there.*

I hung up the phone.

I knew how to lose a sister.

At the doctor's, I stared, stunned, at the pages of health issues on the screen, spanning years.

The blood-rotten, bone-weary, dead-woman-walking truth of my body: silence is not silence.

Trauma doesn't go away because you bury it—it roots.

The truth must be purged like the vomit of a demon-possessed girl: if it's not, it feeds from the inside.

98

I want to speak now.

I want to say no.

I want to say to the people who think they were raped because they weren't good enough, because they were defective in some way: no.

What happened to us was darkness. It came to us because darkness needs light.

It can eclipse your light, swallow it in its hot mouth, but ultimately light has the power.

Light can make darkness vanish completely.

Heal it or become darkness.

Tend it like a bonfire on a damp, fall night. Conjure it so high it could burn a demon. Watch dark shadows slither from your ankles— fleeing, evaporating.

We can drive this from our world.

We only have to set our pain aflame to the heavens, burn eternal.

Come.

Let me show you how darkness almost eclipsed me.

Until I learned to walk through fire.

99

Between celibacy to breakdown are years in which I was a castaway, flailing against a tempest that made the waters a swirling vortex, a centrifugal pull that I felt too weak to wrench myself out of.

My health deteriorated. Cystic acne appeared all over my face. I gained more weight. My hair thinned and became brittle, easily falling out. The bacterial infection was relentless.

My past lovers wormed their way out of the crevices of my crumpled past regularly, reaching out with new profiles to attempt to reconnect after being blocked.

I knew my body could only take a man like a rat trap: one light touch and I'd detonate and snap a spine.

That was the kind of rage I buried.

In order to get myself to orgasm, I imagined I was a man.

I looked for porn of men jerking off to women's pictures, of men having sex with dolls, of cartoon wolves having sex with women, of men waking women from a slumber with dicks in their mouths, of men coming all over women's faces and bodies.

I looked for sex that was obsessive. I tried to untangle it in my brain: why would someone who's been raped have fantasies like this? Why do I imagine I have a penis? Sometimes, I could feel it like a phantom limb.

Perhaps I was envious of men's power. Maybe I was on the LGBTQ spectrum.

Maybe turning fear into desire is the only way to live with it.

But my deepest desire was to have sex with a man who loved me. Tenderness was the kink I sought.

I made an effort to save my life.

I got a job in Texas.

Few places in the country ranked lower on my list. Yet Texas offered an escape route. I was only at that job four months before I realized it was a trapdoor.

That job was so toxic that I filed a lawsuit and took a gag order for a settlement, preventing me from saying anything else about it. Suffice to say, I learned more about how dark the world is.

It was January 2020. The news was abuzz: Pandemic. Covid-19. Shut-down.

I was broken into shards, but a heel was about to come down and turn me into dust.

100

"Ladies, love yourself cause this shit could get ugly."

—Megan Thee Stallion

In July 2020, Megan Thee Stallion, who'd dominated airwaves during quarantine, made headlines for a shocking reason: she was shot.

After an argument with rapper Tory Lanez about leaving a party, he pulled out his gun, aimed at her feet, and said, "Dance, bitch!" Megan was shot in the foot. With her hands in the air to police, she told them she'd stepped in glass.

Social media thundered its lightning flash of memes like "Shot Girl Summer." Celebrities jumped the bandwagon, stating that they had a joke about Megan that "needed to be twerked on" or wishing that they had someone who liked them so much they wanted to shoot them. Transphobic jokes that framed Megan as a man further fueled hatred, a not-so-subtle reminder of who experiences patriarchal violence at the highest rates.

In March 2020, Breonna Taylor, a young black woman, was asleep when police mistakenly entered her residence and shot her dead. No charges were filed, and the summer of 2020 became the largest Civil Rights protest in both U.S. and world history.

Statistics about black women and violence are grim. It's estimated that 40% of black women have experienced rape, stalking, or intimate partner violence.

One would expect that logic should dictate our sense of propriety, that we should be able to see the way black women's humanity is rendered invisible while their pain is put on display for entertainment.

What 2020 taught more than anything is that we live in vastly contradicting realities.

Where I saw black women whose traumas were steamrolled by the hot iron branding of a looming historical shadow, others live in a reality in which they hate women.

Especially black women.

Others live in a reality in which they beat women.

In which they rape women.

In which they cheer for those who do the same.

In which they blame the victim.

Some live in a reality in which hatred means power.

And power alleviates their pain.

Their pain comes from the fact that they hate.

Because it's unnatural to hate what made you, to crush what you should love.

Megan Thee Stallion couldn't tell police the truth about her assault because she feared the police would kill her, her friends, or her assaulter.

Yet, the first thing any woman who's been assaulted will be asked is if she went to police, ignoring the fact that police are a traumatizing force, ignoring the fact that men who want to exploit power are drawn to careers like police and the military, ignoring the horrifying statistics about how many police abuse their spouses, ignoring the racial police brutality statistics, ignoring the truth that most assaulters never see a day in prison.

This is a culture that laughs when women get shot.

This is a culture that does nothing to protect women when they ask for help—the only victim that'll ever get love is the one who's fully silent because they're dead.

This is a culture that only cares for the "perfect victim," the victim who shows up in blurry home videos on late-night true crime television—lily white and young as a bud—lovingly rendered by the narrator as a "beautiful girl who loved to laugh and wanted to be a mother someday, who didn't deserve to die."

This is a story about ghosts.

101

But this is a story about girls.

V and Anne.

Six years of sisterhood—memories sprawling across the country, around the world.

When Sandra exited, V took up the extra space.

The only person I ever met who matched my anger was V.

We were angry at the world: the inhumanity, the disrespect of human rights. We were angry about our childhoods: the ignorance of adults who raised us, their neglect and abuse, the psychological brainwash we'd endured. We were angry at our exes: the false hopes, the inability to see our worth. We were angry at the friends we'd lost: the bereavement that abandonment trails in its wake.

I loved her madly.

It's a thing that wounded girls do.

They sniff each other out, cling, love madly.

They make you feel unique and special.

They make you feel you're chosen to be loved so madly.

They take up a lot of space.

When they leave, you struggle to stand after realizing that space wasn't all they took.

V and I could struggle to handle conflict, as she reacted with sudden cold shoulders, hanging up the phone, or threats to end the friendship. This led to a sense of walking on eggshells, of always trying to please her.

But who was I to hold anything against my friends? I recognized V's issues. V's childhood had been extremely traumatic. When both her brothers would regularly land in prison—one of them for murder—V would unravel and take on a shame that transformed her. I couldn't help but cry when I'd see her in that state: she was a wild cub, shrieking, so unbearably animal and alone.

In 2020, as Minneapolis went up in flames after the murder of George Floyd by a police officer, I watched the news and called V.

"Shit is going down in Minnesota. You ready?"

V and I protested daily. We treated the blisters and the thigh rashes. We bemoaned the backlash and the ignorance. We shared information to educate and got people involved.

The 2020 uprisings were astoundingly large, and witnessing it in the south was new—I saw the radical and brave young minds that emerged from such harrowing histories. I looked at the graffiti and broken windows and felt the distinct feeling of seeing a pressure cooker explode: this was the remnant of slavery's legacy, its devastation and longstanding impact on full display, threatening to ruin us entirely, as it always has.

In order to build anew, something must burn.

As the election came, I felt depression rooting like something terminal.

When a handsome man standing in front of "Free Palestine" graffiti slid into my DMs, I was vulnerable.

We'd video chat for hours; he seemed a hero. His life was devoted to rescuing women from gender violence worldwide. He was smart about foreign policy—it evolved into sexting.

It was the closest I'd had to a sexual partner in four years.

I told myself at least it was with a good man this time.

I told myself that I could do it without any feelings.

Soon, the familiar pattern: he didn't respond for days; he'd be moody and say something to hurt me; he stopped asking about me; he mostly talked about himself and seemed responsive only when praised; when I asked to chat, he reminded me how important his job was; he told me he had a new therapist and was flirting with her.

But just one sext could set me aglow like a dusty old lamp.

He was the drug.

I didn't even know I was using. I convinced myself I wasn't.

My drug of choice was abuse.

One of V's flaws I suppressed discussing was hypocrisy. Sometimes the values she discussed didn't match her behaviors. This came to a head before the election. She was traveling a lot despite the pandemic. I felt I shouldn't question it, but when she told me she was going to travel again, I asked: "Why do you say you care so much about Covid-19 affecting the disenfranchised but you continue to travel?"

She hung up the phone.

We never spoke again.

She texted and said our friendship had come to an end: nothing I could say would change that. No closure, no opportunity to apologize.

She made me feel as if there were no redeeming qualities in me.

It was as if all the love I gave, all those nights of tears and support, didn't exist at all.

V once said maybe I was too judgmental of Sandra's sex life and that's why our friendship ended.

I said, "After I went celibate, I became judgmental of toxic men."

"I think you've always been judgmental."

"What?"

"That's how it seems."

"I was just like Sandra sexually. I don't sex shame. We enabled each other, if anything."

"I feel like you judge."

"How? There was only one relationship where I told you that you were moving fast. Ever since, I've supported every relationship. Have I not?"

"Okay, I'm going to leave."

"V! You can't just address this and tell me? I feel like you hold something invisible against me that you don't say. Just say it, V!"

She looked at me hard, her lip quivered. What was that expression? I've recalled it in my head many times.

Fear.

After a long moment, she responded carefully, "You're not the first person who's said this. And…I can only say I'm working on my

255

mental health. I can't think of any other time you judged me, you're right. Maybe I'm carrying that one time."

My drug of choice was abuse.

I was looking at my crush's Facebook when I noticed all the people who posted on his status misspelled their swear words.

He misspelled his swear words.

I went to each profile—beautiful women, with no friends, pictures, or followers. I reverse image searched the pictures: they were models.

They were all *him*.

I found 29 fake profiles that told him how smart he was, how handsome, how he was the best writer, how he should be running the world.

Another narcissist.

And ghosts must do again what gives them pain.

102

I'm in the bath thinking about how no cut could match the inner pain. I have a razor and I slice my thigh. I know my skin will forgive me the way others won't.

I see Sylvia Plath sitting on my toilet. She's dressed in 1950s garb. She's holding a baseball bat.

She's showing me the spike of her heel. She's threatening to stomp my spine.

"You don't respond to violence unless it's from your own hand, right?" She lifts her brow to mock me, "You suicide." She spits the word.

Then I hear her voice again, but it's coming from behind me: "The bully in your head isn't me."

I turn to look behind me.

Nothing.

I turn back to the toilet.

Mother.

103

In August 2020, Daisy Coleman died by a self-inflicted gunshot wound.

She'd raised awareness through the documentary, *Audrie and Daisy*, which detailed the horrors two young girls experienced being raped, videotaped, and left for dead by teenage boys: the bullying at school, the community vitriol, and the slut shaming. Audrie, tragically, took her own life shortly after her assault. But Daisy, the film's champion, advocated for mental health care for rape victims and for cultural awareness around misogyny.

Then she killed herself.

Later that year, her mother also killed herself.

We aren't meant to survive this.

It's lethal, even if it kills you slowly.

104

Just shy of 40, I'd made it further than I thought I would.

I sunk my head underwater in the bath and thought of Virginia Woolf, drowning herself with piles of rocks in her pockets.

Then, as if a mouth pressed to my ear: "Anne."

I jolted from the water.

I knew that voice.

I hadn't heard it in 23 years.

"It's time," he said.

That's how the voice of C.D. shattered my grey world.

By morning, it was technicolor.

My life was saved.

I heard his voice again: "It's time to know why our paths crossed. Read your journals."

I wrapped myself in a towel and gathered my teenage journals.

I'd avoided this girl. I buried her.

What I found:

1) C.D. loved me.

2) When I lost my virginity, it was rape.

I'd said no, but he was violent, threatening, and I blamed myself after.

Both of these revelations collapsed me and healed me the way only the flaming knife of the divine through the heart can.

I cried, long and hard. I realized I'd been so physically ill because I had unprocessed grief inside me. I said into the darkness, "Why'd you wait all these years? I was begging for a sign."

I heard him once more: "You needed to come to my door."

The suicide door.

His last words: "Now write the book."

106

Feeling lovable came like a gasp, a near drowning. Every moment after was miraculous.

I was aghast: all my life there was this well of love, this pure feeling of light, and I'd never felt it before? I felt my own love for others intensely, and I thought the love you got from others was something you simply understood in a cerebral way, something you chose to trust.

I didn't know you could *feel* lovable. It struck me how sad it was that I'd never felt loved. It struck me that many other people must walk through the world feeling unloved too.

The dominant feeling was relief: even as friendships stretch, bend, or break, love was going to live in me permanently—I only have to recall love like an old video tape; the memories thunder followed by flashes of light.

Let each lightning flash capture love in the midst of the storm that you didn't know you'd survive. *Gasp.* Let it fill you like a first breath after the shelter of the womb. *Gasp.* Scream like a baby if you have to— split the silence with your cries. *Gasp.*

Until the breathing comes easy.

Gasp. It's going to take a while.

107

O r I'd lost my mind completely.

As a child, I saw a woman on TV with silky ringlet curls and vapid doe eyes collapse into the arms of a vampire who draped his erect fangs over her neck.

I've been hooked on monstrous men ever since.

That's roughly the extent of my understanding of my life after years of therapy.

I understood I'd been raped—I counted both the go-go dancer and Santiago as rapes. I understood that a lot of my physical health problems were connected to trauma. I understood that some lovers had crossed boundaries about consent. I understood that some of them were obvious narcissists and therefore abusers, but I understood very little about Narcissistic Personality Disorder, even with a psychology degree. I understood I'd been abused, especially by my mother, and that I had cPTSD.

After I heard CD's voice, I was afraid my therapist would think I was delusional. I very much needed CD's voice to be true.

I held my breath waiting for her to condemn me to psychosis. To my relief, she was moved by the experience and said she didn't think I showed signs of delusion. She assured that visitation was a common experience for victims of grief, and it's not up to her to assign negative meaning to that, especially when it has a positive effect.

I believed wholeheartedly in God. I believed in miracles. I believed I'd never be suicidal again: nothing could convince me that this heartbreakingly beautiful life wasn't worth fighting for.

I was ready to write the book C.D. told me to write.

I thought I had something to say about rape.

I had no idea the abyss I was falling into.

Because that's what real healing is—an abyss.

All the most chilling horror stories eventually take you to the origin story.

The origin story goes straight into the mouth of Hell.

108

If my first experience of sex was abuse, and I didn't realize it, was that because I had no concept of consent?

If my first experience of sex was abuse, and I didn't realize it, did that mean I wanted it?

Did that explain the kind of men I've attracted?
Is that why I've been raped more than once?
Why were all my lovers obsessive?
Why did they always come back?
Why the rape dreams?
Why was I so attracted to the LGBTQ community?
Why didn't any men love me?
Why did I lose friends I loved?
Was C.D. the only boy who ever loved me?
Why did C.D. commit suicide?

C.D. said it was time for me to know the reason our paths crossed. I hadn't thought of my life as a path, only a dead end maze I couldn't find my way out of.

Not being lovable enough to stay alive for.
Not being lovable.
Not being loved.

What had C.D.'s mother's abandonment instilled in him?
Not being loved.

Not being lovable.
Not being lovable enough to stay alive.

C.D. loved me—the girl who looked like his mom, who'd been, like many, thrust out of her own heart, incapable of self love.

The reason our paths crossed was trauma: like magnets, we're dragged unconsciously towards others whose demons mirror the ones that grip us.

When C.D. decided to flip the abandonment, to be the one to leave, he thought he escaped, but he passed it onto those who loved him —a life-threatening disease made purely of pain.

It's taken many of us.
What's its name?
C.D., why did you die?

I'm on my knees in the dirt looking for it, C.D. I'm digging over your grave with my nails. I'm wild and ravaged: I'm pure animal, pure anger, hunger, instinct, and teeth.

I've found you, the bare skeleton of you. I'm gripping a bone in my palm: what curse is this?

If you speak the name of the demon, you'll cast it out.
Say it.
Name this venom.

C.D., were you raped too?
C.D., were you gay?
Was Logan gay?
What curse is this?

There's something parallel about our experiences.
There's something this ghost has to teach me.

C.D., are you my ghost or my demon?

109

Don't let doubt creep in with its slivers of shadows whispering under a door. C.D. was my angel.

He was a boy, so to a girl he was a god.

I did meditation, yoga, therapy, healing. I smiled daily. I loved my students. I had time to write.

He was a boy, so to a girl he was a god.

I got signs.

I wrote to Jason and he replied: he was getting out of prison that day. The timing seemed guided.

I had a dream that C.D. was throwing pennies at Jason. He said, "Jason never looks for signs." I told Jason; he said C.D. used to sit outside the trailer flicking pennies at people. His grandma believed that pennies were a sign from him.

Jason and I started finding pennies everywhere, even in our homes; we didn't carry cash. When I meditated for my 40th birthday, my journals toppled off my bookshelf and an old birthday card fell out. I took that as another sign.

It seemed God was everywhere once you realized where to look.

Jason said C.D. never had girlfriends. He questioned why he started dressing like Logan before he died. Jason admitted he called C.D. a faggot as his last words to him.

"Jason," I gasped, "what if that's a reason he died?"

"Don't think I don't think about that every day of my life, Anne."

266

Jason told me another crucial truth: everyone thought C.D. was nice, but he had serious rage. From the age of a young child, he beat Jason. Jason thought the rage was at his mom for abandoning him.

I prayed for answers, leapt into reading journals, and wrote.

Then the devil himself came to my door.
He had all the answers.

110

Most horror movies have a moment you can pinpoint as the nightmare's beginning—some lapse of good sense where some naive girl let the ghosts in.

Maybe she was the girl who thought the Ouija was a harmless toy. Maybe she was a powerful witch lashing out at a rival for her lover's affection. Maybe she was the serial killer's next victim, an airhead who stumbles towards strange noises rather than away. Maybe she's the love interest of a vampire, eager to collapse into starved arms.

Maybe she's just the girl who spread her legs—that's the easiest way for the devil to enter.

You watch the madness and keep that moment in your head as the nightmare reveals potholes: if only she hadn't let the ghosts in.

I'm at that point. He's at the door. I know that I have to open it if I'm going to tell the story.

Ahhh, he's handsome.
I think he's just a garden snake.
It turns out he's a python.

111

His knuckles meet wood: that's all it takes.
A soft sound that will spring you from your couch, change your life.

You open the door.

You can't take this back.

Even if you could, would you?

Because when you open it, he stands before you and takes the breath out of you the same way the sun shimmers across the horizon of a lake and beckons you to enter.

He *glitters*.

You smile.

No, you crack like a glowstick and beam neon.

He does a double take, smiles, "They said you needed a new fuse."

"That's what they say..." you sing.

He smirks, lifts his eyebrow, steps inside.

Sometimes a man walks into your life looking like he'd fit the exact shape of all your wounds, looking like he just might be an artificial limb—the match for the parts of you lost in a war long ago.

Some men walk into your life looking like their lips will cauterize the bleeding.

With tattoos climbing his arms like vines you want to scale; with his slow Texas drawl, punctuating his sentences with an electric shock as

269

he calls you "mama," "love;" with his dirty hair hidden under a dirtier, backwards hat—when you meet a man like that, and he walks away, it's as if the shape of him was the only thing plugging up a dam inside from bursting.

Then he's gone and you're drowning.

112

Anne: "I thought these men hated me, that they didn't even think of me, but they kept coming back. They always asked if I loved them. But sex and love are opposite to me."

Therapist: "Why?"

Anne: "I've never been loved by someone who had sex with me. They didn't know me. I wasn't giving any of my vulnerabilities: I was giving those to girlfriends."

Therapist: "When you don't give your vulnerable self, they can project whatever they want onto you."

Anne: "I just tried to perform—be whatever fantasy. For some, their projections got dark. Obsessive. I thought I wasn't good enough. I kept trying to be better, more seductive, with no emotional needs, but the truth was they were obsessed *because* they didn't know me. They were obsessed with whatever they made me into for their own traumas."

Therapist: "You put these men on pedestals. Each one had something you praised and thought you lacked. You put up with a lot of poor treatment because you didn't see yourself as worthy of the thing you had them on the pedestal for."

113

He was a handsome man who turned heads. He wore four shirts: a blue buttoned collared shirt with the name of the apartment company, a black shirt that said, "I'm going to piss some people off today," a plain orange shirt, and a blue polo shirt. He had an orange hat and a blue and tan hat. He wore an Apple Watch with an orange band. He wore skinny jeans that still looked baggy on his scarecrow legs. He was Mexican but could pass as white. He smelled like dust and fresh dirt. In the picture I took of him, he has a smudge of grease across his cheek—he always looked like a man wrestling with earth and machines.

He was my maintenance man.

I was smothered before he ever touched me.

He was a boy, so to a girl he was a god.

114

Anne: "He's covered in red flags. Tattoos, hyper-masculine, bad boy vibe, flirtatious, former Marine. But I saw him and it was like a rush of energy washed over me, like I knew him in a past life. Why do I always attract men covered in red flags?"

Therapist: "It's what's familiar."

Anne: "The men I attract have trauma too. How much of my pain did I bring on myself because I choose traumatized men?"

Therapist: "You aren't responsible for your trauma responses. It's not your fault this is the one dance you know."

115

His name was Lewis.

When he came to replace the fuse, he said the real problem was my hot water heater. He installed a new one.

He asked for a lighter, followed me outside.

"How long have you lived here?" He draped his armpits over my fence casually, leaned his head on his arm, fixated like a charmed snake.

Whenever I think of him, I see the beaming smile he'd flash with the devious sparkle in his gray eyes that looked like storm clouds.

He had chiseled features, thick dirty blond hair. He reminded me of James Dean.

When something sparked his interest, one eyebrow would slither upwards stealthily.

When he wanted something, it slithered.

When he was surprised, it slithered.

The rest of him stayed as stoic as the dead, his movements and mannerisms carefully controlled. His body language expressed a general ease, confident in his superiority, supremely unbothered.

His voice was deep, rural, southern, full of questions.

He wanted to know everything about me. He noticed every detail.

He was a boy, so to a girl he was a god.

Healing is nothing but channeling magic in the dark. You have to find your inner child, turn her cages into carousels, pretend that death doesn't have its hot breath on your neck behind you.

As he left, dragging the hot water heater, I called out, "What's your name?"

His smile. "Lewis," he sang.

"Nice to meet you. I'm Anne."

"Nice to meet you, Miss Anne."

I thought he was a garden snake.

It turned out he was a python.

116

Anne: "My dad never showed emotion. Only anger. I always thought he had a lot of emotions but was too prideful. I figured it was military brainwash."

Therapist: "You never had a man who you could express your emotions to safely. The men you've dated have been similarly repressed."

117

You look in the mirror; your flaws etch across your face like a cracked china doll in an old, haunted house.

You paint over every one carefully, methodically.

If you're perfect, if you're the doll, then you might attract the sex that proves you're alive.

It's late. He's coming again. The hot water heater keeps breaking.

It's been breaking every day for…how many days?

It's a mystery. He says he loves a mystery.

You do too. Especially one that looks like him.

You stand outside smoking and see him strolling up the walkway in basketball shorts and a t-shirt with cut off sleeves.

Your voice lilts into teasing, "You said you were 95% sure it was fixed!"

His smile. It invades half his face and all of you. He stumbles against the wall with a chuckle like a dumb baby being praised for his first step.

"I think you're breaking it because you wanna see me, mama."

You don't think of it then because you're too busy staring at his skin, at how the sleeveless shirt and shorts make him seem much more bare, much more touchable. You don't think of it then because you're thinking of all the demon tattoos you can see that you couldn't see before, of if you'll ever trace them with your tongue. You don't think of it then because you're thinking of the right things to say to keep him laughing, because his smile is the sun that makes something in you thaw.

277

You don't think of it then but you think of it later and for a long while you won't stop thinking of it:

Often, what liars accuse of others is their own projected truth.

I think you're breaking it because you wanna see me, mama.

118

Anne: "Why did Noah confess to sleeping with a server right after my dad attempted suicide?"

Therapist: "Because you were vulnerable."

Anne: "He wanted to hurt me worse?"

Therapist: "He needed to be the center of attention."

Anne: "I'm reliving the emotional pains from childhood."

119

His voice was deep, rural, southern, full of questions.
He wanted to know everything about me.
He noticed every detail, asked about my art, my crystals, the smell of weed in my apartment.

If I said something was a gift, he wanted to know about who gave it.

He stared at my appliances but he excavated me.

If he could have *really* seen me, who'd he have seen?

Someone smart, independent, cheerful, kind, quirky—with bright purple hair and flowing sundresses: when I met Lewis, I'd never been so optimistic.

I wanted to believe he saw that. He was just a friendly maintenance man who happened to be so handsome it was hypnotic. It wasn't his fault I'd been isolated, and suddenly he was the most interesting thing in my bubble.

I wanted to believe that when he had knowledge of my crystals, he really just happened to watch a lot of nature documentaries, like he said.

I wanted to believe he happened to read the books I'd read. To watch the same shows. To not want children. To have the same values.

We talked about aliens and space and horror. We shared thoughts about ghosts and past lives. He said his mom was a bruja.

Like you, mama.

He was so casually seductive.

After the umpteenth time looking at the mystery of the hot water heater, he said, "I guess I'll just have to hang out with you today and be your guest." We sat for hours; his energy was eerily familiar, safe. I asked what I should've asked before I answered his questions, "Did you move here with a partner?"

"My wife, well…"

So it began.

"We're not married. But we've been together since we were teenagers, so she's basically my wife."

I nodded.

"Everything I love, she hates. Everything she loves, I hate. We stay together for the dogs."

The power went off again.

He finally pulled out the heating rod—it was bent at a ninety degree angle, covered in calcite. "But it's a brand new heater!"

"Everyone is out to make a buck. They sell faulty heaters."

I wanted to believe that.

Just as I wanted to believe that Lewis saw me as a person.

But Lewis saw me the same as he saw that heater: an object.

He could wreck it if he wanted to.

"You must have angels, mama, because this should've exploded."

The last part kept repeating in my mind: *This should've exploded.*

120

Anne: "Married men talking badly about their wives trigger me. Quitting Brad was like quitting the best drug. It was *physical*. I was in withdrawals. Do you think I'm addicted to sex?"

Therapist: "There's something called Trauma Bonding—when the thing that gives you pain is the same thing to give you relief from pain, you become addicted to that, which happens to be your abuser."

Anne: "People are always shocked by how frankly I discuss trauma. Sandra said I always courted danger—like with Palestine. I just thought everyone else was a coward, but I think there's something wrong that I don't respond with fear. I can see genocide in front of my eyes, and it's not fear that I feel. It's grief. But I have no outlet. It just burns inside, like it's killing me."

Therapist: "There may also be people you should fear who you don't."

121

He was full of questions.
He wanted to know everything about me.
I wanted to know everything about him.
When I want a man to talk to me, I fawn.
It's instinct with a certain kind of man.

Lewis loved to be told he was a genius.

The day we met, he remarked that he was already at 84 hours, but it was okay, because "a genius only needs six hours of sleep."

I put that knowledge away and flashed it whenever I needed to see him smile. When he said he failed English after learning my career, I leaned towards him, made a show of his height by staring up wide-eyed, achingly, "Well, your genius lies elsewhere."

His dominance rolled off his spine like a tense wolf. He put his hands in my face, smiled, "It's in my handsssssss, mama."

I told him he was the best on staff, the best we'd ever had, how he'd never be unemployed, how only a genius could deal with this dump. I told him watching him work was like watching a chess player. I asked him to explain what he was doing, then told him it sounded impressive, like another language, one I was too dumb to understand.

Lewis loved to be told he was a hero.

He said in a past life, he was a knight. He loved stories with monsters to be slayed. He loved tenants who treated him as if their angel arrived. When I worried that giving my cats a flea bath might result in my murder, he said, "I'll come check on ya." When I worried that my heater would still be broken over the holiday, he said, "I'll come save ya."

I said, "It's amazing I'm alive all these years never once changing my air filter."

"When you buy property someday, I'll do house calls."

Lewis loved to be told he was a Good Man.

It was a term he used repeatedly: "I'm a good man. I *try* to be a good man."

He carried himself as if he were the most reasonable, chill, friendly, moral, innocent man.

His co-workers loved him. His bosses loved him. Tenants loved him.

He didn't break rules, he said. "I don't even speed."

Lewis loved to be told he was a victim.

Once you got him talking, a list of complaints came at you so swiftly you couldn't keep track of why they all mattered. His boss had a tone he didn't like. His wife wasted money on a vacation in 2007. His last boss' husband jumped him for flirting. His dog had puppies and they smelled. His siblings had too many children and wanted to bring them to his birthday. His boss hadn't reimbursed him. He got sprayed by a broken toilet. He forgot to clock in that morning.

"No rest for the wicked, huh?" I said.

"I *am* wicked."

"How so?"

"I just think I must've done something really bad in a past life to deserve this life."

"What plagues you in this life, Lewis?"

His smile.

"I like talking to you, mama. You feel like therapy."

122

Anne: "I can't believe the amount of violence I'm finding in my journals that I blacked out."

Therapist: "When the brain blocks trauma, it's doing what it's supposed to. It's helping you survive."

Anne: "I'm noticing that many lovers put me through the same cycle of abuse—the only difference is that some seemed really nice to the rest of the world."

Therapist: "Covert narcissists can abuse in ways in which you have no idea you're being abused."

123

On the vampire classic, *True Blood*, the main character is a sexy, smart half-fairy, half human with a fetish for vampires. She thinks it's because some vampires still have their humanity, but she later discovers that the vampires want her solely because her fairy blood is full of delicious light—a light so intoxicating that vampires get stoned and can temporarily walk in sunlight. Her blood is so addictive it takes incredible will for vampires not to kill her violently in a single feeding.

Why does the fairy fall for vampires?

Unlike with humans, fairies can't hear vampires' thoughts.

They consume her, but she can't feel their emotions.

She can never truly know them. The most she can ever really know them is when they feed on her, leaving her half-dead.

If she never knew them, it's as if they were never there. If they were never there, what's there to grieve when they're gone?

Who was Lewis?

He was an eclipse. A covering of darkness.

He was an apocalypse. An uncovering of darkness.

He'd been raised in poverty—the floor of his shack in rural, nowhere, East Texas was dirt. He was the eldest of five children. His dad was, in his words, "an abusive alcoholic," and he never drank, because "someone in the family had to break the cycle," he said with a bitter shrug. In reality, he was an alcoholic too. He said his dad was the reason he never wanted kids: "Parents don't know what they're doing."

"They fuck us up pretty good!" I replied.

His eyes shot me a sideways glance of momentary fear when I said that.

His grandmother, dying of Alzheimer's, raised him. He said his mother predicted he'd go to prison as a teenager. He mentioned prison casually, saying that sometimes people judge him for his tattoos, for having been to prison.

"You've been to prison?"

He nodded his head no. Then looked at me sheepishly, leaning forward and gripping the stove to steady himself, the shame a palpable weight, slowly nodding yes.

"I don't judge," I said quickly, moving towards him. "I don't believe in prison." He raised one eyebrow, looked at me sideways, leaned his body next to mine until our skin touched. I flinched: he felt like an electric shock. "I have penpals in prison."

"I wish you were my penpal in prison."

"What did you go for?"

"Deadly intent. I was in the car during a drive by."

"Did you know there was going to be a shooting?"

"I thought we were going to a party."

"How old were you?"

"15."

"That must've been traumatic."

"I think I was more butthurt to lose my girlfriend. I still have her name tattooed."

His wife never wore makeup, never wore her hair down, always wore the same t-shirt and jeans, always looked sad, walking around on trash duty. She was a cleaning lady; he was her boss. The one time I saw them interact, he jumped out of his truck and pitched a set of keys at her face. I was shocked because his angry body language was different than anything I'd seen. When it began to get cold, his wife wore a jacket matching his.

He had a friend that moved with him; he was his friend's boss too. Something his wife and friend had in common was that they were both obese; they both were people who seemed, on glance, to be depressed.

Lewis had only traveled to Colorado and Mexico. He rarely did anything for fun. He worked, went home, got high, turned on the TV, and zoned out, according to him.

I thought we had this in common.

But trying to know Lewis is to gather crumbs scattered after someone else's gluttonous feast.

What I know is that my light fed him, and I almost died.

Without realizing, Lewis snuck inside me like a tapeworm. To try to explain who he really was is to wrench a parasite from a vital organ.

I rattle off facts I collected only to prove that he was human, as if he was knowable: he had four dogs; he rarely kept a job for more than a year; he and his wife both had affairs; he dreamed of building tiny homes; he wanted to save $2,000 a month for two years to have enough money to start his own business; he fantasied about living in Colorado and working for a weed dispensary.

He said the best vampire was Lestat in *Interview with the Vampire*, the one with no link to past humanity, the vampire who'd gleefully rip your throat out, marvel at his predatory skill. Lewis rooted for the most evil characters. In an eerie coincidence, my cats and his dogs were both named after *Game of Thrones*, but I named mine after heroes and his were after villains.

"I like witches best," I said.

"It's your voodoo that keeps bringing me back to your apartment."

"Am I your favorite tenant?"

His smile.

"Yeah. That's why I always answer your requests last."

"You're my favorite maintenance man."

"If you think I'm handsome, you should see my brother. He plays for the other team, but he's handsome," he said. "Anyway, I'll be back tomorrow with the part. What time do you work until? 12:30?"

I nodded. I didn't say what I was thinking.
How does he know I think he's handsome?
How does he know my work schedule?

288

124

Anne: "Every interaction feels so…charged. I want to be friends, but I wonder if I'm lying to myself and I want to sleep with him. The other night, I got home late visiting a friend and his truck was there. He came out, seemed anxious, asked where I'd been, smoked with me, asked to look at my hot water heater. He got in my face and was teasing. I thought we'd kiss. Then he bolted so fast I could barely say goodbye. One of the things I noticed in my journals about every man I've been with is they were insecure. It's ironic because they're all egomaniacs, but I can think of a million ways they revealed their insecurities."

Therapist: "People like that are afraid of abandonment."

125

A dream. I'm at the sea. I ask the waves, "Have I figured it out?"
A goddess emerges from the water, touches my cheek,
"Almost." She transforms into a mermaid.

She tells me that when I drown men in allure, those men were already drowned.

I'll drown too if I try to please dead men.

I ask what I'm supposed to do. She says, "There's much wreckage to explore when you're drowning."

A nightmare. My sister's come to live with me. She's growing weed with Lewis. She gets in his truck.

Later, Lewis texts me a picture of her stabbed to death.

The world collapses.

A nightmare. My doorbell rings. I find Lewis sprawled on my doorstep.

He's dead.

There's a teabag in his throat.

I pull it out, a message: "You're going in circles."

A nightmare. I'm in a shadow of corridors. My most violent lovers appear—

Miguel, Peyton, Santiago, Noah, Dwayne, the go-go dancer.

Then, C.D.

He says I can free him when I free them.

I say I don't want to let go of him or Santiago.

C.D. looks at Santiago, "Your inner child needed him once, but you don't anymore. Just like me."

I say, *I do need you.*

C.D., don't leave me again.

This is a story about ghosts.

126

Anne: "I read that in idealization phase, a covert narcissist may not use gifts or grand gestures to woo you with lovebombing."
Therapist: "They mirror you. They present themselves to be just like you."

Anne: "Instead of grand gestures, they give…emotional vulnerability."

127

How strange it is to be human, lusting.

Tiny particle of the universe, mere Earth matter, no more than dust, that, magically, is able to think about itself.

When planetary dust thinks about itself, it's full of wanting.

One mote of dust finds another and it's as if there's no other dust in the universe. That speck is singularly special.

What do humans yearn for when they fixate on each other?

Something about our parents.

Something about fear.

Something about something that hurts deeper than you have words for.

Something about something that hurt you before you even had words.

Something that can't be named so it must be touched.

You want to smash your bones against each other in an ancestral chant.

You want his skin cells on your body like bread crumbs you can follow back home.

You want his teeth to take you by your scruff while you go limp under the thrust of instinct.

You want and you want and there's nothing more infantile than a body, wanting.

But what we need and want are different.

You need a lover who understands that the work of healing is learning to live and struggling to thrive with a blade lodged in your side.

Because if you show up on his stoop in a trench coat and begin to seductively untie it, he's not going to marvel.

He's going to ask about that cleaver to your gut.

"This is my mother," you'll explain.

You'll point to the mangled stump of your thigh and say, "My dad. He just vanished."

Then he'll see the bubbling tar pouring out of your womb, blistering your thighs, enveloping him with steam. You'll lick his earlobe, whispering, "This is my rage."

It was nearly Christmas. Lewis sat on a broken footstool on my balcony. He'd been at my apartment for hours: my heater wouldn't turn off. He was stumped, spending most the time staring aimlessly into the closet with the electrical wires, asking questions about me.

I noticed how little he actually worked.

I noticed how long he stayed.

I noticed how suddenly everything in my apartment seemed to be breaking.

I just didn't care.

Every time I saw his face, I thought, *Stay forever.*

No man ever wanted to know me as much as Lewis did.

His barrage of questions felt like an annoying child pressing tacks into your arm. I'd never noticed how palpably painful it was to talk about myself.

I didn't realize how little most men knew me until I met a man for whom no amount of knowing would ever be enough.

Lewis lit his cigarette, took a deep inhale, looked at me skeptically through half-closed eyes, "So, this is what you do? Just hang out alone with cats?"

"I read, I grade, I talk to friends, I get stoned, I watch TV. Yeah, I'm pretty boring. I write," I shrugged.

"What are you writing?"

"A memoir."

"About what?"

"My life."

"Your whole life?"

"Just some traumas."

"What kind of traumas?"

He looked earnest. Trustworthy.

"It's not interesting."

"I think you're interesting."

He looked honest. Kind.

"Sexual traumas."

"When you say sexual traumas, what do you mean?"

"Um." It felt like he was asking me to jump off a cliff, "Rape."

He looked pensive. Serious.

It was as if you'd opened that trench coat and he saw the blood and the tar and he realized that those weren't your wounds: those were your powers. Only something supernatural could heft a weapon like that.

It was as if it was possible to show a man your wounds and have him crash his body into yours without making them fatal.

It was as if maybe he knew something about wounds too.

That was the day he installed surveillance in my apartment.

This is a story about ghosts.

128

Anne: "My deepest desire is to experience sex with someone who loves me. But the porn I watch is sex that's hate."

Therapist: "We desire what we think we deserve."

129

I t took him seven hours to install the microphone, the most time I spent alone with him.

I was *drunk* on him. The way he coaxed my darkest traumas out of me had me in hypnosis.

He wanted to know everything about me.

He said we had so much in common.

He was beautiful.

His accent, a serpent's flute.

An old pain rattled, hissed, bared its fang.

Lewis wandered my living room, looking at the books I'd published on my shelf. He said my name in Spanish repeatedly, "Anne Campeón, Anne Campeón."

I loved hearing him say my name.

I wanted to exist in his world.

"*Reluctant Mistress?*" He raised his eyebrow at one title, looked at me sideways with a smirk.

"You know how it goes," I teased.

He nodded. "Fun."

I laughed. "Until it's not!"

"That's right, mama. Until it's not."

"Do you ever have tenants hit on you?"

"All the time. The lady next door answered the door fully naked."

"You should come smoke with me sometime. I promise I won't hit on you."

He flinched, looked away, paused. I quickly tried to reassure, "Just as friends," I said.

He sighed wearily, "My wife and I have both cheated." He looked at the floor, "If you have an itch, you're gonna scratch it. It just depends on how bad the itch is."

"I'll be good," I said.

He tensed, hesitated, walked away, looked out my window with his hands in his pockets. It felt like he was afraid, as if something was tormenting him. After a moment, he reached into his jeans, handed me his phone.

"You ever lose your job over sex?" I asked.

"No. You?"

"No. I used to work in restaurants. Everyone slept with everyone. One big, incestuous family."

His neck snapped.

It turned so fast that my stomach flipped, knocking me slightly off kilter—had I said something wrong?

I quickly tried to save myself, "It was a long time ago."

He relaxed and told a story about having an affair with a co-worker: they both promised not to have feelings. However, she got feelings. He discarded her.

I thought to myself, *I know his type.*

What I didn't know yet: the word that made his neck snap was *incest.*

Before he left, I told him he was the coolest person I'd met in Texas.

He smiled, "By now, we're friends, right?"

I thought he was a garden snake.

130

Anne: "I've been celibate for 6 years and I've had several exes still text. They don't like me enough to love me, or be kind, but they obsess enough to remember me years later? To check my social media? I used to think that was love. What brings them back? It's not my looks. That's not enough to get consistent sex. It's not my personality or accomplishments. They ignore that. It's not how good I treat them. They're never grateful."

Therapist: "It's your lack of boundaries."

131

"Desire is despair with sex mixed in."

—Elisa Gabbert

You have a picture of Lewis the day he installed the microphone. You took it covertly. He had no social media. You were tired of trying to recall his beauty from memory when he wasn't around.

You still look at it sometimes. You try not to, but you're searching for something.

You want to understand why he colonized your mind.

What do we yearn for when we fixate on each other?

Something about our parents.

Something about fear.

Something about something that hurts deeper than you have words for.

Something about something that hurt before you even had words.

He's nobody from nowhere, Texas. Even in the picture, he doesn't seem impressive—a grease stain across his cheek, dirty spots all over his shirt, his hair in need of a cut, hand combed, stuffed under a faded hat.

He's over 6 feet tall and said he was "170 soaking wet:" the amount of times he called attention to how thin he was made it clear that was one of his insecurities. You'd suspected that even his weight was an exaggeration: he looked skeletal.

What is it that kept him burrowed in your mind like a tick?

Why is it so hard to stop thinking about abusers?

What do we yearn for when we fixate on each other?

Something about our parents.

It was Christmas.

You're alone every Christmas. It's been this way for years.

You usually take as much weed and Xanax and melatonin that you need to sleep through the day.

That Christmas, the Texas chill took on a metallic smell that you can still recall which sends euphoria down your spine. You cooked comfort food casseroles and watched two full seasons of *The Witcher* because Lewis recommended it. You relived his conversations.

Like when he asked what TV you watched. "Have you seen *You?*" He asked.

"About the stalker?"

"Yeah."

"Yeah, dark."

"That's my *favorite* show."

You thought about the way he talked about how crystals had ancient knowledge stored in them. You'd never believed that, but you're a sucker for mythology, so you loved that he knew that. You asked if he felt anything holding one of your large smoky quartz wands. "It feels cold."

He told you he wanted to go to Mexico and visit a crystal cave. "That's my dream!" You exclaimed.

When you started EMDR therapy, you had to imagine a safe space. Yours was your altar space. Lewis was the first man you showed your safe space to.

You thought this meant perhaps you were healing.

Abusers have a way of doing that, making you feel like your best self before wrecking you.

They can't drop you into darkness without first giving you the sun.

How do they do it?

What do we yearn for when we fixate on each other?

Something about our parents.

Something about fear.

You've been on this carousel since you were born. The carnival music keeps playing its tinkering piano notes until they become warped and menacing. It starts as unicorns and laughter and ends in dizziness and vomit. It never stops spinning unless you can throw yourself off.

A few months previous, you woke up to do yoga when you got a shocking DM. "Hey sexy," it said. It was from Santiago.

You did yoga in a trance.

Then you did what every person with good sense knows not to do: you responded to your rapist.

You didn't say a word about the rape.

He sent you voice notes. They said what you needed to hear.

Not *I'm sorry.*

What you *needed* to hear: they said you were still beautiful.

Because what you felt when Santiago and his cousin raped you was unbearably ugly.

He said he'd do anything to see you again. He said he'd travel to the moon and back. He called you his love, baby girl. He said you were wild and he had no regrets.

He said he had no regrets.

You told him you were no longer sleeping with anyone. You blocked before he could reply.

It may make little sense why someone would speak to their rapist.

The problem is you think a rapist is a monster.

But a rapist is a human.

A rapist is just an abuser.

How do abusers get you to take abuse and still want them?

What do we yearn for when we fixate on each other?

Something about our parents.

Something about fear.

Something about something that hurts deeper than you have words for.

The problem is that you don't know how abusers work.

Who do they get you to fall in love with?

When Lewis played with your crystals, when Santiago and you played on the swings, those weren't abusers you played with—who were they?

Children.

Specifically, you.

Abusers get you to fall in love with yourself—as a child.

Abusers get you to love them by becoming you, but not just any version of you—they become the most innocent, curious, vivacious, hungry, mischievous, funny, quirky, adorable version of you.

They love what you love—things you've cultivated love for all your life. They humor you in all things you say. They give unprecedented attention. You look up, dizzy in adoration—that camouflage jacket, that rugged masculinity—you think, "Pay attention to me. I'm just like you. I can be anything you want."

Just like you did as a child.

They pull this little girl out of you like a zombie rising from the dead. Once she's out, she's voraciously hungry, wounded, stumbling around like some dumb wound-up toy looking for daddy.

They touch you and everything feels better. It's almost as if that little girl inside of you wasn't dead. Because here's a boy—just like her—he's lonely and looking for his mom. You'll never find your parents, but you found each other. And you're children, so you're innocent and all your intentions are only to make them happy, because when they're happy, they touch you and love you, even though deep down you know you're a bad child, you know you'll make mistakes and be punished. You hope this time, you'll be able to prove that you're good enough, you'll be able to make someone happy. Maybe then, they'll not turn on you and make you sad.

What do we yearn for when we fixate on each other?

Something about our parents.

Something about fear.

Something about something that hurts deeper than you have words for.

Something about something that hurt before you even had words.

What do abusers do after you've fallen in love with your inner child through them?

They vanish.

It might start subtle—a text is ignored or there's a ghosting. Or they just callously reject you. Or they criticize you. Or they show no reaction to something that makes you happy.

Maybe it escalates, maybe they cheat on you, hit you, rape you.

Each abuser has their weapons of preference.

One way or another, they vanish, repeatedly. You slip into addiction, feigning for your next fix, because whenever he goes, he takes that little girl inside of you with him.

Now you're yourself, a lonely adult, desperately looking for yourself, a happy child, and she's gone.

It's as if she's dead. It's as if she doesn't matter. It's as if she's not good enough. It's as if she's not lovable. It's as if it were all her fault.

Now look what he's done.
It's almost as if he was your moth—
...
It's almost as if he was your fath—
...

This is a story about ghosts.

132

Anne: "I saw him three times yesterday. He said he was going to come over after work to hang out, but he never came. At night he texted, 'I'm at home lol.' He said I should meet his wife. That was confusing. He always talks badly about her. What do you think?"

Therapist: "Narcissistic abuse."

Anne: "You think?"

Therapist: "We have clear warning signs: confusion, triangulation between you and his wife, lovebombing with emotional vulnerability, a sense of instant connection…"

133

After Lewis installed surveillance, he started to vanish, and I started to ache.

Over the holidays, I ached most, wondering what he was doing, if he was thinking about those hours as much as me, if he was going to text, if I was fooling myself to think we could be friends.

The more he wasn't around, the more he was a rusted penny rattling in the tin can of my brain and I was a beggar.

"His hair is getting really long," I complained to a friend.

The next time I saw him, his head was shaved.

"He shaved his head. I hate it," I complained.

I never saw him again without a hat.

"I don't know why I'm attracted to him. The guy has four shirts."

The next day, he had a new shirt.

It took me some time to realize these were not coincidences.

When I'd smoke, it would only be seconds after going outside in which he'd appear. He might not talk to me, but he appeared, maybe across the street or next door or coming from around the corner. He always looked in my direction.

Look for me, I thought. *I'm looking for you too.*

He came to chat irregularly. Every time he talked to me, with only a few minutes of interaction, I could live on that loop all day.

After the holiday, he appeared across the street when I went outside and looked at me, then started to walk towards my porch.

"How was your holiday?"

"Terrible," he shook his head.

"Oh no! Why?"

"So many maintenance calls."

"Awww, I thought you got some time off."

"I ignored them. What did you do?"

"I started to watch *The Witcher.*"

Truthfully, I'd finished it. I didn't want to admit that.

"Season 2 just came out."

"I started it. Did you?"

"I finished it," he said.

"So fast?"

"When I like a show, I binge."

It took me a long time to realize that the things I was watching, Lewis was watching with me.

The less he was around, the more I ached; the more I ached, the more he was actually there, invisible, a python spiraling up my leg.

Caitlyn visited over winter break. She was seven years sober, attending college, pursing goals that alcohol had temporarily eclipsed.

But Caitlyn's alcoholism ultimately lit her path forward brighter. On the other side, Caitlyn's inner light shone more strongly in its depths of compassion, faith, and her intelligence about pain. You could say Caitlyn was transformed, but it's more like when an antique is restored: she was the same person, but polished, vibrant, functional, inspiring of reverence and awe.

It was the one year anniversary since I'd heard C.D.'s voice. I deemed it my rebirthday.

When I picked Caitlyn up, I told her about Lewis' behavior. We got to my apartment and I said, "Let's go get my mail. Maybe we'll see this maintenance man and you can tell me what you think."

"Does he normally hang out at the mailbox?" She laughed.

"No, he's just...around. I even ran into him at the gas station."

When we walked to the mail room, there was Lewis, leaning against the door, casually smoking a cigarette.

"It's my favorite professor," he smiled. Then he saw Caitlyn and immediately put out his cigarette. "Oh, you're here! She's been so excited for you." He rushed up enthusiastically and held out his hand.

He was warm, thoughtful, welcoming. He made her feel special, and, in doing so, made me feel special. He almost made me feel like I lived somewhere where people cared about me. He almost made it feel like home.

Caitlyn laughed at his charm. I began to think that everything about his behavior I'd blown out of proportion.

"What's your name again?" Caitlyn asked.

"Lewis. I could give you my Spanish name, but I keep it simple for my Caucasian friends."

"What do you want me to call you?" I asked.

"You can call me," he hesitated, then smiled, "the maintenance man."

How strange, I thought, *I do call you the maintenance man.*

"What'd you think?" I asked Caitlyn.

"I think he's a genuine, kind man."

"I think I got myself worked up because I don't trust men. Do you think he's cute?"

"Very, yes."

"What do you think that was about when he invited himself over?"

"I think he's a good guy and didn't want to cheat."

134

Anne: "The most sex I had always happened when I lost someone. After C.D. died. After my divorce. After my dad attempted suicide. After my boss. After Cassie left. After Brad's cheating."

Therapist: "Which continued to reinforce you weren't lovable."

Anne: "So many of them were narcissists. They hurt me, lied to me, ghosted me, cheated on me, raped me—but they always came back. I read it's called a hoover when a narcissist comes back. The abuse is their supply. It doesn't matter if the supply is positive, like praise, or negative, like abusing. Both of them make them feel superior. I took them back every time. Thinking, *I'm unlovable. But touch me, please, someone—someone beautiful and interesting.*

135

Have you ever felt invisible?
I'd been celibate for 1,998 days.
For the most part, I spend time entirely alone.

To sleep, I have to wrap myself tight in a blanket and pretend someone's holding me. Yet the thought of a lover makes bile churn: will I be able to be the lovable girl that never disagrees or upsets or bores them with my opinions, personality, or accomplishments, who's able to make them stay?

No one can hurt me if no one's here.
No one can leave me if no one's here.

Then, I start to wonder if I exist.

I feel my body overflowing with ideas, dreams, longing, creativity, jokes, wonder—like sparklers shooting off tiny beams of fire held by a terrified and awe-stricken child watching them burn down to her thumb.

I want to make them fill the sky.
I want someone to see them.
I want someone to see me.

When Lewis left after installing the microphone, he said the thing I've always wanted to hear a man say: "I can't wait to read your book."

It's the same thing as saying, *I want to see the fireworks inside you.*

When I told men I had successes, they usually seemed indifferent: I wondered what I'd need to do to impress them. I assumed they must've written me off as having no talent or they just weren't interested in how I processed life, because I wasn't interesting.

Even my sister didn't read my books. She stopped writing after my first book was published. Sandra also didn't support my books. I asked her to be more supportive because it hurt me—I felt enthusiastic for her work. She stopped writing poetry too, stopped reading it for pleasure.

So when Lewis said that, the ground I stood on fell sideways like a Tilt-a-Whirl.

"My memoir?"

He nodded.

"It could be a couple years."

What Lewis gave me in that moment was the most kind-hearted smile I'd ever seen. I mean that: it's singed into my brain. He looked so earnest and loving, "Well, I'll be around," he said, "I live here."

I felt like a toddler being praised for saying its first word. I beamed and nodded. I wanted to give him all the words I had.

In the end, he used them all against me.

The weeks after Caitlyn's visit went back to the pattern of him being around for brief conversations in passing. Then days without contact, even if I'd see him working. On a couple occasions, he came to my door unannounced—I let him in without hesitation, but he never stayed long and never had a good reason to be there, leaving me perplexed about his motives. Every time I saw him, he called me his "favorite professor" or "favorite tenant."

That alone was enough of a drug fix to keep me aching.

The ache got worse, but I vowed to see him only as a friend.

I realized: you don't ache for friends like that.

Then Lewis made it clear I didn't have him as a friend.

I'd gotten home from work. Lewis was near the maintenance garage a short distance away: he looked at me long and lingering, but didn't wave. A man with a full ski mask approached. He asked me to help him jump his car, parked right next to mine. I said I didn't know how. He said he could do it.

311

As he opened my hood, I saw Lewis stop what he was doing, look at me, and smile big. I decided to text him: the man made me nervous. I asked if he'd help me.

I watched Lewis dig his phone out of his pocket, look at it, and put it back. I watched him walk away.

I told myself, *He must be busy.*

The man jumped his car; I went inside. I texted Lewis to disregard my text.

No response.

I told myself, *I guess that doesn't warrant a response.*

I'm very skilled at telling myself why I deserve treatment that's less than what I give.

Then I had an epiphany: there's no scenario in which Lewis would text that I wouldn't text back. If I was busy, I'd text and apologize.

It dawned on me: he's not my friend.

I decided to quit smoking. Smoking allowed me to interact with him; it was self-harming behavior. I needed to love myself. I needed to stop needing to be seen. I needed to see myself.

I needed to quit the addiction.

In my journal, I counted how many days I'd gone without cigarettes and without Lewis.

I made it to 34.

I didn't know that Lewis had his own addictions—ones I was entangled in—that he had no intention of quitting.

That man put a tracker on my car.

I didn't know how seen I was.

I thought he was a garden snake.

136

Anne: "He genuinely seems like a good man."

Therapist: "If you were his wife, and you saw how he acts, what would you think?"

Anne: "I'd be upset."

Therapist: "Maybe his flirtations devalue her. Not responding to your text could be devaluation too."

Anne: "I read that in the narcissist cycle of Lovebomb—Devalue —Discard—Hoover, covert narcissists devalue in ways that you can excuse, like hiding your keys or pretending not to hear you. You just eventually end up feeling like shit and don't know why, but it can't be your partner, *a saint*. They destroy you without you even recognizing. Christmas could've been a lovebomb. And then the tactic they do between devaluing is called breadcrumb: they give you only glimpses of the lovebombing. Ever since Christmas, when I've seen him, it's only been for minutes."

Therapist: "It keeps you addicted."

Anne: "He moved here with two people. They're both people who seem vulnerable. Narcissists love vulnerable people as supply. I'm overweight and I live alone. I saw his friend on trash duty and I asked, 'Why'd you put your bestie on trash duty?' He said, 'Because he got a promotion to the better complex next door.' I didn't get it. It's a complex owned by the same owners and he still lives here and helps Lewis; it's not like he left."

313

Therapist: "People with Narcissistic Personality Disorder have jealousy as a baseline emotion."

Anne: "But I can still find ways he seems like the nicest man in the world."

Therapist: "Regardless, it's a good idea not to talk to him. Definitely good to quit smoking."

Anne: "When it comes to anyone, I think, *Please don't ever leave.* Even with Lewis, in speculating if he's a narcissist, there's a sick part of me that thinks, *That means he's coming back.*

137

I made it 34 days without interacting with him.

That's not true.

I saw him.

I just thought it was a dream.

Early 2022: the trending topic was a famous person with Narcissistic Personality Disorder.

Kanye West and Kim Kardashian were embroiled in a divorce, and Kim moved on to Pete Davidson.

Kanye aired his thoughts.

He'd recently transformed his style, favoring black face masks and bulky boots. From Instagram to music, Kanye showed us what happens when a person with Narcissistic Personality Disorder feels rejected: *narcissistic rage*.

I'd spent my days going to work or staying indoors. I put myself on the nicotine patch, didn't get mail until it was dark.

I channeled my energy into learning about Narcissistic Personality Disorder. Anytime I thought of him, I searched the web, picked up a book.

When I got my degree in psychology, I knew NPD fit my mother. I wasn't invested in learning about her mental health. I was invested in moving on with my life and forgetting her.

315

I thought the disorder rare, though I could generally spot an overt female narcissist. They were the "Karens," spewing their toxicity loudly and irrationally with surprising pride, not a hint of shame. My mother was the lady arguing with the cashier about a 50 cent coupon, terrorizing her kids behind closed doors. She projected misery everywhere.

She could be near euphoria after raging. She'd go on about how *right* she was, how much *smarter*.

Anyone that's raised by a narcissist knows this: their sense of superiority is a lie. Their insecurities are bullet holes through a straw man, spilling out their wretched truths.

They betray themselves often.

As Kanye posted rants, a new documentary captured his rise to fame and mental health struggles. I must've watched it 10 times.

Most fascinating was the fact that Kanye's fantasy worked: he told his friend to film his life because he was going to win Grammys—that's exactly what happened.

But Kanye West has always been an abuser— that's his notoriety.

From the slut shaming of his ex, Amber Rose, to the insulting of 19-year-old Taylor Swift as she won an award: when Ye has a narcissistic injury, America feels it.

I watched the documentary with new eyes, able to name so many of the signs. *Look, he's devaluing his best friend by calling him the wrong name on TV. Look, he's blameshifting after saying something sexist. Look, how he can't apologize. Look, how he compares himself to God.*

Look. Look at the patterns.

Kanye West released *Donda 2* through a performed event. His growl came over the speakers—a child feigning the rev of an engine. A simple melody began to haunt my apartment, the kind of unsettling, menacing simplicity and repetition that belongs in horror movies. On stage, Kanye skulked aimlessly as black shadow. Behind him, his childhood home was on fire. A string of fascists began to walk across stage, protecting the fire with their might. Kanye raps,

Pop's home, I ain't gettin frisked. I'll put your security at risk.
I'll put your security at risk...

Over and over, he threatens.

His childhood home on fire: how unsafe his inner child is.

The fascist police: the desperation, the violence needed to guard a vulnerable pain like that.

Him, the shadowy figure: the unmasked narcissist with no identity, standing in the truth of his wound:

A predator now.

I've seen many narcissistic rages.

They're motivated by the most unbearable fear.

Yet the overt behavior of my mother that I could spot easily in women went by nearly undetected when it came to men. I could spot overt ones: misogynists, racists. Beyond that, I missed it entirely.

When Brad would meltdown and climb up my fire escape after I'd discovered him cheating, when Peyton raped me during an argument or stalked me when I left, when Noah threw dishes around the kitchen, when Dwayne would choke me during sex, when Santiago raped me with his cousin…

I could finally see how many narcissists I'd endured. My memories morphed as I began to reject self blame and name the abuses —gaslighting, lying, blame shifting, projecting, devaluing, bread crumbing, hoovering, smear campaigning, cold shoulder, word salad, neglect, future faking. Mental abuse, physical abuse, emotional abuse. Overt abuse, covert abuse.

I had a lot more abuse than I'd realized.

I finally had a map out of a maze I'd been in lifelong.

Strangely, I didn't see Lewis at all. I used to see his truck parked places or him walking around. It was like he hadn't existed.

No, I saw him.

I just thought it was a dream.

317

138

Anne: "I'd thought narcissists had a conscious understanding of what they're doing, chose to be abusive."

Therapist: "It's very difficult to treat because it's unconscious."

Anne: "Emotionally, they never mature past toddlers, so they can't grasp emotions like empathy or guilt. Many of my exes seemed childlike. They only saw things as "all good" or "all bad." They deny a lot of obvious truths. It helps me to think of it as an emotional disability. Due to frontal lobe brain damage from childhood trauma, whenever anything happens that gives shame, their brains automatically redirect it to make shame disappear. When they hurt you, they're taking their pain and making you feel it. That's why when you fight with a narcissist, the things they accuse you of are the things they've done. It's also why when they get caught, all of their abilities of logic and reason disappear: you start to get gaslighting and word salad. Their brains need to do that to survive. They become predators because any sense of shame makes them feel like prey…The more I learn, the more I see how often I had people with NPD close to me. The hard thing is realizing they hated me."

Therapist: "It may be more appropriate to say they're jealous."

Anne: "They believe the mask, even while consciously lying—it's baffling."

Therapist: "When the mask comes off, they go into collapse. They can be dangerous."

Anne: "But they bounce back as if nothing happened. I've seen it. I worry because I'm no angel. I have emotional empathy and deep guilt, and I don't abuse in the ways they do, but with them, I felt toxic: did I become a narcissist?"

Therapist: "Narcissists lack self-reflection and don't experience guilt. They can't hardly consider that question. It'd give them too much shame. That was reactive abuse, a trauma response from a lifetime of narcissistic abuse, defense tactics you learned."

Anne: "What happens if they have no supply?"

Therapist: "It's their life blood. This is why they move on immediately; it's why they'll never want to let supply leave, even when they hate them."

139

I'd been seeing snakes everywhere.

Online, on billboards, in dreams, on television.

Red and yellow kills a fellow.

I had an irrational fear of snakes. I feared since childhood that I'd wake and a snake would be under my covers. I'd wrap myself in blankets like a mummy, so no snake can slip under.

I started having dreams in which I awoke and there was a snake tangled in the covers. When I tried to figure out how it got there, I realized the snake was me.

I wasn't safe from myself.

I'd thought I was a snake charmer, that men slithered towards me with their open wounds disguised as open jaws. I'd thought I unveiled my body and it sang, a flute they writhed helplessly towards.

The truth was I was descending into a snake pit.

They used to lower insane people into snake pits, hoping that what would drive a sane person insane might drive an insane person sane.

This world flung me into the pit: now, a python slithered between my legs, hissed, bared his fangs at the object of his obsession.

He wants my body, no, he wants my entire being, no, he's just a snake, he just wants and wants.

I felt thrust back into the pit, but I was ready, testing my reflexes as he snapped, jumping back, taunting, wondering if I'll get well or if I'll become one of the snakes.

When I met Lewis, a hiss began to hum through my days, a rattle punctuated everything I said, a snake in me wanted to coil.

I prayed to shed the snakeskin, step out of its jaw and run.

But I also feared that I'd hissed at Lewis in the Eden of my inner childhood, and if he doesn't eat the apple, then what am I worth?

Look, all these snakes flying out of my head.

Watch as I cast my gaze on a wretched man and he turns to stone.

Another childhood phobia came from a recurring dream I had: the faceless man.

I'd be looking out my window and the faceless man would walk up. I'd be watching a plane land and the faceless man would step off.

He always came towards me.

He looked at me without being able to see me.

Now, the dream returned.

I ran through forests chasing men disguised as monsters. I'd tackle them and claw at their faces until I pulled off the mask: *who are you?*

What was under it was my face.

I kept clawing, pulling my own face off, enraged: *who are you, really?*

The faceless man.

Another dream: my father at my door. He's angry.

What happened? What have I done?

He says boys are coming to my window.

Hunting.

Who is it, dad? Who's coming to my window?

Some scrubby kid from your childhood.

C.D. He's not...

He's rotten. He's hunting.

No, dad. Who else?

Some other rotten boy.

Some hunter.

He's just like the other one.

I'm sorry, dad. I'm a broken girl, I go with the broken boys.

I spent those days without cigarettes pulling words from my wind-whipped lust, the kind of storm you aren't sure you'll survive. The writing was like plucking the tightly wound string of a harp to let sound puncture silence, the same way an orgasm punctures loneliness.

I kept journals, making sense of why I'd been attracted to Lewis, what that meant about my pain.

I felt like I wrenched the crush out of me like a tumor, and the thing had roots and its own pulse. I carefully studied to see how it grew. I could see the ways that fixating on how great some man was made me ignore the only truth that could heal me: how great I am.

I set out to suture the wounds. I had no idea what I was about to discover.

At day 30, I prayed: Show me the truth.
At day 31, I started to get sick. Fainting. Vomiting. Brain fog.
At day 33, a hiss in my kitchen.
A snake in my bed.

No, my dishwasher broke.
A flood in my kitchen.
Time to face off with the snake.

140

When he came to fix the dishwasher, I saw him differently. From friend to predator.

With a predator, I should run. I should be afraid. I should defend myself.

I couldn't.

I'd spent my life thinking narcissists didn't want me; I wasn't good enough.

Now, I saw how badly they needed me.

I saw a deeply wounded child.

As he started to mirror—talking about reincarnation, books he's read, my tree of life keychain—as his personality morphed into mine, I knew he needed me.

What did he need?

What's behind a narcissist's core wound? What do they lack?

Love. They need my love.

My wounds match theirs: I think I'm unlovable and worthless. I survived by accepting that as truth and giving love while feeling starved, incapable of receiving.

A narcissist feels unlovable and rejects that feeling, builds a delusion, feeds it by finding ways to maintain it.

They need love to feed their facade.

They need love because breaking it in others is the key to power.

They absolutely need that to survive.

They live in a terrifying, loveless void.

I realized that being able to give love made me powerful.

Finally, I looked at a narcissist, and I found my truth.

I saw his bare need, reeling me in. I fed him.

I saw he wasn't working; I let him stay and chat. I answered personal questions.

I saw red flags as he bashed his wife; I humored him.

I heard him brag about his job; I praised him.

A narcissist's favorite subject is the self.

My favorite subject is anything but the self.

But especially, especially a narcissist.

My fantasies involved teasing the snake, pressing myself up against him like I'm going to make a move, then retreating.

Or just bluntly unmasking that I know he's a snake. Watch him wither.

But let's be honest.

No, *really* honest.

I wanted him to grab me by the waist, pull me to him, kiss me passionately, bend me over, take me in my kitchen.

And ghosts must do again what gives them pain.

As a child, I thought I'd write sexy novels about vampires. I realize this was a prediction.

But it's not a romance. There's no love here.

It's a haunting. It's a hell. It's a story about ghosts.

141

Anne: "He didn't park outside. He didn't want anyone to see him here. That's calculating."

Therapist: "Being at your apartment after work hours devalues his wife too."

Anne: "I said that men like him never leave their wives. He got agitated."

Therapist: "Be careful. We don't know what he's capable of."

Anne: "I've been woozy, had a bad headache. He never even opened the dishwasher. He fiddled with something under the sink, then said he'd need to let it run. It didn't flood again…"

142

I woke in a puddle of sweat and my teddy on the floor.

I've slept with a teddy lifelong.

The day C.D. died, I woke and my teddy was on the floor.

I thought it was a sign, a bad omen. I became increasingly superstitious, clutching the bear in a tighter grip, fearful that if I let go, the fumes of love I'd been able to muster out of this world would dissipate again.

Then I awoke at 40: my bear was on the floor. Something died that day.

Lewis had promised to come the day before with a new dishwasher. He hadn't. That evening, I stood and my ears started ringing; I got dizzy. I clutched my stomach, ran to the sink, vomited.

I crawled into bed and passed out for 12 hours.

I thought of the dream I'd had.

Was it a dream? It felt so real.

I woke to the sound of clanging in my kitchen. I thought to myself, *He's here. How late is it?*

I got out of bed and wandered to the kitchen, disoriented.

Lewis stood with his arms crossed, hip cocked to the side as he leaned against the dishwasher, staring intently with a half grin and dead eyes.

"What are you doing here so late?"

He didn't answer. He uncrossed his arms and held them out.

I'm dreaming…

I walked into them and kissed him. He reached into my bra and fondled my breasts.

Then he put both hands on my hips and flipped me around so I faced the stove. He shoved me into it and pressed himself into my back, putting one hand on my neck.

Next I woke in a puddle of sweat and my teddy on the floor.

The sheets were drenched, worse than any night sweat I'd had. I wondered if I had Covid, grabbed a test.

That was a dream, wasn't it?

I went to check the dishwasher. I looked around the kitchen, touched the stove.

Wasn't I just here? Wasn't he just…

I shook my head, looked at the deadbolt. He has a key but he couldn't get in through the deadbolt or put it back.

Just a very vivid rape dream. Anyway, who'd rape someone and tuck them back in after?

Covid test: negative. I went to scoop the cat litter, to take my vitamins, to scoop the cat litter…

Wait, I already did that.

Went to take my vitamins.

I did that too.

What's wrong with my brain? It isn't working….

I vomited more, changed my sheets, picked my teddy off the floor.

Lewis didn't bring the dishwasher that day. He didn't bring the dishwasher that week.

I had rape dreams about him every night.

I'd wake in wet sheets daily.

Driving to work, I felt so stoned I feared an accident. When I came home, he'd appear behind me, startling me.

"It's my favorite…." he'd coo.

One day, he asked, "What are you working on in your book?"

"Writing about some dark days."

"Is it when you were in the gay clubs?"

How did he guess the exact thing I'd just written?

327

"Do you really believe in reincarnation?" He asked.

"Sometimes. Do you?"

He nodded.

"Why?"

"Sometimes kids talk about past lives and can remember with exact detail."

"I've seen that documentary too," I laughed.

"Watched it back in January."

I saw it with Caitlyn when she visited. In January...

"How long are you going to make me handwash dishes *Little House on the Prairie* style?"

"I put in the order—just waiting for them to approve," he gave an apologetic shrug.

Plausible deniability.

Lewis noticed all kinds of details, but so did I. One thing I'm locked in on is the nuance of body language.

With Lewis, I noticed the deadness of his eyes when I challenged him about badmouthing his wife.

His body stayed lax, his face completely blank, but his hands— clenched and unclenched, clenched and unclenched, until he snapped, thrusting them both in my face, saying, "I'm not married! Do you see a ring?"

He was flustered, walking straight to the closet, thrusting his face inside so I couldn't see him.

Something gives him comfort in that closet.

"You know how many times I almost came by to take a picture of this? I fixed it in a special way."

"Sounds impressive."

What's in that closet?

"You have spring break soon?" He asked.

"Next week."

"You gonna hit up some Texas beaches?"

"I'm not much of a partier. I'm old."

"How old?"

"40."

"You don't look 40."

"We've had this conversation."

"So I shouldn't act surprised about your age anymore?"

He was acting surprised the first time?

"I never get time off," he said.

"You need time to rest. You can't spend your whole life fixing dishwashers."

Shame passed over his eyes like storm clouds, turned his face into a broken little boy.

"I only mean you work too much," I stumbled, "I just mean it's important you have time for…fun…you know?"

"I know what you mean," he nodded, sounding regretful, "I live in a bubble."

I kept having dreams of Lewis raping me. Sometimes I dreamed I was waking up mid-orgasm, and he felt so real, and those orgasms were unlike anything I'd ever had before: they started in my toes, traveled up my legs, lasted impossibly long. At the same time—night sweats, vomiting, exhaustion, fog brain, sleeping for 14 hours.

Is it PTSD?

A dream: I walk into a dark, empty room. When my eyes adjust, I see a girl huddled in the corner. It's me. I'm four. I have pigtails. I'm covered in bruises. I can feel her fear: it's the terror of floating in deep space, flung far from God. I kneel. She flings herself into my arms and clutches so hard that her nails dig into my back. My sister used to grip me that way after my mom hurt her: I suddenly remember her tiny body in my arms, shivering, the way she'd grip like she hadn't believed she'd ever be held safely again. The little girl—me, Cassie, me, Cassie—sobbed on my chest. *Don't give me to the monster again. He's trying to kill me.*

And ghosts must do again what gives them pain.

143

Anne: "Without attention and praise, narcissists look for someone to blame. The scapegoat, a container that holds the shame."

144

J OURNAL ENTRY
3-1-22

The paranoia is intense.

Today I woke and my ass was sore. My vagina too, but that faded. Ass, still yes, and bleeding.

I was on my back. I sleep on my stomach. My breasts were out of my bra. There was a leaf on my floor. I was disoriented, felt like I was high. <u>Very</u> high.

Is he drugging me?

Is he coming in when I'm asleep?

Then I saw him outside. It looked like he was looking for me. I said hello and he didn't say it back—he just smirked, menacingly.

I saw him again and he definitely was looking for me. He peered around the corner and found me smoking. He smiled, said he'd unloaded the dishwasher Friday and was knocking on my door. I said, "You should've rang the doorbell. I was napping. I had a headache."

"I did. Twice!"

<u>Why didn't I hear the doorbell?</u>

Now I'm drinking bottled water. Avoiding my Brita.

I was just outside—it's late—I heard someone walking. I got spooked, stood, and saw someone walking away, <u>fast.</u> It looked like him.

Something metal clanged, like he dropped something. It's some little tool of sort...

Is it PTSD? Or...?

But he did come by with the new dishwasher today.

331

He was lovely. It's not hard for me to pretend all is normal: it's not pretend. My body just does it. I just love that guy. I love that face. But I was on watch, throwing supply, remarking, "Wow. I've never seen anyone carrying a dishwasher like that." He laughed, "Thanks, I needed to smile."

I inquired about his day, was at rapt attention. I told him more than once he's the best maintenance man and watched him light up.

But I did, maybe not the wisest, press him on why he didn't call my cell when I didn't answer the door.

When I reminded him he had my number, he said, "Oh yeah…I forgot."

Then I kept on—"Why didn't you call?"

"You know what it is? My wife deleted it."

"Why didn't you tell me?"

"It's embarrassing."

"Did you fight about it?"

"No. We didn't talk about it."

"How do you know she deleted it?"

"Because 1+1=2."

"Why would she be suspicious of me?"

"Probably because she knows I have a type."

"How would she know I'm your type? I could be an 80 year old lady."

"She knows you."

"How?"

"Cause you're the only professor."

"How does she know I'm a professor? How does she know what I look like?"

"She knows you."

"HOW?"

"I've talked about you."

"You made her jealous?"

"She wants to meet you," he shrugged.

"So bring her."

"Then I have to worry about her wanting you."

"She's bisexual?"

He nodded. He kept his face to the dishwasher, avoiding eye contact.

"I never texted you anything inappropriate."

He sounded warm, "No, I know. It's not you she suspects."

"But nothing's happened."

He looked like he was thinking about his words carefully. "Here's the thing: if I could get away with it, with no consequences, and no one would know, I'd do it."

"Cheat?"

"With you, yeah."

He got on the floor as he was installing the dishwasher. His head was inside so I walked around and stood over him.

"Do you normally fuck tenants?"

He knocked his head on the dishwasher. He came out and stood on his knees and said, "What the WHAT?" Looking wide-eyed and frazzled.

"Is that why your wife's suspicious?"

He looked relieved, "No."

"You don't cheat?"

"I didn't say I didn't cheat."

"Co-workers?"

"One, yes."

He kept trying to change the subject. He seemed uncomfortable, on his back on the floor. I said, "You're squirming like a worm, Lewis."

"You're making me nervous! Asking about affairs."

"You ask me questions."

"I feel like I'm being interrogated."

I said, "Tell your wife I'm a eunuch."

"What's that?"

"A person with their genitals cut off."

"How does a woman…"

"Cut off her clit."

"But there's still penetration."

"Yeah, but you can do better, Lewis."

He looked stricken with sudden grief, as if he was unsure he could do better. I assured, "You can do _WAY_ better."

He put his hand to his heart. "I'm a good man. I try to be a good man."

I asked if his wife was gonna beat me up. He said, "I don't think that's on the menu."

He asked if I had a knife. I said yeah. He asked where. I pointed. Then he said, "Actually, do you have a bucket?" I said, "What do you need? A knife or a bucket?"

He said, "Neither."

He asked if I was capable of violence. I said I'm not a violent person, but I feel capable, because I have so much rage, especially about things like racism. I asked if he's capable. He said, "Very capable." I asked how he knew. He chuckled, "This charming man in front of you isn't who I always am...But I don't like violence. It gives me a bad feeling in my stomach."

Then he asked, "When did you decide to stop putting off your dreams?" It felt like a strange question, because I didn't ever put them off: I've always been trying. I wonder if that's why he hates me. Then we were talking about dreams, his life ambitions. He asked me when I started to write and what I wrote. It's so unusual for a man to want to know me that it's intoxicating.

I'm going to sleep like shit. I'm jumping at every noise. He's not drugging me, right? This is TOO crazy an idea.

What if all those dreams weren't...

I pray, pray, pray.

145

Anne: "I went to school and taught the same lesson I'd already taught until students reminded me. I felt so high I could barely stay awake. I slept 14 hours. My vagina has been sore, and yesterday I woke and my ass hurt too."

Therapist: "Oh God…"

Anne: "Those dreams…"

Therapist: "You said they felt real."

Anne: "I'm texting you a picture. I thought, *If he anally raped me, then there'll be a stain.* I checked my sheets…"

Therapist looks at her text.

Anne: "But there's a deadbolt. I thought—*unless he came in through the screen door.* I went outside and…"

Anne texts a photo of crow bar marks. Therapist puts her hand over her mouth.

Anne: "I stopped drinking my Brita. I was outside and heard someone behind me; I stood up and he bolted. It looked like him. When he ran, he dropped something. It's this metal thing. To flip a screen door lock."

Therapist: "Have you thought about a rape kit?"

Anne: "What if this is all PTSD?"

Therapist: "You have a lot of physical evidence that makes me think you shouldn't be so quick to blame yourself."

Anne: "He still seems like the world's nicest man. But then there are the weird things, like *If I could get away with it, and no one would know…*

335

Like even *I* wouldn't know? He also talked about getting into a fight with his boss. He said, *I try really hard never to break character, but I broke character.*"

Therapist: "He knows he has a character."

Anne: "When he was here lying on the floor and his shirt was clinging to his ribs, I was standing over him, thinking, *I know that body.* You know how you feel like you just know a person's body when you've had sex with them? Like how it *feels?* I could even see it naked."

146

I stood at the shore holding dead daisies and carnations.

A psychic told me my inner child loves daisies. She said when I felt afraid, I should cast them in the sea.

That Valentine's Day, I'd bumped into an old student carrying a bouquet, "There you are!" She exclaimed, thrusting the bouquet at me. "Happy Valentine's Day!"

I'd been teaching for 15 years—I had cards all over my office from students. Why couldn't I find love in my friendships or romances, but when I walked into a classroom, love bloomed? I loved them with the same intensity I loved everyone: an all consuming inferno. They loved me like a tidal wave, saving me every time my own love threatened to turn me to ash.

I couldn't get over the thought that this young girl woke up on Valentine's Day and, of all people, thought of her old English teacher. I couldn't get over my gratitude for that: this was a holiday for people who were loved.

When it comes to real love, I'm so sensitive that it takes me out at the knees.

I stood with my bouquet at the water. Flower by flower, I named all the people I'd loved who couldn't love me back. Leaf by leaf, I named all my griefs. Stem by stem, I prayed for my rapists. Breath by breath, I conjured my ghosts.

I called to the water as it lapped my ankles, "Take this from me. I don't want to carry it anymore."

337

On the drive home, I imagined scenarios of catching Lewis on camera. I practiced plunging a knife into his chest and killing what I wanted so badly to love.

I set up the camera.
I hadn't slept more than 3 hours in 3 days.
What does it matter if he raped you? I thought. *You wanted him.*
Then another voice entered: *Why would he rape you? You're not good enough to rape.*

Before bed, memories of V floated like passing clouds.
I had a toy growing up called a View-Master.
Click, I see her bright lips in her myriad selfies; click, I see her throw back her head and erupt into joy like a volcano; click, I hear her tell me to fuck off about her girlfriend; click, the money I loaned that she never returned; click, the ferocity of her breakdowns; click, the married couple she triangulated; click, the $25,000 she owed her ex; click, the cold shoulders; click, her ex's mental decline; click, the trips during Covid, the sudden discard…
Click.
Knowledge took me out like a sniper bullet.
V had Narcissistic Personality Disorder.

147

Anne: "I texted her ex. He said, *Yes, she abused me, and it wasn't even covert. She uses her wokeness to hide it. I try not to think of her.*" I looked at her Instagram. She had pictures holding *The Bell Jar*. We read Plath's letters together. How could she be reading that and not love me?"

Therapist: "They absorb parts of your identity: they don't have a stable identity of their own. They were trained to mirror their narcissist parent for affection, so mirroring is all they understand."

Anne: "Every time we argued, it was over her feeling criticized. She gave me the cold shoulder when she got rejected to NYU: I said NYU was an elitist institution that didn't deserve her. She hung up."

Therapist: "Walking on eggshells."

Anne: "I'm thinking about V's sexuality. No pattern, no preference. I thought back to some of my lovers and all of them were men who people suspected were gay—some of them questioned their sexuality or had rumors of past relationships with men."

Therapist: "Some of the examples I know were closeted."

Anne: "Think of how many trans people get murdered. Or how the Proud Boys are so obsessed with harassing LGBTQ people. I wonder if NPD, homophobia, transphobia, and closeted sexuality due to shame are linked? Maybe their sexuality is motivated by power. People who were molested sometimes become rapists."

148

LETTER TO A GHOST: V
Remember when I had that psychic reading? She talked about the close friend, practically my sister. She told me we had a soul contract: it was one of the hardest contracts.

We both laughed, "That sounds exactly like something our dumbasses would sign up for!"

Something in us said we were here to push this world forward.

We talked about this. We talked about our lack of fear.

Do you remember, V?

The psychic told me we had to never abandon each other.

I got a matching tattoo with you.

You abandoned me.

I had cystic acne all over my face for two years. When you abandoned me, it cleared.

My body knew what you were doing, but I didn't.

Did you?

We Facetimed daily, texted all day, spent hours on the phone.

When you left, only a miracle could save me.

If I'd died, would you have been happy?

When your ex-boyfriend from high school killed himself, you said, "Why do so many people close to me kill themselves?"

Like you knew, maybe, you hurt people who love you.

What did we have most in common?

Our rage.

We survived our anger by boiling rapidly—a bubbling, steaming, untamed choreography of rage.

I can see our cycle clearly.

Idealization: the instant chemistry when we met. How you mirrored all the things I said, how similar our mannerisms and values and knowledge. I loved your tattoos, bold makeup, bright hair. I loved how you said the truth no matter how it upset people.

Since we were babies, we learned that authority was bullshit, didn't we? We had that in common too.

Devaluation started as soon as we came home. When we returned, you marked yourself as my sister on Facebook, you liked my posts, but you didn't speak to me for six weeks.

Finally, a response. You said you and your boyfriend were struggling—that's why you'd been absent.

All forgiven.

Sisters.

I never registered the abuse.

But it kept happening. Whether you were giving me the cold shoulder over a disagreement, or taking a condescending tone in an argument, or projecting your behaviors or feelings onto me so that I'd be defensive.

In those seven years, I'd been discarded and hoovered more than once. You always said it scared you how easily you could cut someone out. It scared me too.

The discards were the worst.

You made the choice each time: we need a break.

Each one was a kill shot.

After the last discard, all this time, I've been waiting for you.

What did you say when you discarded me?

You drive everyone who loves you away.

Projection.

You do that, V.

I'm sorry. I shouldn't have said that. This is why we can't talk.

It's like you knew.

It wasn't true what you said, but I took it like a bullet. It's been lodged all this time.

Every time a partner left, you went into collapse. I'd be on the phone assuring you they were wrong, they weren't worth you, you were going to find someone better. I reminded you that you're beautiful, brilliant.

Then you'd bounce back as if those exes didn't exist.

With each partner, new aspects of your identity blossomed. New hobbies. New fashion. New ways of speaking. When I got braces, you got veneers.

It's all so clear now.

But the tears were real: those weren't manipulation.

When you cried, you shattered.

When your brother murdered someone, I'd never seen someone so broken. You kept saying it could've been you.

I said you aren't your brothers. You aren't responsible for their choices.

You said something I buried and held for you: as a kid, you molested your brothers.

You thought maybe that's why they turned out bad.

No, I told you. *A child who molests is a child who was molested.*

But why'd I have to become a fucking sexual predator?

You were a child, V.

You were a child with a mental illness.

You had to project it, the shame.

You couldn't carry it. You gave it to your brothers.

That's how sexual predators are made.

It's still not your fault.

It's a disability.

Even now, I want to excuse you.

When you collapsed, I met your inner child: she's profoundly afraid.

The emotional labor of our friendship felt like holding a pile of shards.

Other memories: the teeter totter at the Tent of Nations, overlooking miles of Palestine from high in the hills as the sun went down. Up and down in glee—we'd come so far from what hurt us. I thought we were the luckiest girls in the world.

That's still true, isn't it?

What about that island we sailed to covered in seals in South Africa, that beach and the waddling penguins?

We were happy, weren't we?

Tell me I made you happy, V, if only for a moment.

How about when you shimmied in that wet suit, first in line to get in the diving cage to face sharks? You were determined to get a selfie with a shark. I always joked you were happiest doing things that felt as close to death as possible.

Were we escaping our childhoods, V?

What about standing in front of Nelson Mandela's jail cell? Or the Tomb of Yassir Arafat? Or the shrouding table of Jesus Christ? I have a picture of you kneeling, praying.

I wonder what you prayed for.

For a year and a half, I've prayed for you.

I've prayed you would forgive me for not being enough.

I've prayed that you would realize that nothing can override love.

I've beat myself up wondering how you could forget.

I think the psychic was right. We had the most difficult destiny.

You're my soulmate.

Your mental health does not change the truth:

You were a great love of my life.

We walked through fire together. You taught me how to be brave.

When you left, you taught me how to survive.

You're still inked on my skin: an olive branch, reminding me—the only way forward is to forgive.

I couldn't have survived without you.

I didn't want to survive without you.

I loved you something primal—an instinct, a blood bond.

Just like my mother.

We're born of the same root.

343

Just like my sist—

…

Just like my sis—

…

Oh my God.

149

Anne: "I can give up every man on this planet. I can give up my mother. I can let them all wallow in their misery. But I can't give up *my sister*. That's my sister! She's the only one who knows me, who knows what happened! How did this happen? I…"

Anne puts her head in her hands.

Therapist: "Breathe."

Anne: *"NOT MY FUCKING SISTER."*

150

"Hey Cassie. Do you have time for a phone call?"

"I have 20 minutes."

"Okay, I need to tell you something."

"Okay."

"For the past six months, my stuff has been breaking in my apartment. There's this new maintenance man. I thought he was my first friend here."

Cassie remains silent.

"Um, lately I've been feeling disoriented and have been sleeping a lot, and the other day, I woke and had anal and vaginal pain…I think he raped me."

"Oh." Her voice remains flat.

"I just want to tell someone in case something happens."

"Okay."

"I told my therapist and a few others, but I thought I should tell you."

"Okay."

"I sent the picture of the crow bar marks to my apartment managers and asked to break my lease because it's not safe. They haven't responded."

"Oh."

"Okay, well, I'll let you go."

"I still have a few more minutes."

Anne hesitates. "Are you happy?"

"Sure."

"How's your marriage?"

"My husband probably would like more physical affection."

"Why don't you like affection?"

"I'm just emotionally closed off. It's our childhood."

"Yeah."

"It takes every bone in my body not to abuse."

"Is that why you're cold to me?"

"Sometimes. You're the same way."

"How?"

"You're never happy for me."

"When?"

"When I got the vaccine."

"I was happy for you. I was just stressed myself. I was teaching in person."

"You never support my accomplishments."

"What? I have your art all over my apartment. I have every journal you've ever published in. You're the one that never supports my accomplishments. You never say anything."

"I don't like poetry anymore."

"In therapy, I've learned about trauma bonding, that I'm addicted to abuse. Why do you think we turned out so differently?"

"Oh, I don't know. You've always been emotional."

"Cassie…"

"Well, you've always been a bit crazy."

"Cassie! I called you to talk about my mental health and my fear that I may be having a PTSD episode or being raped! And you call me crazy?"

"Poor word choice."

"I feel like you don't have empathy for me."

Cassie remains silent.

"Do you think we'll ever be close again?"

"You ask that all the time."

"You always say yes, but it doesn't happen. You don't call me. I call you. You don't see me for Christmas. You don't know one person I've dated in 15 years. You never even ask about my life."

"It's hard for me to talk to you."

"Why?"

"Because you know how to hurt me."

"I never want to hurt you. Everything you accuse me of are things that you've done to me. I don't know why we do this anymore. This isn't love, Cassie. It doesn't feel like you love me…I think you need to get help for what happened in our childhood."

"What are you saying?"

"I've been learning about Narcissistic Personality Disorder to understand mom and what happened. Now I see that you discarded me 15 years ago."

"I'm emotionally cold, Anne, I'll give you that."

"It's more than that, Cassie. You even said, it takes every bone in your body…"

"You're the same way!"

"I stress that I may have unintentionally hurt someone. I'm not a saint. I've been abusive. But I admit my wrongs and imperfections. I apologize. I get therapy. I seek to educate myself, heal. I'm trying so hard to break the cycle."

"Whatever." She hangs up.

Anne walks outside for a cigarette. She sees Lewis across the street. He turns and looks, a smirk on his face.

It's as if he knows I'm miserable, and it makes him happy.

Does he know?

What's in that closet?

Anne walks inside and looks in the closet. She fiddles with the cover to the electrical panel, starts to remove the screws.

I'm going to get electrocuted.

Anne fills a glass of water from the Brita she's been avoiding.

I'm being crazy, like my sister said.

After 20 minutes, she goes to bed. A dream. Lewis' face. An orgasm. She wakes. Pain between her legs. Nothing's on the camera.

It's impossible. Unless…

She goes to the spare room, checks the windows. One of them has no screen; the lock is busted.

This is a story about ghosts.

151

Anne: "I got an app that detects wifi devices. There's a strange device. But who'd go to these lengths?"

Therapist: "Rape and stalking are about power."

Anne: "That anal pain jogged a memory of my ex-husband. About a year after we broke up, he called. He wanted to hook up. During, he got agitated and said he couldn't orgasm; he put it in my ass. I cried. I just realized that was rape. I thought I ruined my marriage to a perfect man. I also noticed how many of these men were Jrs., named after their narcissist parent, or their names rhymed or they had the same middle name as them or their first name as a middle name."

Therapist: "It's amazing you say that because the narcissists in my life were Jrs. too."

Anne: "I've been reading about how narcissists are made. It said that narcissist parents have golden children, scapegoats, and invisibles. Cassie's name rhymes with my mom's and she has the same middle name; my mom wanted her to like all the things she liked. She'd say, *You know you're my favorite.* But my sister was abused too."

Therapist: "People think coddling alone causes narcissism, but it's the cognitive dissonance between spoiling and abuse."

Anne: "And I was scapegoat—I was never spoiled; there was no dissonance."

349

152

LETTER TO A GHOST: CASSIE
In high school, I had to write an article reviewing horror films. I rented *The Exorcist* and had a meltdown when the possessed girl took a crucifix to her vagina, stabbing mercilessly, screaming, *Let Jesus fuck you.* You wanted to see what terrorized me. I let you watch.

For weeks, you slept in my bed.

We were afraid of waking up and discovering a demon residing inside us.

We thought maybe being together could prevent it from rooting.

When you were born, Mom gave me an orange teddy in a bonnet named after her. She said she was going to the hospital to have another baby. She said the bear would take her place forever. I cried. I've slept with a teddy all my life.

I remember dad coaching me to hold you. You were so small and so was I. I shivered in the chair in the hospital as he placed you in my lap. My arms were jello and you seemed so fragile. You had mom's face. You slept soundly and wriggled, nestling close to my belly.

I *loved* you.

It was all I'd ever wanted.

Sister. I said the word repeatedly as if I didn't believe it real.

I remember the first time you hit me.

You were maybe two years old; I was six. Mom was beating me. She turned to you and said, "C'mon Cassie, get her!"

Your tiny fists landed on my back, my belly, my face. Mom said, "Kick her! Pull her hair!"

Your fists and feet landed like feathers.

But it hurt more than anything.

I always said, "My sister's a bull. If you upset her, she'll charge."

When you beat me, everything transformed: you turned purple faced and bestial, growling, screaming, clawing, biting. Once, you bit my cheek so hard I had an imprint of your teeth for weeks.

When you attacked, I believed you wanted me to die. It was a rage that passionate. The only thing that saved me was being stronger than you.

But I hated to hit you.

I'd always wanted a sister.

You understand, right? You know how lonely it was being in that house, right?

Mom dressed you in pink and had you watching Disney all day, telling you repeatedly about how she went to Disney World in high school and all the boys wanted her. You had shelves of Barbies. You propped them on stands. You told mom you'd be just like her—you'd never stop playing with Barbies. You played with them so long you got bullied for it.

I once watched you get off the bus and get knocked into a snow pile. I dropped my bag, jumped the girl, and hit her upside the head with my lunchbox.

It didn't matter that you hated me.

My instinct has always been to defend you.

You had your own language only I could understand. You couldn't pronounce your r's: when words seemed difficult, you replaced them with words you could say.

"Namby!" You'd yell at our grandmother.

She'd look helplessly at me, "What's she saying?"

"She wants a banana."

But I couldn't be your translator always. In school, it became a problem. They put you in speech therapy.

Mom sat you on the living room floor, "Say run."

"Won."

She'd slap you across the face.

"Say run."

"Won!"

Slap.

"Are you my daughter or are you a retard?"

"I'm your daughter!" You'd cry helplessly.

"Then say run."

"Won, mommy!"

Next time it was the fist.

"Are you fucking stupid? You're an embarrassment."

"No, mommy, I'm saying it! Won!"

Another fist.

You'd collapse on the floor, heaving, "Won, won, won."

The memories that haunt me most are not what Mom did to me, but what Mom did to you.

Nothing terrified you more than being alone. I took being locked away as a reprieve, but the mere threat made you collapse. Mom or Dad would drag you up the stairs by your arms and shove you into your room kicking and screaming. Like a terrified animal, you'd curl your little body into the door and claw, knocking your head against it for hours.

Mom and Dad seemed at peace when you screamed. They'd turn up the volume on the TV. I'd ask, "Can I get her yet?"

When they finally let me, your body would be curled against the door frame. As soon as I unlocked it and pushed it, you'd leap into my arms.

I can still feel it, Cassie—every bone of you shivering against every bone of me.

You held me as if you thought no one was ever coming back, as if no one was ever going to hold you again.

"Sissy," you'd sob. I can still feel the raw heat of you, the damp hair against your scalp, the trembling.

I'd whisper, "Someday we're gonna get away."

Those were your first narcissistic collapses.

As we got older, your hugs got weaker. The last time I hugged you—years ago—you hovered your limbs inches off my body. I thought I must revolt you.

I've been alone for so long, Cassie.

They say that people who don't get touched experience what's called skin hunger, a withering starvation.

I can't describe the force of this craving, how I've fantasized that you'd soothe my shivering body the way I did for you.

Idealization phase began when you were 12, all those nights in my room as I taught you how to be a teenager. "Your life is like a movie," you'd say, awestruck.

You became obsessed with taking my picture. I'd buy disposable cameras and you'd snap me unknowingly or ask me to pose.

"That doesn't look like me," I'd say.

"Yes it does."

"I look pretty."

"You *are* pretty. I hate that I look like mom. Nobody'll ever kiss me."

When you got your first kiss, you came to my room only to find I hadn't come home. I went on a date with a boy who'd already hurt me. You wrote me a letter: "You're the dumbest girl in the world. I got my first kiss today. I'm so mad at you."

My devaluation phase began then too.

But it didn't register—in my mind, I was, indeed, the dumbest girl in the world.

Unlovable.

Skin hungry.

Starving.

After you decided to study poetry—a competition I didn't know I was in began, and you refused to read mine.

One time, inexplicably, while you were on summer break, you came to my room with a sheet of paper. "I wrote you a poem," you said.

My heart filled with love to be worthy.

Then I read it.

It was about a girl who got fat, sneaking away in her room to eat pastries, because it was the closest she could get to feeling sweetness.

Those that have experienced loving narcissists have common stories: how they ruined holidays and special events, disappeared when times were hardest.

When I got a kidney infection, you came with me to the E.R. You picked a fight, stormed out, left me alone for 12 hours. I cried in the hospital bed. A nurse asked what was wrong. I said I couldn't get a hold of my boyfriend or sister, that I was scared I was dying alone. She asked if I wanted to borrow her phone.

I said it's not that; it's that no one will answer.

It took me so long to see because in my mind, we were little girls who'd just watched *Swing Kids*, attempting to dance in the kitchen, sliding across the tile in our socks as I took your arms, slid you between my legs, and lifted you up over my head as you giggled. In my mind, you were the little girl at the kitchen table with a box of crayons drawing contently for hours, because even now, you paint every day, and your sketch books are full of leaves you picked up, plants you observed, mushrooms you found on a hike, trees and streams and landscapes so accurate they look like photographs. How could I doubt that your hands were capable of love when I looked at the beauty that poured out of them? In my mind, we were in our 20s at some hole in the wall bar, and Ol' Dirty Bastard blasted from the speakers and you took to the dance floor alone, spinning and gyrating, your curls bouncing in perfect choreography as your skirt blossomed, and you looked like an orchid, a slim stem rising from a florescent bloom.

I've always had trouble living quietly in untruths.

After our conversation, you emailed.

I do love, Anne. I just love differently than you.

Is it true, Cassie? Is there any shred of love inside you for me?

Then you said what I'd always feared.

"If we weren't sisters, I wouldn't tolerate you."

Not love—tolerance.
The kill shot.

I was in a motel, homeless, running from my rapist when I read it. I'd never felt more alone.

Trauma is a forest fire: it wrecks anything in its path for generations.

Losing you after losing so many others was like surviving a war only to wake up and realize your entire platoon is corpses on top of you in a ditch.

I don't want to live in a world in which happiness isn't possible for you.

Sister.

I'll never love anyone more than I've loved you.

"We can live without limbs unless they are our siblings."
—Megan Fernandez, "Tell Me What You
Know About Dismemberment"

153

Anne: "It's generational trauma. My grandfather on my mom's side got remarried after my grandma died of cancer within months. My grandmother died young. I'm sure her health had to do with abuse. On my dad's side, my grandmother. They all died of Alzheimer's. I looked it up and there are scholarly studies linking NPD and Alzheimer's."

Therapist: "Have you had any more clarity about Lewis?"

Anne: "Hardwire surveillance takes 6-8 hours. That's how long he was here in December. It also said that surveillance will mess with your TV—I've been having trouble getting my TV to work. I wrote the apartment complex about wanting to break my lease over the crow bar marks, but I didn't name him. I said I was uncomfortable with the belligerent racist neighbors with the confederate flag who yelled at me the other day. They haven't replied. I'm avoiding the Brita. I looked up my symptoms. If he drugged me, I fit all the symptoms for GHB. It even explains the intense orgasms."

Therapist: "I've taken G recreationally. You can be conscious, but you have no memory. Plus, in the midst of trauma, the brain will go into denial to restore safety."

154

Let me tell you what happens when a girl like me loses someone.
She starts to feel like she doesn't exist.
Then something reminds her that she does exist, and she starts to feel she shouldn't.

Why should an unloved thing exist?

Then, a bandaid appears: an abuser.

A rattle in her brain.

Yesssssssss, her brain hisses, *yesssssssssss.*

That's what you need.

But she doesn't want to be punished. She thinks he's just skin to touch, a mime of love.

But her body knows. Her body knows because it's all her body's ever known.

To be relieved of the pain of abuse, you need someone who treats you like rot to come back and touch you because if only they'll touch you, if only you can convince this one abuser that you're lovable...

...then maybe you'll close the cycle forever.

My face was puffy from crying in therapy over my sister as I stepped outside for a cigarette. I looked to my left to see Lewis coming out of the neighbor's apartment.

What I saw next, I'd never seen before.

357

His face transformed. *A scowl.* He looked like a wolf growling. He snapped his neck quickly to turn away from me. He turned back, and there was Lewis again.

But my body registered that scowl like an animal running into an electric fence.

"Hey Lewis, I have something of yours."

He looked hesitant, "What?"

"A business card I found on my floor."

He started to slowly walk towards my porch. "For what?"

"I'll get it."

I came back, handed it to him, taunting, "I know you have a habit of losing numbers."

"Aww man."

"How've you been?" I asked.

He couldn't have…Look at that face.

"Terrible," he moaned. "My birthday's this weekend. Everyone wants to bring kids, so I had to cancel."

Narcissists complain about everything and ruin birthdays.

"You can't just say, no kids?"

He shook his head.

"Your wife will do something."

"Ha," he rolled his eyes. He draped his wrists over my fence, "So, uh, what blue truck was it with the confederate flag? Who yelled at you?"

The email about breaking my lease.

"You heard about that?"

"I was sitting in the office when my boss read your email. She has a habit of reading while moving her lips."

That must be the largest crock he's said yet.

I pointed to their apartment. "I want to move."

"You should move into the apartments next door."

He wants me close.

"People feel sad here. Don't you feel it?"

"There's cool people here. You're cool."

"I already hang out with me."

Dead-eyed. "I'll be knocking on your door in 20 mins."

"Why?"

"To hang out."

358

Rattle. Hiss.

I thought he was a garden snake.

A knock. I opened the door, surprised.

"You thought I was bullshittin?" He breezed past like he lived there and washed his hands. He walked into the living room. My cat ran up to him. He bent down to pet her, "Where's the orange one?"

"He's terrified of people."

"He likes me."

I looked hard at him: *What do you mean he likes you?*

"Sit."

"I'm really dirty." He paced my hallway aimlessly.

"You're making me nervous."

He sat. "You look like you've been crying. Rough week?"

I nodded.

"Let's watch *Ancient Aliens.*"

"Okay, let me try to get this remote to work. My TV's been acting up."

"It's because of your crystals."

Is it?

For the next half hour, Lewis was Lewis again—the sweet, charming, boyish man with the irresistible twang explaining evidence of aliens in Mayan Ruins.

"You left Andrew alone? Way to treat your best friend."

"He's not my friend."

"*WHAT?* He talks about you all the time."

Lewis shook his head.

"Who's your best friend?"

"A buddy from prison. That's my only friend in this world."

"Why?"

"Because you can't trust anyone," he spat the words bitterly.

"Why do you trust him?"

"Because he's just like me."

"What does it mean to be like Lewis?" I mused, "Let me pull you a tarot."

"*No,*" he flinched. "That shit's real."

"What about this Animal Spirit tarot?"

He looked skeptical, "Fine."

I shuffled the deck, spread them in front of him. He closed his eyes and pulled, handing me the card. "The bat!"

His eyes gleamed, "I'm a vampire."

I read the card: darkness, the unknown. "The light's coming. Everything's going to change."

Lewis remained stoic and nodded. He jumped up and started pacing as I drew mine, seeming agitated.

"The Fire Ant," I said. "The part of you that's attracted to what's bad for you. Don't pretend the heat isn't getting to you."

Lewis stared intently, "What do you think?"

"I feel called out."

"Yeah, me too," he said. "I'm going to check on Andrew. I'll be right back."

I knew he wasn't coming back.

The next day I came home and stopped as I walked inside. A leaf.

I thought about the day before, Lewis pacing the living room.

Fuck. Anne. Fuck. How'd you miss it?

What did he do right before he stopped pacing?

He peered behind the TV where the camera is.

He knew I installed a camera because of his surveillance.

He knew I was onto him.

The scowl.

He was looking for where it faced to determine if he could come in through my front door when I'm not home. It faced the screen door.

I looked at the app that detected Wi-fi devices.

The suspicious device was gone.

My camera had picked up shadows moving, a loud metal clanging.

He'd been here. He took out the microphone.

That meant:

Those definitely weren't dreams.

I thought he was a garden snake.

It turned out he was a python.

155

*A*nne's sobbing hysterically.

Anne: "My dad's a narcissist too. I was his invisible child, my mom's scapegoat. How do I miss *everything*? How did I not know I was covered in snakes?"

Therapist: "You were trained to excuse abuse."

Anne: "I spent all these years thinking he was emotionally repressed, not covertly abusive. Now—I let a rapist into my house."

Therapist: "There's four trauma responses: fight, flight, freeze, or fawn. When you meet a narcissist, your instinct is fawn."

Anne: "My mom—she's not just a narcissist. She's an antisocial… She killed my cat."

Anne puts her head in her hands.

Therapist: "Okay, yes, this is a different level. Is this a recovered memory?"

Anne: "No. It's just too painful. I didn't have anybody. This one beautiful Persian favored me and…There's no way I got out of this childhood without a disorder too. *What's wrong with me?*"

156

I locked myself in my room reading about Cluster B personality disorders.

What happens to children in a toxic family?

What happens to a girl pummeled lifelong, addicted to trauma?

My trauma was bigger than me. I felt the weight of an inherited generational trauma from the wounds of colonialism and patriarchy. The people slitting each other's necks, feeding each other to wild animals in death games, cloaking themselves as missionaries, luring slaves, casting nets, shackling chains.

Then they cracked the whips, raped the women and children, simulated drowning when the whip would render them worthless for work.

And then the student shot up the school.

And then the police officer kneeled on a neck.

And then the white child walked into a protest with an assault rifle.

And then the drone fell on the preschool.

And then the mother hit the child.

And then the husband beat the wife.

And then the boyfriend killed the girlfriend.

And then the inmate raped the inmate.

And then they polluted the rivers, the oceans, the air, the soil.

And then...

Am I crazy? Or is this world crazy?

A world with no empathy.

Will this be our story? Or will we let the ghosts in?

I closed my eyes: I saw myself walking into a circle of rocks under the moon. The rocks began to heat. A wolf watched in the distance.

Who's my pack?

How do I reclaim the territory of my body?

The rocks erupted into flames.

I knew that I'd walk through this fire and wouldn't burn.

I turned around and there was Lewis.

All the lovers.

All the friends.

My sister.

One by one, I unmasked them: narcissist, histrionic, antisocial. I'd always attracted to Cluster B's.

What am I?

I turned to the fire and walked through it towards the wolf.

I knelt down and I knew—

Borderline Personality Disorder.

C.D. appeared in front of me. He held out his arms—the cigarette burns.

A mirror descended between us.

Brother.

I turned around and all my loves were burning.

I blew out the fire.

I knew they were burning anyway, forever, regardless.

157

Therapist: "I hesitated to say Borderline—there's a stigma."

Anne: "It makes everything make sense. My sexuality, my addiction to narcissists, my addiction to abuse, my smoking, my eating disorders, my cutting, my suicidal ideation. I even read that Borderlines are often creative, that we can sense other's emotions with our empathy, and that we report lucid dreaming. We always have a favorite person we intensely enmesh with, another Cluster B. I've done that since childhood."

Therapist: "This is a huge step. What about the apartment situation?"

Anne: "If he removed the mic, do you think he's planning to leave me alone?"

158

Every person I'd loved was a fire that had tried to consume me, so healing meant nothing short of supernatural transformation: I had to rise from ash transformed, a Phoenix soaring above the hellscape that made me.

Every morning, I woke in drenched sheets, vomited several times showering. I thought my illness was breaking trauma bonds. I couldn't think clearly: my brain was a fog I could barely navigate.

I received suspicious friend requests on social media that I was sure were Lewis. The first was obviously fake with no followers and two followed: Elon Musk and Tesla, Lewis' hero. The account was called Bibliophile_Space—tailored to two of my interests. The poor grammar matched the emails we got from maintenance.

I googled why a narcissist would make fake accounts and read that it was a result of losing power and trying to attain it other ways.

His microphone.

I got out of my car and looked up to see Lewis in the distance. He spotted me and raised his hand hello, flashing a big smile.

I stared defiantly.

I'll never talk to him again, I vowed.

He was already wrapped around my neck, squeezing.

I'm driving to work, disoriented. I pray to get there unharmed. I'm thinking about all the people I loved. Very few are left to hold onto.

I'm still the girl C.D. loves, I assured myself.

C.D.'s face flashes in my mind's eye as clear as if he's in front of me.

Expressionless. Emotionless.

You're just like me.

C.D.'s face returns. A mirror descends between us. It shatters. I feel like I've been shot.

No, I'm going crazy.

When I get to work, I can barely walk. I sit down, close my eyes.

I had a toy growing up called a View-Master.

Click, Jason says, "Everyone thought C.D. was nice, but C.D. had some rage;" click, C.D. beating up Jason, the same way Cassie beat me; click, Jason saying, "His mom abandoned him for an abusive man. His dad was in and out of prison;" click, C.D. says, "I go by C.D because I'm named after my dad, and I hate that asshole;" click, C.D.'s shift to skater fashion, mirroring Logan; click, C.D. says, "Anne's obsessed with me, and she broke my heart," a projection, a smear campaign; click, C.D.'s anger; click, his meanness; click, his sudden discard; click, his discard of Logan; click, his body in the casket, Logan's body in the casket.

I see it, C.D.

I see what curse this is.

Baby narcissist with so much pain.

I carried your shame all my life.

I almost died for it.

That haunting echo: *not lovable enough to save him.*

I see your face. I reach for it.

I don't want to do this, C.D.

I peel off your face.

I see *my face.*

All this time, the person I loved behind the mask was…*me.*

You mirrored *me.* I'd fallen in love with myself.

I wrap my arms across my stomach and heave a sob, looking frantically for a sign.

Tell me you're healed.

Tell me you're not discarding me again.

Tell me you didn't save me to leave me alone like this.

Then I hear your voice, and I know it's for the last time:

"What heals you, heals me. We're not the same, but we are. Who pulled you from the suicide, whose love did you finally feel worthy to stand in the light of?"

My own.

"Now you have the truth. What will you choose? Stay trauma bonded to my ghost? Or will you choose to live?"

I get home from work.

I go outside for a cigarette. I see some maintenance workers run from the building across the parking lot. One of them says, "Lewis got zapped!"

Lewis walks out. I quickly turn around to face my screen door. I see him reflected in the glass.

He turns his head towards me. He stares several beats too long.

His expression is clear: pure hatred.

159

Anne: "I went to the office and they said Lewis got fired. I assumed they must've figured out he's nefarious, so I told her. But she was defensive as I tried to tell her my apartment had been broken into and that he knew of the emails I sent. I asked if he still lived here. She said no. Then I saw Andrew and asked what happened. He said they drug tested Lewis because he got injured. He's still here four more days. I went back to my journals and I found passages that were crossed out that I'd never cross out. He crossed out when I speculated he's lonely and when I wrote that friendship is better than sex. He crossed out a few other things too. And then I'd found where I'd written that even though I suspected he had NPD, I still wanted him to take me in my kitchen: that's exactly what he did the first time. I wonder if, in his sick mind, enacting that allows him to tell himself I wanted it. Then, something told me to look in that closet. I turned off the power and finally unscrewed the cover, and look—his wire cutters were in there."

Therapist: "Oh my God."

Anne: "Andrew said he's moving two hours away and that he'd never seen anyone cry that much, that he screamed for two days."

Therapist: "Narcissistic collapse."

Anne: "Also, those neighbors with the confederate flag moved. Andrew said Lewis told him they pulled a gun on him. But what narcissists accuse is confession: that means *he* pulled a gun *on them*. Because of my email, because he's territorial over me. Also, his brown pride tattoo. I remember when I told him how much racism upset me,

368

and he stared with such a deep grief in his eyes that I thought he'd cry. The cognitive dissonance makes my brain hurt. I feel sick."

Therapist: "I...have no words. I know you don't trust police, but..."

Anne: "I read that a narcissist's collapse feels like a borderline's baseline, which is, *I'm unlovable.* And a borderline's collapse feels like a narcissist's baseline, which is, *Where's the predator?* Imagine the kind of narcissistic injuries I gave him talking about NPD with you."

160

I'm at the beach, watching the waves march forward in obedient formation. I find a grey feather in the sand. I pick it up and write the word, "Free."

I pray for Lewis, for protection, that I can heal the shame he filled me with when he raped me, that I can remember his shame isn't mine.

I walk back to my car. A man's on the pier. He's staring. I think he's just a creep, bracing myself as I walk past.

I'm sitting in my living room and look up.
A man is at my screen door.
The same man. He's staring. He's on his phone.
I walk to the window and stare back, shutting the blinds.
I go to my bedroom window.
He's standing at my bedroom window.
Lewis isn't letting go.

I'm in the management office of my complex crying. I have Lewis' wire cutters, my journals, my soiled sheets, the tool he dropped, the broken screen door photos.

His boss says she believes me. She says Lewis got in her face and threatened to hit her, that his wife said he beats her, that he's egotistical and lazy, that the maintenance costs skyrocketed and he'd be constantly going back to the same apartments, not having fixed anything. She says he'd fooled many.

I say, "I need to break my lease."

She says, "He doesn't live here anymore."

"I'm still being stalked, the door's still broken, I'm sick, I'm stressed, I can't sleep, not where he raped me. I have to flee tonight."

She says, "That'll be $700."

I'm in a hotel with my cats in another city. A knock on the door.

"Who is it?"

"Maintenance."

My heart stops.

"Why?"

"We got a call that your room flooded."

"My room didn't flood."

"A man called and said it did."

"There's no man here."

"He's staying downstairs."

"Well, my room isn't flooded."

I look at my phone. An Instagram request. Another fake profile. I screenshot and block it. One of the posts says, "I had to forgive someone who wasn't even sorry."

I call my friend. Urgently, he says, "Anne, *he has your phone.*"

161

Anne: "The Apple store confirmed: he went into my settings and shared my phone to his. He had access to everything."

Therapist: "Where are you now?"

Anne: "I went to another city, another hotel. I won't say where on the phone."

Therapist: "Did you talk to police?"

Anne: "Yes, she said I could file an incident report. But I don't want to file until I have a safe place to stay, not when he's sending people after me. Can you write me a letter for work that says I'll need a leave of absence for mental health?"

Therapist: "I'll do that right now."

Anne: "I can't do a rape case. They'll rake me over the coals for my mental health, for having a crush on him, for being in denial and drugged when I realized he raped me."

Therapist: "Rape cases are traumatic and rarely result in conviction."

Anne: "I feel like I'm in withdrawals. Like how it feels to try to quit smoking without the patch but even worse. Then I thought, if he came back in to take out the microphone, then he had access to my Brita again. I'd still been drugged after the camera. I'm so dumb. How am I still alive?"

162

LETTER TO A GHOST: LEWIS

"I point to my body and say, 'Oh, this old thing? This is where men come to die.'"

—Warsan Shire

My first rape put me in a deep sleep. You raped me in a deep sleep and I awoke.

I keep thinking of Eros and Psyche, how Eros came to her invisible nightly. Everyone said, *Your lover's a monster.*

She dropped wax on him to make him visible, and he fled.

She wanted to know, *What does obsession look like? Is it monstrous?*

It was, but not because Eros was a monster.

Because he was a coward.

You needed me in a coma to rape me.

Sometimes I imagine if I saw you again, how I'd carve out your eyes as you watch me one long, last time.

A month passed. I moved. I thought I'd lost you.

After calling a lawyer, I sat outside smoking. A green trucked pulled up, no license plate.

I knew it was you.

Out walked…Peyton. The heroin addict from 17 years ago.

For a moment, I thought I was going crazy.

Then he looked at me, smiled, waved in sadistic glee.

I was writing a book about my ghosts, and you resurrected one. I realized I was imprisoned inside your sick brain no matter where I fled.

The message was clear: you know my core wounds. You know where I live. You're always watching. You'll make me go crazy or look crazy. You'll have me killed before you go back to prison.

Peyton is your kind—insecure, giddy to hunt old prey.

I felt fear momentarily. Then I realized that fear was yours, being projected into me, so I rejected it.

You're not stronger than me: we're made of the same stock.

I discovered you: a narcissist.

I discovered me: a borderline.

A match of childhood trauma made in hell.

We're the children of sociopaths.

We're the bad seeds.

I filed a stalking report, detailed the rapes, but I didn't want you to go back to prison. Justice means different things to different people.

If I thought vengefully, I'd be as shameful as you.

And I'm not naive to how this world works for a victim.

We live in a world salivating to bite down on a girl.

I chose not to use our justice system in order to give mercy to myself, as well as you.

The only real justice is truth anyway.

You seek power relentlessly to make up for your pain.

But the only real power is love.

I have that. That's why you wanted to break me.

Love is generative. The absence of it is destructive.

Hatred isn't power: it's self sabotage.

You came to my body to die, didn't you?

I can feel it—what you tried to bury here.

I learned that whatever narcissists accuse others of is projection —essentially, confession.

You said your wife's bisexual. So, you're bisexual.

Why did your lonely friend move to a terrible complex in a city he'd never heard of? Why did he seem to flirt with you? I remembered how you shaved each other's heads, how I saw you spend the night at his apartment. For him to see you in collapse would be intimate.

Your sexual arousal comes from power, shame, and abuse.

Once, you told a story: "You know how they say, 'don't drop the soap' in prison? Well…it happens….when I bent over, I saw this guy's dick. It had a full demon tattoo. I stood up, raised my eyebrows, impressed."

I thought, *Why the awe?*

I laughed, "Imagine having sex and putting that demon inside of you." Your head snapped and you looked afraid, as if you were thinking, *Does she know?*

After you got out of prison, your brother came out: you said you had to beat him. You thought he wasn't accepting homosexuality as a phase.

Was it really that he had the power to heal the shame you couldn't?

You had a wife you beat.

A secret homosexual lover.

A girl you were drugging and raping.

Your nieces and nephews lived in the complex too.

I researched the cause of stalking: childhood emotional neglect, taking an emotional connection that mirrors your parents and putting it on steroids, violating all boundaries because the connection is so charged: no amount of knowing can ever fill the void of despair.

Rejection hits your core wound: abandonment.

Something awful happened.

Something about your parents.

Something about fear.

Something about something that hurts deeper than you have words for.

Something about something that hurt you before you even had words.

In a collapse, people with NPD reveal their emotional intelligence. From Cassie to Sam to Brad to V, they became childlike. When they rage, the vengeance they enact projects the trauma they felt.

What did your rage feel like? As if I was never safe; as if I was hunted, terrorized, hated; as if my worst pain will be used against me; as if I'll never be free; as if I might die; as if I'm full of sexual shame; as if I can't trust anyone; as if I'm going crazy; as if I need to think ahead of the threat.

That's how your parents made you feel.

I recognized those were your feelings, and I could reject them. My mother may have pulled out my spine like filleting a fish, but I've reinforced it with steel.

Can I look at the rapes as a reflection of your pain?

Can I look at my desire as a reflection of mine?

Can I forgive both?

I remember how I'd see you walking in the distance. I wanted you to come closer, to know you. Now I think of how enmeshed you were to me without me knowing. I think of every violation: the drug, the crow bar, standing over my bed, unwrapping me from blankets, taking my teddy, flipping me over, crawling into bed, taking off my panties, putting them back.

I keep seeing you putting your hand to your chest, professing, *I try to be a good man.* I wanted to erase my body so I could believe that.

I still want to convince you not to hate all of me.

Because that's what I always wanted from my parents.

I still want to believe something was real. Was there ever a time we were just two humans, not predator and prey? Did our inner children connect? Deep down, do you recognize me, your sibling?

I hold you up in my memory by the scruff, a terrified baby wolf, abandoned to the wild, snarling. I see why the world feels hostile, why you need to hate me.

If it makes you feel better, hate me.

Do you remember me talking to you while you raped me? You never said a word. What did I say? Was it the truth? That I wanted to love you? That you were my parents? That you were C.D.? That I thought you were beautiful? That I thought you were terrifying?

But I could've never imagined *this* from eyes that looked like yours. You left no bruises but you made me wretched.

Rapists who were raped as children reenact their own rapes. Did raping me give you your power back, expel your shame?

I can still feel the weight of you, your thin build, your ribs through your shirt. You're so small. You felt…fragile.

Did it give you pleasure to see me ugly, helpless, dumb? That's how you wanted me, because *that's who you really are.* The truth you can't bear to face. The part of you that came to my body to die.

You lured me with a mirror of all that's lovable in me.

I transformed into a mirror of all that's unlovable in you.

I'd sacrifice myself if your pain could be alleviated. I know how unbearable your shame, Lewis. I wake up with it every night.

I've known your kind since I was a kid. A ghost like you haunted my life, exposed your dark truths.

You're a part of me now. I'll drag your corpse along.

Come, brother.

Let me bury you in the family mausoleum.

The truth is…

I really hurt and scared you.

That's why you needed to really hurt and scare me.

If I terrified you, ironically, that means you must've *really* loved me.

Love is what a sociopath is phobic of, because the first person you loved suddenly turned predator and killed your inner child.

It's why your nickname for me was *mama.*

It's why I have one memory that'll haunt me always: you're raping me and sobbing, "Mama, mama, no."

I've always wanted someone to fully see me. You did, then you used it all against me.

But Lewis, my body's already been trespassed—that's a well-worn path. There's no game to hunt there. I was raised to be violated, but my inner child isn't dead, so I found a place to hide, a place to grow, a place no one can touch.

My soul.

You can't break it. Everyone already tried.

I needed to understand you to survive the genuine affection I had for you, so I had to dissect the darkest pain, which took me to the brightest wisdom for healing. Like Persephone, I got wed in the underworld and returned to a spring with intimate knowledge of wintering.

Are you still watching? Do you see what I've done?

I swallowed your poison, transformed it to nectar.

The only power is love.

The only justice is truth.

163

L ETTER TO A GHOST: C.D.

"And ghosts must do again what gives them pain."

—W.H. Auden

When I broke my bond to your ghost, I felt as if my skeleton shattered and I was frantically rebuilding my bones.

The similarities between you and Lewis are uncanny: abused by criminal fathers, abandoned by narcissistic mothers, raised by narcissistic grandmothers, emotionally abandoned, raped. The iceberg of pain he carried, alongside his beauty and tenderness, reopened my deepest darkest wounds with the precision of a surgeon.

What did you accuse me of after discard? Obsession.

What were you? What was Lewis?

We're siblings in pain. Yin and yang. Dark and light fraternal twins. Golden child and scapegoat. Predator and prey.

The borderline always thinks this time they can close the cycle: they can prove their lovability.

When I was about to die, the only thing that saved me was an abuser.

The borderline attracts abusers like magnets because our hearts are capable of unconditional love. We have no need for a mask. We wear our shame.

When an abuser has no one to blame, they experience an ego death: if they have to face their shames, they'll realize they're the predator and become suicidal. This is why sociopaths become obsessed. They need to project their feelings of unworthiness to survive.

I figured some things out about you, C.D.

What happened between you and Logan put you in a narcissistic collapse. He discarded you. You said Logan said it was okay for men to suck each other's dicks. Projection, smear campaign—you said that.

Another thing you and Lewis share.

After Logan, you collapsed, afraid you'd be outed, forced to face your shame.

You reverted to how you felt as a child—you projected that pain: you felt *dead*.

Your pain followed my life. It came through my door decades later, almost killed me again.

In confronting your inner child through the grief I carried, I solved the mystery of why you died, why Logan died.

Now I see: vision from the underworld is a gift if you're chosen to come back from the fire, if you learn to rise from the ash.

The only power is love.

The only justice is truth.

What pain you must've been in to take those pills.

It turned Logan into you: dead. Me: near dead. Jason: imprisoned.

After Lewis, I looked in the mirror and I was you.

Drugged. A ghost. I had to flee or I was going to overdose.

You were my first love, my destiny, a haunting, a core wound. If you hadn't committed suicide, you'd have become Lewis.

Brother, we're the bad seeds.

I'll drag your corpse along. I'll lift your shame. I'll lift it by lifting it from myself.

I'll love us back to life, C.D., back to perfect.

C.D., Anne

You were perfect children.

Anne, V., Jason, Logan

You were perfect children.

Anne, Cassie

You were perfect children.

C.D., Lewis

You were perfect children.

None of you deserved what happened to you.

Come, siblings, let me bury you in the family mausoleum.

This is a story about ghosts.

There's no exorcism.

The key to survival is love, and love is the hardest war.

You have to love every chipped tooth, every vomit-covered nightgown, every beastly snarl. You have to love every rotted foundation, every dusty cellar, every cracked mirror.

Don't let the girl become the ghost—hunted.

Don't let the house become the girl—haunted.

The horror ends when you face truth.

Sit with your ghosts long enough, and you'll see that what haunts is a different threat altogether. A toxic poison in the atmosphere.

Its name is shame.

We're its corpses, its living dead.

Heal your light or you'll become the darkness.

Set your pain aflame to the heavens, burn eternal.

Come. See how darkness almost eclipsed me until I learned to walk through fire.

I rise from this ash and my plume of feathers snuffs out flames in a single soaring swoosh.

164

L ETTER TO A GHOST: DAD
"Daddy, daddy, you bastard, I'm through."

—Sylvia Plath

I realize this is the shame that'll kill you.

As I interrogated my past, I saw the patterns, I learned the serpent, I studied how it moves.

I learned to spot their confessions.

I remembered my ex-husband. He accused me of being a lesbian. He urged me to kiss my friends, then accused me of liking it more than I liked sex with him. He accused his friends of being weird, of being closeted homosexuals.

So many memories shivered clear. Once I could see it, it seemed astonishing I'd missed it. There were so many signs.

He was a closeted homosexual. I was his mask.

C.D., Lewis, Sam, Pedro, the M.C.

Even Santiago, raping me with his cousin.

Why did so many of my lovers have secret relationships with men?

Why was I so attracted to the LGBTQ community?

What did *you* confess through accusation, dad?

You said mom's friendships were secret lesbians.

You said all feminists were lesbians who hated men.

382

You said I'm a kinky n***** lover.

You said all black boys will rape me.

You said black men think I'm holes for their dicks.

You *cried* when you flung these accusations. Your voice became shrill: a hatred so viciously dark it paralyzed me.

You'd stare out the window at the black neighbors. One day, you saw the boy playing with his sister. You called the police: "There's a black boy having sex outside. Like an animal," you spat. You laughed watching police interrogate the crying boy.

Where was it coming from, your venom?

Your friendships were closeted affairs.

You're a misogynist.

You raped black boys.

You thought they were holes for your dick.

You raped outside, like an animal.

There, daddy.

I've staked you.

I won't hide your truth by believing the mask you made out of my face to hide behind. I'm taking the child you used back.

After Lewis, I cried in therapy, "Who writes a book about rape and gets raped while writing?"

Why was I raped so many times?

Because nothing felt more comfortable to me than a rapist.

Why did Lewis feel like the most powerful magnet?

Nothing could feed my void more than a covert, closeted serial rapist and predatory stalker.

One who needed to control me compulsively.

One who wanted to kidnap my inner child.

You're the reason I could look at him and see a broken, unloved boy.

Lewis is Mexican but passes as white. When he first met me, he told me his name was a white sounding name.

The day he installed surveillance, he told me he had some "tattoos he regretted," like his brown pride tattoo.

"People say I'm a bad guy, I've been to prison, I'm like the KKK," Lewis explained, "But *they* take it too far."

You're white but look Mexican. You'd go places and people would speak Spanish to you. You have black, wavy hair. People always called it an afro.

You hung a confederate flag in the basement. You said there shouldn't be anything wrong with white people having pride.

I knew not to argue or face a torrent of disorienting rage that you'd take too far.

Lewis grew up in the shadow of a colonized country, in an area that used to be Mexico. Yet, as a Mexican native, he grew up with a dirt floor.

He looked white, yet he couldn't have what white people had.

He joined the military to attain the respect he craved.

Battered by his country, battered by his parents.

To solve this, Lewis nurtured his hate and ego.

You grew up comfortably middle class. Your parents often found arrowheads in the yard, delighted at evidence of natives who hunted there.

You were white, yet you didn't get the respect white people got.

You joined the military to attain the respect you craved.

Betrayed by your country, battered by your parents.

To solve this, you nurtured your hate and ego.

Neither of you could nurture your healing, because doing so would require you grieve, and your brains cannot process shame because of your illness.

Your mother was a lot like mine, which is why you married mine.

When I was little, grandma used to complain about mom. I said, "You two are exactly alike." She exploded.

Whenever mom wanted you to beat me, she'd say, "You're not man enough." Then you'd beat me with such a fury, you'd be crying.

I imagine this is the same fury you have when you rape, this outrage that you might not be man enough, that you might not be superior or perfect, the same outrage Lewis took out on my body.

I didn't deserve it. No one does. But you have to find someone to blame. You need someone to hold your shame. You tell yourself they deserve it.

That's what Lewis meant when he said he had a type.

When my first book got published, my professor invited me to read at the college.

You and mom came. I walked into the auditorium and saw my childhood friend, Tom, in the audience. I was ecstatic, but I also felt panicked. He's black—my father would be upset.

I walked up to Tom, "I thought you didn't live here anymore!"

"I'm visiting family. I saw you in the paper."

Tom had known me when C.D. died. After he moved to Chicago, he continued to write. We speak fairly often.

After the reading, with knots in my stomach, I introduced him to you. To my shock, you were jovial. You suggested a restaurant. When I came home, you said, "Your friend looks like he could be in GQ."

Never in my life had I heard you say a kind word about a black person. I was shocked it would be about his appearance but relieved you didn't spew vitriol.

You were attracted to him.

That makes you angry, doesn't it, dad?

Because if that can be true, then what are you?

Daddy, what've you done?

You have to feel better than them: they have to deserve it. Otherwise, with the simple, split thinking of a child, that'd mean you deserved what happened to you, and worse.

Your ego is all that shields you from the pain you carry.

You can't be cast off from God if you *are* a god.

A god can cast anyone into Hell if it pleases him.

This is the truth of what you made: in order to hold you and mom's shame, I had to be strong enough to process what you couldn't. In order to survive such truly dangerous people, I had to recognize you as a child, and I had to love you, because I was *actually* a child, and children need love to survive. I had to heal each ugly truth you dumped into me to survive all the self loathing and blame as I denied your accountability.

I thought my gender made me inferior, so I learned feminism.
You taught me racist ideas, so I learned history.
Each poison I swallowed and I transformed.
Eventually I had to face mental health and generational trauma.

I remember asking you if God exists. You sighed heavily and answered, "I've thought about this a long time…and I don't think so."

I know now why you couldn't think so. What God would allow what happened to you as a child and the curse of your mental illness? I'm sure you must've prayed to heal, and it wasn't answered.

It's a question I've wrestled with too. Because nothing breaks my heart more than what I now know happened to you, the generational trauma that runs in our family.

This poison—it's a killer.

I have a photo from my wedding. During our dance, you couldn't look at me. You kept looking at the floor. You said, "People are going to think I'm a sap."

In the photo, I'm looking at you with such tenderness, like you're my child.

I'm smiling with genuine happiness, assuring you. Now I see what made you cry.

It was with shame that you couldn't look at me.

Being next to me reminded you, always, of what you didn't deserve.

You had to hold back your tears, because if you faced *this* pain, this *love*, then the thing you fear most would come true: *your tears would never stop.*

Had I been a boy, my name would've been Casey Wayne.

I can see the mark of the golden child—the first name mirrored mom's—it rhymed with hers, gave them the same initials. Wayne was your best friend from the Air Force. Scapegoat children are always named after someone dead or former supply of the narcissist; I noticed that pattern as I studied my disorder. Therefore, I'd have been golden to mom, scapegoat to you. A sociopath.

One day, a strange man showed up on our doorstep. He said he knew you from the Air Force. You never had friends, but then we were at dinners regularly, going to air fields as you flew together.

One night, drunk, you said something racist.

Your friend grimaced. He gently said he didn't agree.

Disgusted, you looked at mom, said it was time to leave. You never spoke to him again. You said he turned out to be an unpatriotic fag.

I understand now that this was a man you loved, that this is why you told me that no white man would ever love me—because every time you got close to one, they saw your truth, and they couldn't love you.

You tried to give me that curse. You flung it at me like a hatchet.

Once, during a collapse, you woke my sister and wept at her bedside, apologizing for what you did. All my life, I wondered, *Why didn't he come to me?* I was the daughter who loved him.

What were you apologizing for, daddy?

And why, when you attempted suicide, did she say she couldn't have your blood on her hands?

Daddy, what've you done?

If I had to choose my father, over and over, I'd choose you. If I had to save you from suicide, over and over, I'd save you, because to lose you would mean to lose myself. I see your illness, but I also see your efforts as a father, and the good things alongside the horror of your secrets make my brain hurt and heart break, just as Lewis' hate marred me with cognitive dissonance.

Why should I feel empathy for you? You didn't often tell me you loved me. You didn't protect me as a child. You weren't proud of me. We haven't spoken in years.

Some soul ties are just very strong: I wish you all could feel the blood bond and unconditional love I feel for you, then I wouldn't go through this world orphaned, grieving, and looking for your replacement to make my tragedy end differently.

Because I was a girl, I was named Anne, after Anne Boleyn, a queen decapitated by her husband. Only my gender saved me from your fate, but the cost's been enormous.

I'm here to tell you: you're the one who's decapitated. You've been dead all this time. Something killed you long ago. Like the tales of vampires or *The Strange Case of Dr. Jekyll and Mr. Hyde*, you're cursed. Like Lewis, you sit in the wreckage of a festering history, a deep crater of a spiritual wound. It's not your fault, but you've been wandering this world as a ghost.

So have I, daddy, and it's you who killed me.

I loved you more than anyone.

Come, daddy, let me bury you in the family mausoleum.

EPILOGUE

As I healed, I decided to look at childhood videos of my grandmother. I opened the case: the disc was gone. Lewis had taken a souvenir.

I took a deep breath, remembered that he can't take my love. He only wanted to steal what was stolen from him: childhood.

Abusers hate those who threaten their egos and grandiosity with truth and love. Deep down, they hate themselves. That's also why they're often racist, sexist, transphobic, homophobic, etc.

Deep down, they know the fact their scapegoats can process shame makes us strong. Every time someone abuses me, I study the shame head-on, cast it aside as wreckage that's not mine to carry, and *grow*.

No one in my life has been as noxious as Lewis. He sought to bury me, but what I found deep within was the battered inner child I'd buried. I brought her back to life.

On the one year anniversary of the rapes, I wrote this:

Lewis,

Thank you for the opportunity to sit beside the wound in your core. In the past year, I've walked through fire, into the underworld, and seen the truth: a demon is just a broken-hearted child. Hatred is just a love that's in the anger stage of grieving. Evil is just the void of empathy.

By grace, I've sat with the fire of your shames and let them torch my entire foundation. You projected your pain into me, and the fire illuminated so many truths.

I felt impregnated by your pain. Your pain was a seed of the most creative fertility in my life. I had to process it *somehow*. It's unbearably heavy. You once told me you must've done something terrible in a past life to deserve this life.

I believe you.

This life hasn't been kind to you. This isn't the life of someone who knows love.

When I found your old social media, you had only nine friends, not even your own family…I remember how you winced when I said your marriage sounded "toxic."

The shame: of being a *poison* of a person. A predator.

Not like that…not like…your father.

I'm sorry for what happened to you as a child. You didn't deserve it. I didn't deserve what you did to me either.

I'm sorry this world failed you at every turn.

I learned a lot from your pain, but I pray your pain harms no one else, so I pray for healing for you.

According to the National Institutes of Health, 6% of the population has Narcissistic Personality Disorder, 5% of the population has Borderline Personality Disorder, 2% of the population has Histrionic Personality Disorder, and 4% of the population has Antisocial Personality Disorder. That's 17%—over a billion people on the planet—in the Cluster B category. However, a survey of psychiatric disorders conducted among 43,000 Americans found that 5.5% of men and 1.9% of women had sociopath traits, lacking in both empathy and conscience (NESARC). This study excluded the prison population, which houses many people with this disorder. Therefore, this much larger estimated research reveals the broad-scale public health crisis of sociopathy, estimating that it affects 7.4% of the population or more. I believe it to be higher than this.

This makes sociopathy the most common mental health disorder in America after general depression.

All cluster B's are under diagnosed: we operate heavily in denial, and there's no special pill to solve our symptoms. We often get treated instead for misdiagnosed disorders or comorbid disorders: cPTSD, eating disorders, depression, autism, etc.

80% of people with BPD attempt to kill themselves. Our average life expectancy is 39, and the majority of our early deaths come from health issues that result from abuse, such as cancer, stroke, and cardiovascular issues.

Popular culture has maligned borderlines as irrational, overly sexualized, manic pixie dream girls.

An often overlooked detail of all Cluster B's is that we're most often birthed from the same root: parent(s) with Narcissistic Personality Disorder. But many people with BPD can't identify their covertly abusive parents or that their Favorite People and lovers had NPD because we internalize abuse, idealize abusers, and were raised as scapegoats.

We're your Amy Winehouses, Britney Spears, Marilyn Monroes, 2Pac Shakurs. Women have BPD more often than men, with a ratio of 4 to 1. This is due to boys more often being golden childed, which is linked to the wound of patriarchy. Cluster B disorders are synonymous with generational trauma and linked to societal ills.

The true danger of NPD/ASPD is bigger than a cheating ex, as narcissistic abuse recovery spaces would have you believing. A lack of empathy is linked to climate change, income inequality, genocide, sexism, racism, rape, mass shootings, police brutality, incest, child abuse, animal abuse, and more.

The wound of NPD is massive, historic, dangerous, and largely ignored. It's the least funded disorder for research. It shouldn't be presumed that psychologists and doctors can't have NPD as well: they typically seek careers with power and access to vulnerable supply and believe their own brains are without flaw or superior.

NPD is also a leading cause of suicide; it's why 75% of suicides are men who never sought treatment.

What I'm saying: it's deeply rooted and it's killing us.

What I'm also saying: it's our brothers, sisters, mothers, fathers, lovers.

How can we abandon our family?

On the anniversary of my rapes, I feared for Lewis. Given that he collapsed twice during those times, he may have anniversary PTSD, but since he can't process shame, it could manifest as violence, either towards himself or others. I googled his name for obituaries or arrests, plagued by paranoia and my own PTSD.

One day, he appeared on a Facebook search. It was like a hive's nest was stirred in my brain. He looked gaunt, impossibly thin. His wife left him; she'd posted he attacked her.

His Facebook was eerily full of my interests: pictures of the moon, spirituality, mental health awareness, poems, even Borderline Personality Disorder.

If I read all his posts as projections that were confessions, he fully confessed all he did, including taking a person's worst pain and using it against them, something he said only "trash people" do.

Then, some surprising confessions:

"What's really behind a person's rage is that they love you and that makes them feel scared."

"Whatever they did to you, you didn't deserve it."

"If you completely break a person and they still wish you well, you've just lost the greatest person to ever walk into your life."

"If you ask God for wisdom, He'll show you the darkest pain."

After death comes resurrection.

Then he posted artwork of a girl with pink hair. I had pink hair when he raped me. She was sitting underneath the moon, grieving with her whole body, sitting atop a grave.

I realized the girl was me; the grave was Lewis.

As I heal, I'm grieving for the death of his inner child, murdered by his parents.

That's the pain he projected into me.

He had many posts about his romantic desire for love; about feeling suicidal; about hating women; about women being insecure, weak, jealous, needy; about women being in need of love but unwilling to give respect.

More projections of his truths.

Then he posted a video of accused sex trafficker Andrew Tate saying that transgender people molested kids, that they wanted to put people in prison over pronouns.

I recoiled, recognizing Lewis was projecting his own crimes and that *he was transgender*. Just like the homophobia of the narcissists I've known, his phobia was a fear of his *true self* he masked. They accuse scapegoats of their own shames to get ahead of their secrets. I blocked. The profile no longer exists.

Lewis' transgender identity was a revelation. Sitting in the tub, I began to cry for him, once again.

Then truth struck like a gong as more of my life began to make sense. Lewis seemed my mirror in opposition. I'd said since childhood I felt like a boy. When I masturbated, I imagined I had a penis. I passed out at the gynecologist. I loved gay men and gay clubs. Many of my lovers were closeted. I never wanted kids. I always felt my hyper-femininity was performative drag. I've always known my hyper femininity is a fear I'm not *girl* enough. Though I never desired changing my body, I'm phobic of and disgusted by my vagina. Lewis even remarked that I wasn't like a girl, as if I was "gender free."

In the most shocking turn, facing Lewis' repressed shame freed my own. I began the process of grieving my gender trauma and reading about my own gender queer identity.

In seeking to understand Lewis, I found mercy for his childhood trauma, shame, fears, and wounds. In finding mercy for the most difficult type of person, I found forgiveness. In finding that, I found unconditional love.

When I could finally forgive and love my enemies, including my family, I could finally forgive and love myself.

We are one. We always were.

Unraveling C.D.'s tragic pain and writing his story as I continued to grieve and heal was a miracle. His ghost has been with me all along. I still find pennies all the time.

I had a dream that I was a deer, wounded, writhing on the side of the road. Suddenly, Lewis' truck pulled up. He stepped out, sighed, then took my head in his hands and snapped my neck.

That felt like what he did in real life too. He gave me considerable pain in order to finally put me out of my misery.

The thing that finally snapped my neck was looking at the full, ugly truth. I can see why so many avoid, numb, or deny it.

But the cliché is true: the truth will set you free.

I still suffer the consequences of the trauma of rape, narcissistic abuse, and my BPD. I believe I'll grieve these pains for life. But processing the grief and taking away some of the internalized blame has healed me in ways that no therapist or medication did.

Understanding my own BPD opened up much self awareness, and understanding the disorders of those around me helped me process a lot of pain: I wouldn't have done any of those things were it not for how Lewis brutally attacked me. Through his hatred and my persistent survival, I began to finally see and understand my own strength and worth. He also led me to understand the mystery of C.D.'s tragedy—as much as that hurt, it relieved so much grief. I took no task more seriously than to attempt to tell his painful story with love.

As I healed, my writing became more successful and impactful than ever. My gratitude for life and my inner peace deepened. My faith and belief in magic and miracles became solid. My empathy expanded rather than contracted. A lot of pain in the world began to make sense.

Despair and pain are still parts of my struggle, but hope is now my guiding light in the storm.

What's the toxic root of Cluster B disorders?
Shame.
Where's shame wielded as a weapon?
Everywhere.
The inner child of America bore witness to the horrors of slavery and the birth of white supremacy, which was sired by a wounded father: patriarchy.

But who are we without our abusive fathers? Orphans?

Eyes shut to abuse, our narcissistic culture makes us feel terrible. We doubt if we're attractive enough, hardworking enough, smart enough, thin enough, sexual enough, chaste enough, white enough, man enough, woman enough, powerful enough.

By the time our brains form, it's already broken our self love, leaked its pollution into our neural pathways, turned us predatory to each other, making us our own worst enemy, trauma bonding us to lies.

So you want to be a freedom fighter?
To break the cycle, you're going to have to heal.
You have to learn to dissect shame.
Healing generational trauma means you have to dig deep, uproot the gnarliest roots, face painful truths, and grieve.

Do you know how much strength that takes?
Are you prepared for how dark it gets the deeper you dig?